P9-CMY-404

Buy It, Fix It, Sell It, PROFIT!

KEVIN C. MYERS

Dearborn™
Trade Publishing
A **Kaplan Professional** Company

This publication is designed to provide accurate and authoritative information in regard to the subject matter covered. It is sold with the understanding that the publisher is not engaged in rendering legal, accounting, or other professional service. If legal advice or other expert assistance is required, the services of a competent professional should be sought.

Vice President and Publisher: Cynthia A. Zigmund
Acquisitions Editor: Mary B. Good
Senior Project Editor: Trey Thoelcke
Interior Design: Lucy Jenkins
Cover Design: DePinto Designs
Typesetting: Elizabeth Pitts

©1998, 2003 by Dearborn Financial Publishing, Inc.

Published by Dearborn Trade Publishing, a Kaplan Professional Company

All rights reserved. The text of this publication, or any part thereof, may not be reproduced in any manner whatsoever without written permission from the publisher.

Printed in the United States of America

05 10 9 8 7 6

Library of Congress Cataloging-in-Publication Data

Myers, Kevin C.
   Buy it, fix it, sell it : profit! : a comprehensive guide to no-sweat money-making home rehab / Kevin C. Myers.—2nd ed.
      p.   cm.
   Includes index.
   ISBN 0-7931-6938-0 (pbk.)
   1. Real estate investment—United States.   2. House buying—United States.   3. House selling—United States.   4. Dwellings—Remodeling—United States.   5. Housing rehabilitation—Economic aspects—United States.   I. Title.
   HD255.M93   2003
   332.63′243—dc21   2003006387

Dearborn Trade books are available at special quantity discounts to use for sales promotions, employee premiums, or educational purposes. Please contact our special sales department to order or for more information at 800-245-2665, e-mail trade@dearborn.com, or write to Dearborn Trade Publishing, 30 South Wacker Drive, Suite 2500, Chicago, IL 60606-7481.

Dedication

To my lifelong sweetheart and lovely wife Sharon—the 30+ year adventure continues and gets better with each passing year. To my daughter Nicole and her husband Aaron, who have both just graduated from the University of Oklahoma (go Sooners!)—I'm very proud of both of you as you begin your own exciting life journey. And finally, to my youngest daughter Tiffany who has become a world traveler and academic wiz kid—always remember that the Old Man will always love and support you wherever your journey takes you (even if it's liberal politics—ouch!).

Contents

Preface

Take this job and shove it! We've all dreamed of walking up to the boss and shouting this little phrase at the top of our lungs. The problem is we haven't won the lottery yet, so we need the money. Looks like we're stuck in the squirrel cage for the long haul.

I've written this book for those of you who feel trapped in a dead-end job and want to do something about it. I am of the opinion that unless we create our own future, someone else will create it for us, and it probably won't be very rewarding.

Investing in real estate rehab projects offers just about anyone the opportunity to break the chains of servitude and create a comfortable future for themselves. Each house you buy, fix up, and sell will generate a *minimum* net profit of $10,000. Working part-time, you should easily be able to complete two to three houses over the next year, as you learn the business and develop your skills. Does an extra $20,000 to $30,000 sound attractive? This isn't hype—it's for real. Many people all across America are learning the techniques and are generating huge cash flows for themselves. You can do it too, with a little knowledge and a little effort, focused in the right direction.

I've designed the book to take you through the whole process, from beginning to end. You will learn numerous techniques for finding bargain properties, negotiating a wholesale purchase price, financing your projects with little or none of your own money, getting the rehab work done by skilled craftspeople, and quickly selling the properties to convert your paper profits to cash. Get in, get out, and move on to the next project.

Quick-turnaround real estate rehab is a time-tested formula that consistently generates an excellent stream of income, regardless of external economic conditions. Unlike the buy-and-hold strategy, you are *not* dependent on price inflation to earn profits. And best of all, you are *not* getting yourself into a long-term landlording job.

As you consider whether this investment opportunity is right for you, two thoughts have probably crossed your mind—*Where am I going to get the money?* and *When will I have the time to do all of the rehab work?* Good questions!

As to the money required to buy and fix up properties, let me assure you that this business can be conducted with little or no money of your own. The basic concept that I emphasize in this book is: *Find the good deals and the money will come.* All the money you will ever need to do the deals is out there and available, if you get good at finding the good deals. I will show you how to find the good deals and how to attract money like a magnet!

What about the time and skills needed to get all the rehab work done? You will need a little of both, but keep in mind that the work will be done by skilled professionals. You will learn to be a project manager, not a worker bee. You will be rewarded for orchestrating the process, not for doing the work. Even if you are a talented handyman, you will learn that doing it yourself is a losing proposition. Your time is much better spent working *on* the business, not *in* the business.

Real estate rehab is not a get-rich-quick scheme. It is a solid investment opportunity that requires knowledge and hard work, like any other worthwhile endeavor. The knowledge you need is in your hands. Opportunity is knocking at your door—seize it and enjoy the fruits of your labor!

And let me know how you're progressing. I'd love to hear from you.

Kevin C. Myers
StreetSmart Real Estate, Inc.
Albuquerque, NM
E-mail: rehabwiz@rehabwiz.com
Web site: <www.rehabwiz.com>

About the Author

Kevin C. Myers is president of a diversified group of companies in Albuquerque, New Mexico, involved in real estate investments, real estate appraisal, and real estate education. He has rehabbed numerous investment properties during his 20-year-plus real estate career, specializing in single-family homes. Kevin has an MBA degree and is a former officer in the U.S. Coast Guard. For leisure, he enjoys riding his Harley-Davidson motorcycle, fly fishing, and skiing with his family.

Handyman Properties

A Niche of Opportunity

*T*he world of real estate investing is vast and intricate and there are many ways for the small investor to participate. In this book, you will be exposed to one small niche—buying, fixing, and selling "handyman-special" houses for profit. As you know, there are many other investment opportunities in real estate. For example, you could buy rental properties and become a long-term landlord. You could specialize in foreclosures or tax lien properties, or build an income through several lease-option techniques. Other opportunities could include such ventures as buying and selling discounted mortgages, mortgage lending or brokerage, or even new-home building. The possibilities are numerous and often confusing, particularly for the beginning investor.

What is the best opportunity for you? There really is no right or wrong answer to this question. This is something you must carefully consider and decide for yourself, based primarily on what aspect of the industry you are most interested in. In all of the areas I've mentioned, the opportunities are there to succeed as an investor either on a part-time or full-time basis. Clearly, I have a preference for handyman properties. Let me tell you why I think handyman properties are an excellent opportunity for the beginning investor.

Handyman Specials—The Rehab-and-Sell Strategy

The essence of this investment strategy is speed—buy a fixer-upper property at a bargain price, quickly rehab, and then quickly sell the property. Get in, get it fixed up, and get out: a simple yet very profitable and safe strategy, regardless of external circumstances. Using this technique, profits are made when you buy at a bargain price, increased as a result of the renovation process, and converted to cash when the property is sold.

The key advantage of this strategy is that you, the investor, are in control of every aspect of the transaction from start to finish. You are *not* dependent on price inflation or any other external factors to make profits. You will know going into a deal what it will cost you to fix up the property and for how much the property will sell at the end. Best of all, you will know exactly what your profit will be, because you will have included it in your buying decision. Uncertainties, and therefore risks, are controlled and thereby reduced substantially.

Risk management and reduction are two of the most compelling benefits of this investment technique. In many respects, it is a recession-proof business. Regardless of the external economy, people need and want quality housing and will pay top dollar for a relatively inexpensive house in excellent condition.

Are there negatives associated with this strategy? Sure. Just like any other worthwhile endeavor, sustained success comes to those who have created an advantage for themselves. Typically that advantage is hard work and knowledge coupled with a system of doing business—a system that, once developed, can be repeated over and over again with predictable results.

What would such a system consist of? It's really several systems or subsystems: ways to consistently find and buy properties at prices well below market value; methods to get the work done by professionals, without impacting your profits; techniques for financing the purchase and rehab work, using little or none of your own money, if possible; and finally, selling the property quickly and for top dollar and more. The formula for success in any business is:

Knowledge + Hard work + System for doing business = Profits

Do not be misled. Real estate rehab is not a get-rich-quick scheme. The necessary knowledge and a system for doing business is the subject of this book. And never forget the *hard work* ingredient. It is required and is indispensable to make the investment strategy work.

Why is this technique particularly well suited for the beginning investor? There are three reasons:

1. It provides for immediate positive cash flow.
2. The acquisition and rehab work can often be financed without any out-of-pocket money from the investor.
3. The business system that I recommend utilizes skilled professionals (Real estate agents, appraisers, contractors, home inspectors) for the critical elements of the business, thereby significantly minimizing potential mistakes and reducing risk. The investor assumes the role of the *project manager*, leaving the day-to-day implementation in the hands of the various experts who are brought into the project for specialized tasks.

Just the Opposite—The Buy-and-Hold Strategy

In contrast to my preferred rehab-and-sell technique is the traditional buy-and-hold strategy. Let's take a closer look at this investment method and examine the pros and cons to see how it compares.

There are many variations of the buy-and-hold strategy, but usually it entails buying a house or small apartment building with a small down payment (20 percent or less) and renting out the units. The holding period is at the discretion of the owner—it could be one year, one decade, or forever. In the meantime, the owner is making payments on the underlying mortgage or mortgages and managing the property. During the holding period, profits are derived from positive cash flow (if any) and possibly tax advantages.

But the real profits of the buy-and-hold strategy are dependent on price inflation; that is, the extent to which the value of the property increases over time. Of course, the more highly leveraged the property is, the higher the return on investment. For example, let's say you own a $100,000 house with a $95,000 mortgage, which you bought with a $5,000 down payment—a typical deal. Over the next five years, the house appreciates 20 percent or about 4 percent a year. The house is now worth $120,000 and the return on your $5,000 investment is

$20,000 or a whopping 400 percent (not counting any positive cash flow or mortgage reduction). This is the power of leverage at its finest.

But what happens if the market stays flat, or worse yet, if the market goes down? Unheard of? If you're lucky and the market stays flat, you come out even and your $5,000 investment is worth $5,000, five years later. Not exactly a super-duper investment. What if the market went down 20 percent and the house is worth only $80,000? You are now in a situation known as being "upside-down." You owe $15,000 more than you can sell the house for, so you have negative equity. Not a pretty picture.

The point is this: Local real estate prices generally move up and down over time, in cycles. Although the long-term trend may generally be increasing, the short-term trend may be devastatingly down. Where in the cycle did you buy and where in the cycle did you sell? To a large extent, this will determine your profit outlook in using the buy-and-hold strategy. And it is these external circumstances that you as an investor have absolutely no control over. Shake the dice and take your chances.

Consider this from Robert Bruss, real estate expert and syndicated columnist, who wrote in his September 8, 1996, column:

> The quick-buck real estate profits are long gone. With a few "boom-town" exceptions, such as Las Vegas, Nevada, and Palo Alto and San Jose, California, home prices in most cities are relatively stable today. Average home sale prices are appreciating about 4 percent annually on a nationwide basis, depending on whose statistics you believe, keeping pace with inflation. This "get-rich-slowly" economic environment has driven away the get-rich-quick real estate crowd. Instead, it's the quiet low-profile real estate investors who are earning substantial profits today. . . . Successful investors in single-family houses, as well as commercial properties, specialize in fixer-upper properties. Buying property in excellent condition, hoping to somehow earn a profit, is a no-win situation.

A Blueprint for the Novice Investor

Much of this book is devoted to the novice investor, someone just starting out in the real estate investment field or someone new to the rehab-and-sell philosophy. Additionally, it is focused on providing you with detailed information on the various steps or phases of the entire process, so that you can go out and immediately begin work on putting your first project together.

I have organized the book so that it follows the logical sequence of the investment technique: *Buy It, Fix It, Sell It.* The final chapters, *Profit,* are designed to provide some of the more advanced techniques for those of you who may eventually want to pursue this activity as a full-time business. Let's take a closer look at the outline of the book.

Buy It

- Develop a workable business plan for the overall investment process.
- Find and work with real estate agents.
- Evaluate neighborhoods and recognize candidate properties.
- Find bargain properties that have profit potential.
- Research foreclosures and bank REO (real estate owned; properties that have been foreclosed by a bank or other lending institution) properties.
- Determine the maximum purchase price for any property.
- Use appraisals for estimating as-is and after-repaired values.
- Attract partners, investors, or private mortgage lenders for financing.
- Inspect houses and estimate repairs.
- Negotiate with sellers to get offers accepted.

Fix It

- Choose the best renovations to maximize profits and marketability.
- Create fantastic curb appeal.
- Install killer kitchens and bathrooms to die for—cheaply.
- Get bids and negotiate acceptable contracts.
- Get the rehab work done by skilled professionals.
- Successfully manage your rehab project.

Sell It

- Find a top-gun selling agent.
- Develop a powerful and successful marketing strategy.
- Include incentives and protections in your listing agreement.
- Attract buyers with seller financing options.
- Sell the house quickly and for top dollar.

Profit

- Consider the profit potential of a full-time rehab business.
- Incorporate advanced bargain-finding techniques.
- Operate your rehab business for maximum profit.
- Invest your profits in mortgages to skyrocket your returns.

Buying, fixing, and selling handyman properties can be a very exciting and profitable investment technique. For me, it has always been intellectually rewarding because it requires you to develop and use your social skills, analytical skills, and creative abilities to successfully complete a project. It is a niche in the real estate field that offers great potential for those who really want to dig in and learn the business. In the next chapter, I unveil the complete rehab project plan that will guide you through the entire process. You will have a chance to see what this investment technique is all about and whether it is a good match for your interests, skills, and lifestyle.

The Real Estate Rehab Business Plan

Outline for Success

*I*n virtually every aspect of the rehab business, from finding properties through getting them sold, there are many, many different options. It's very important to know what options are available, but it's even more important to narrow your choices and get focused on a specific strategy. Keep this in mind—if you *do* know where you're going, you might just get there!

Here's a sampling of some of the questions you'll need to answer:

- What is your best strategy for finding bargains in your community? Real estate agents, bank REOs, foreclosures, for-sale-by-owner properties (FSBOs), or auctions?
- How are you going to finance your projects? Banks, sellers, government programs, investors, or through private mortgages?
- Are you going to operate solo or bring in partners?
- What price range of house are you going to focus on?
- Who is going to do the rehab work? You, a general contractor, or a handyman?
- Are you going to sell properties yourself or list with agents?
- How are you going to handle multiple projects?

One of the most important things you can do, prior to starting any business venture, is to prepare a business plan. Going through this process is both exhilarating and humbling. It forces you to carefully think through all aspects and options related to the business, risks and rewards, and choose the alternatives best suited for your financial goals and objectives. It also allows you to pinpoint any weaknesses in the system you have devised and to take appropriate corrective action to strengthen your plan of attack.

In the paragraphs that follow, I have prepared a model rehab project plan that is similar to a business plan but outlines a specific approach to a rehab project. It is prescriptive in nature, in that it focuses on those techniques and systems that I feel are most appropriate for a first-time venture.

Keep in mind that this is a summary presentation, not a comprehensive business plan, and some of the terms used or some of the concepts may not be fully explained or make complete sense to you. Don't worry about that now, because I go into more detail on these topics in subsequent chapters. For now, concentrate more on the big picture to get a feel for how this business works and whether it might be something you want to tackle. I'll come back to this last point at the end of the chapter to help you assess your skills and interest level.

Overview of Investment Strategy

The basic investment strategy is to purchase fixer-upper single-family homes, rehab the properties to "doll-house" condition, and quickly sell the houses for top dollar. Only houses that can be purchased at wholesale value should be considered for investment. This will ensure that your profits are secured at purchase and are not dependent on any price inflation in the marketplace.

Success with this investment strategy requires speed in the execution of the component parts: speed in the acquisition of properties when opportunities are found, speed in the rehab process, and speed in selling the properties quickly. You must accomplish these tasks through aggressive project management, combined with the use of professional independent contractors to complete the rehab work and market the properties. This approach will significantly reduce your holding costs and will result in a high-quality finished product that will sell for maximum retail value in the marketplace.

Finding Target Properties

The properties targeted for this investment are single-family homes in need of significant repairs but located in decent neighborhoods. Houses located in marginal or low-demand areas should not be considered. Your attention will be focused on neighborhoods of lower- to mid-priced houses in areas where first-time homebuyers want to live.

Targeting houses in need of "significant repairs" is a paramount factor in your investment strategy. Houses requiring only cosmetic repairs typically are marketed at or near maximum retail value and thus offer little profit potential. In contrast, houses that are in very poor condition but are structurally sound command little attention in the marketplace and often can be purchased very cheaply. These are the properties that can be transformed through a value-added rehab process into a valuable asset, capable of producing substantial profits.

Note, however, that certain properties that have the wrong things wrong will not be considered for investment. These include such problems as severe foundation settling; extensive roof truss damage; soil or hillside instability; obsolete floor plans requiring a room addition; severe drainage problems; and the need for extensive lead paint, asbestos, or radon abatement.

Properties will be located through a variety of techniques. Real estate agents will be utilized to view handyman types of properties currently listed on the market and to obtain information on expired and canceled handyman listings. Real estate agents also will be used to assist in evaluating bank REO properties and government foreclosed properties, such as those available through the Department of Housing and Urban Development (HUD) and the Department of Veterans Affairs (VA). Homeowners offering their homes for sale by owner (FSBO) also should be contacted as appropriate.

Determining the Purchase Price of Properties

The purchase price of properties will be determined by using a unique formula that incorporates desired profits plus all buying, holding, rehab, and selling costs.

The starting point for this calculation is maximum retail value of the property after all repairs have been made. This value will be determined based on recent comparable sales in the neighborhood and will be obtained by consultation with real estate appraisers or real estate agents familiar with local market conditions.

Once the maximum retail value is determined, all of the costs identified previously and the desired profits are subtracted to arrive at the maximum purchase price. For the basic formula, see Figure 2.1.

Buying and Financing Properties

Due to the poor condition of our target properties, conventional bank financing typically will not be available. As a result, financing for your properties will be obtained primarily through two sources or a combination thereof: seller financing and private mortgage lenders.

Sellers of properties that are in poor condition are very often motivated to sell at bargain prices and with flexible terms. Several options of seller financing will be explored within the context of each deal to match the needs of the property owner and, to some extent, your needs as a buyer. However, in order to increase your chances of getting an offer accepted, you must tailor each offer to meet the needs of the particular seller. Some sellers will be in a position to carry all of the necessary financing, with a small down payment. This could be worked into a split-funding deal where the owner would accept a small down payment with the balance due in a 6- to 12-month short-term mortgage. Other possibilities could include your assumption of an existing first mortgage with the seller carrying back a second mortgage, or your obtaining a private lender first mortgage with a seller note in second position. All options will be evaluated with each potential deal.

Private mortgage lenders are perhaps the best sources of short-term financing for rehab properties. Loans are typically available for 50 percent to 75 percent LTV (loan-to-value ratio; i.e., the ratio of the loan amount divided by the value of the house) and are based on the after-

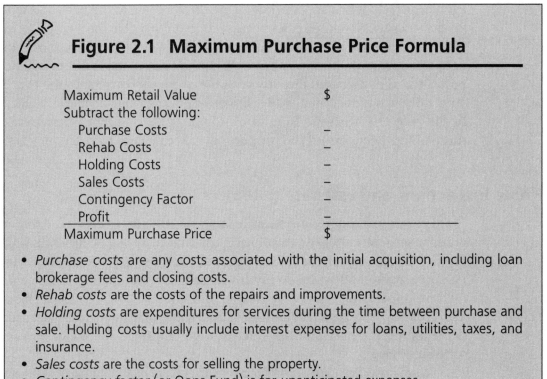

Figure 2.1 Maximum Purchase Price Formula

Maximum Retail Value	$
Subtract the following:	
Purchase Costs	–
Rehab Costs	–
Holding Costs	–
Sales Costs	–
Contingency Factor	–
Profit	–
Maximum Purchase Price	$

- *Purchase costs* are any costs associated with the initial acquisition, including loan brokerage fees and closing costs.
- *Rehab costs* are the costs of the repairs and improvements.
- *Holding costs* are expenditures for services during the time between purchase and sale. Holding costs usually include interest expenses for loans, utilities, taxes, and insurance.
- *Sales costs* are the costs for selling the property.
- *Contingency factor* (or Oops Fund) is for unanticipated expenses.
- *Profit* is the amount you expect to net, after all expenses.
- *Maximum purchase price* is the top dollar figure you would pay for the property. It is essentially the wholesale value of the house.

repaired value of the house. For example, a 65 percent LTV loan on a house valued at $100,000 after repairs would be $65,000. These loans generally can be obtained for up to a two-year term, with interest-only payments at 9 percent to 12 percent interest. Although these interest rates are relatively high, they have no impact on your profits because this cost is accounted for in your purchase price formula. Additionally, the loan should be paid off within three to six months, which is the normal holding period to get a house rehabbed and sold. These loans will be obtained through private mortgage loan brokers located in your community or in nearby larger communities.

In consideration of the two primary financing alternatives, your buying strategy will generally involve making two simultaneous offers on each property (when appropriate). One offer will be for all cash and will be at a steeply discounted price. The second offer will involve some form of short-term owner financing (if feasible) and will be at a price closer to or at the maximum purchase price. Where possible, these offers will be presented and discussed directly with the property owners. In the event your offer is not accepted, you will continue to monitor the availability of the property with the intention of making subsequent offers every three to four weeks until the property is sold to you or to someone else.

Home Inspections and Estimating Repairs

Properties under consideration will be initially inspected using a comprehensive checklist developed for this purpose. Items needing repair or replacement will be noted, as well as upgrades needed to enhance marketability. Based on this information, a repair estimate will be developed using material and labor rates derived from the local market. This cost estimate (including a contingency factor) will be used in determining the maximum purchase price and form the basis of your written offers.

Note, however, that all of your written offers will contain a "subject to inspection" clause. Should an offer be accepted, this will allow you to bring in a professional home inspector to thoroughly evaluate the property for previously undetected defects. This is an important risk management tool that you will use consistently on all houses where an offer has been accepted.

Rehab Strategy

The basic rehab strategy is to renovate each property to "doll-house" condition including the addition of appropriate "sizzle" features to enhance marketability. All mechanical and structural systems will be repaired as necessary to ensure compliance with minimum FHA construction standards. This will allow the house to be financed under government programs suitable for first-time homebuyers, thereby increasing the options available to potential buyers.

The rehab plan developed for each property will pay particular attention to curb appeal, the kitchen, and the bathrooms. These areas of the home are critical to the overall success of each project. All other areas of the house will be cosmetically improved to produce a final product that sparkles. Certain sizzle features will be incorporated into each house to induce interest and increase demand in the marketplace. Unique and unexpected items will be added, as appropriate. Consideration will be given to such things as a hot tub, security system, bay windows, skylights, microwave oven, mini-blinds, garage door opener, and ceiling fans, to name a few.

All rehab work will be completed by experienced professionals from your local area. This will ensure that all tasks are finished promptly and with high-quality work. Items identified in the rehab plan will be competitively bid. The work will either be done through general contractors or through a handyman/subcontractor arrangement. All items will be bid on a materials plus labor basis. In no case will lump-sum bids be accepted. All contracts will require your written approval of change orders for items outside the original scope of work.

Each rehab project will be closely monitored. Work progress and expenditures will be tracked and records will be maintained in a project file. Photographic documentation will be made, as appropriate.

Marketing and Sale of Completed Houses

The marketing and sale of the completed house will be accomplished primarily through local real estate agents. This will allow for maximum market exposure. Agents will be selected on the basis of recent sales performance and commitments made during their listing presentations. Top-gun selling agents will be given priority consideration. Monetary incentives will be given to the listing agent to stimulate a sense of urgency. These incentives will decrease with time and will be eliminated after 60 days of marketing time. In no case will a listing agreement extend beyond 90 days. All listing agreements will contain a buyout provision, which will be used in those instances where you locate a qualified buyer through your own independent efforts.

Subsequent to listing a property, you will keep in close contact with the real estate agent to monitor progress of the marketing plan. Agents will be required to promptly perform all marketing activities agreed to during their listing presentations.

Following acceptance of an offer, you will closely monitor the progress of the escrow process to ensure timely closing of the purchase transaction.

Profit Potential of Rehab Projects

Unlike a conventional real estate investment where profits are based primarily on an unknown inflation rate, profits in your rehab projects will be determined in advance. As discussed earlier, you will specify a profit number in your purchase price formula. To the extent that you can manage the rehab process such that your costs are below projections, you will exceed the profit selected. And the opposite is also true.

Your profit target is a variable that will change with each project. However, you will not proceed with any project that does not contain a minimum net profit of $10,000. On smaller houses in lower-priced neighborhoods, $10,000 to $15,000 net profit will be the normal objective. Larger houses in midpriced neighborhoods usually will allow for higher profits. In general, you will target a 15 percent net profit on houses that exceed $100,000 retail value. Thus, on a house that will retail for $150,000 after repairs, your net profit objective will be approximately $22,500. This is the typical investment criterion that will be used to evaluate potential deals.

Cash Investment Requirements

In most real estate transactions, some amount of cash is required at closing to finalize the deal. The amount of cash varies with how each deal is structured. It depends on the extent of seller financing (if any), down payment needs of the seller, loan amounts, real estate commissions, and other associated closing costs. In addition, some cash will be needed during the holding period for such items as utility costs and loan payments. Generally, cash requirements will range from a low of about $1,000 to a high of about $30,000, depending on the variables previously discussed.

To the extent feasible and prudent, you will attempt to structure deals such that cash requirements are kept to a minimum. With some transactions, all of the cash necessary for the acquisition and rehab work will be obtained from private mortgage brokers. For those deals

Figure 2.2 Sample Rehab Project Projections

Estimated After-Repaired Value	$120,000
Purchase Price	$ 70,000
Private Mortgage at 65% After-Repaired Value (65% of $120,000)	$ 78,000
Repair Cost Estimate	$ 15,000
Investor Cash Required*	$ 10,000*
Estimated Sales Price	$120,000
Loan Repayment	–78,000
Return of Investor's Cash	–10,000
Real Estate Commission	– 7,000
Approximate Net Profit	$ 25,000

*Investor cash required: $78,000 (loan amount) – $70,000 (purchase price) = $8,000 excess. Apply excess to repair costs: $15,000 – $8,000 = $7,000 cash needed + $3,000 in holding costs = $10,000 total investor cash required.

where additional cash is needed, your own cash will be used to the extent available, or a partner or joint venture investor will be located to provide most, if not all of the cash.

The project shown in Figure 2.2 is for illustration purposes only and does not necessarily reflect an actual transaction that would be available for investment consideration. This deal assumes financing would be obtained from a private mortgage lender, with additional cash coming from an investor or partner. In this example, the net profits of $25,000 would be split in accordance with the provisions of your partnership or joint venture agreement.

Pulling It All Together

Those are the basic elements of your business plan. You may want to modify it somewhat to match your specific circumstances and you may want to add a section describing your background and experience. Many of my students have used this rehab project plan to attract partners or investors, and others have used it to help in obtaining financing from private mortgage brokers. The advantage of handing out copies of the plan to these people is that it gives you a certain amount of credibility. It says to them that you know what you're doing, where you're going, and how you're going to get there. You've done your homework and you're serious about getting them involved. It also shows them how they will benefit by funding your projects.

Note that this rehab project plan does not highlight a specific project for investment. It is intended to attract investors or partners by explaining how you will execute your investment activities once a project that meets the investment criteria is found and how they will benefit by participating. It's basically designed to get them to the point of saying, "Yeah, I like your plan and I'm definitely interested. Let's get a joint venture agreement worked out." A further discussion of presenting your plan to potential partners or investors, along with a worksheet for presenting an actual investment project can be found in Chapter 9.

Is the Rehab Business Really for You?

Having read the rehab project plan, you now should have a clear picture of what this business is all about. As you can see, it's going to take a lot of hard work—not physical work (that will be done by others), but a fairly large time commitment (intermittent, spaced out over several months) to coordinate all of the various activities. Without a doubt, the most time-consuming part of the entire process will be the hours and hours spent up front in finding the good deal; that is, looking at properties and making offers. Fortunately, it is an activity that you can pursue in the evenings and on weekends or otherwise fit into your current schedule. Once you have purchased a property, your time requirements will generally be manageable—probably an hour or so each day that the rehab work is ongoing and a few hours here and there to take care of such things as permits, finding your selling agent, and reviewing offers.

In addition to time, you will need to develop a working knowledge of several areas of real estate, including:

- Property values in the neighborhoods of interest
- Basic home inspection techniques
- Repair cost estimating
- Negotiation techniques

- Mortgage financing options
- Contract administration
- Real estate marketing

Let me be clear on this. You do not need to be an appraiser, home inspector, cost estimator, master negotiator, mortgage lender, contract administrator, or real estate agent to execute a successful rehab project. But you *do* need to have a basic working knowledge in all of these areas. You need to know something about all of them because you either will be required to perform them yourself or hire others to perform them. If you hire others, you must be able to evaluate their results.

Where do you get this knowledge? Reading and studying this book is a good start. I cover all of these areas, to varying degrees, in the chapters that follow. If you are serious about real estate rehab as a long-term investment strategy, you must plan on continually updating and increasing your knowledge in these areas through other books, courses, and seminars. Of course, one of the best of all learning experiences is actually going out and doing a project or two.

Knowing what you now know about the real estate rehab field, I would suggest you take a little time for self-assessment and reflection. Ask yourself these questions: Is this really the type of project I want to get involved with? Do I have the time and am I willing to learn what I need to know to carry out a successful project? Am I willing to make the necessary commitment to make this complex venture work?

Getting Started

Before you actually go out and start looking at properties, there are two important steps you must take: Figure out your funding plan and find your real estate agent (in that order).

First, you need to figure out where the money for purchase and re-hab will come from. As discussed in the rehab project plan, the two primary sources of funding for rehab properties are seller financing and private mortgage lenders, or a combination of the two. Can you supplement these funds if necessary, with cash coming from your own savings, from partners, or from other investors that you bring into your project? You might want to jump ahead and read Chapters 9 and 10, which discuss these issues in detail. Then, I would suggest you start your search for private money by contacting private mortgage brokers in your area. Get to know their loan criteria and application procedures. This would be a good time to meet with one or more of the brokers in person and review your business plan with them. Even though you don't have a specific project to show them, you will get to know their requirements and thus your options in structuring a deal.

The reason I emphasize getting your funding plan worked out first is that it gives you, your real estate agent, and sellers the confidence that you can perform. You know, in general, where the money is coming from and this will give you the needed leverage in working with real estate agents and sellers. It's just a waste of everybody's time, including your own, if you haven't identified your funding options in advance. This does not mean that you have to have firm commitment letters from lenders or signed partnership/joint venture agreements. It simply means that you have identified potential sources of funding and know what lending criteria you will need to meet. Once you find the good deal, you will approach these funding sources and get them signed up.

Second, you will need to find at least one good real estate agent that you can work with in finding properties on which to make offers. This critical step is discussed extensively in the next chapter.

How to Find Your Real Estate Agent

*F*inding handyman properties, making purchase offers, and getting them accepted is where it all begins. And finding bargain properties with profit potential is the most time-consuming and often most frustrating aspect of the real estate rehab field. This phase will test your patience and persistence, in addition to your analytical skills. Whether you're just starting out or are an experienced investor, using a good real estate agent to help you find your target properties is a must.

Real Estate Agents—Your New Best Friends

If you have little or no experience in the real estate field, real estate agents are indispensable for their expertise in the real estate marketplace. They know what properties are available; what properties are going to become available; price ranges; financing options; neighborhood characteristics; and how to resolve title issues, negotiate with sellers, prepare and submit purchase offers, and so forth. Even if you're experienced in many of these areas, working with one or several good agents will save you an extraordinary amount of time that you can better utilize on other tasks.

In considering all of the advantages of working with real estate agents, two capabilities in particular make them essential to getting started with this investment:

1. *Real estate agents have access to the listings of properties that are on the market.* On a nationwide basis, about 85 percent of all houses are sold through an agent, while only 15 percent are sold FSBO (for sale by owner). If you're depending entirely on FSBOs to find properties, you're missing 85 percent of the marketplace. (FSBOs are an important source of bargain properties and are discussed extensively in Chapter 5.) Also, if you're searching for bargains in REO properties, many institutions list their properties with real estate offices, so your only access to them is through an agent. Because REOs are one of your best sources of bargain fixer-uppers, finding the agents who have access to them is critical.

2. They have access to a Multiple Listing Service (MLS), a database of properties typically provided through the local Association of REALTORS.® This database is usually available only to real estate agents and real estate appraisers who are members of the local association. Limited versions of available home listings are now popping up on the Internet for many communities. This may be a useful tool in your area, but it does have limitations. For example, many of the Internet databases do not have information on recently sold properties, which is needed to evaluate neighborhood property values.

How to Find Motivated Real Estate Agents

Real estate agents come in two flavors: those you can work with and those you can't. You're looking for an agent you can work with—someone with whom you can establish good chemistry and who will bring you a steady stream of properties to inspect and make offers on.

How do you find such a person? The best source would be a referral from a fellow real estate investor. This might not be easy to get, because you would be competing for the same service from the same agent! But it never hurts to ask. Referrals from other people you know might also be a good starting point.

Let's assume that you're starting from scratch. The town you live in has an abundance of real estate agents, all willing to sell you something. How do you narrow the list down? The first thing is to realize that good real estate agents tend to specialize. Over time, they become experts in certain aspects of their realm. For example, some specialize in high-end properties, dealing exclusively with buyers and sellers of luxury homes. Some may be experts in certain neighborhoods because they have established a listing "farm" in the area and have done a lot of deals there over the years. Others may specialize only in listing properties—they become good at dealing with sellers of properties but may not be particularly good at working with buyers. Of course, there are the selling agents who specialize in working with buyers and all the problems they bring to the table, but can't stand the thought of cold-calling FSBOs to get a listing. The point is, you want to find agents who are good at the things you need them to be good at. Just what are those things? Well, let's make a short list of key attributes. The ideal real estate agent would:

- Specialize in selling handyman properties to investors.
- Have access to listings of bank REO properties.
- Be willing to submit offers on multiple properties, realizing that many of the offers would not be accepted.
- Be experienced in securing owner financing.
- Be knowledgeable about private mortgage sources.
- Be knowledgeable about the neighborhoods you want to work in.
- Be competent in evaluating neighborhoods and in establishing retail market values of properties after repairs are completed (after-repaired value).
- Be agreeable to working with you on a "buyer agency" basis (which is discussed in the following paragraphs).

So now, you've identified the characteristics of the type of real estate agent you would like to work with. Finding one to work with you, someone who has these attributes and is motivated, is somewhat akin to looking for the proverbial needle in the haystack. The best way that I know to identify these people and have them call you is to run a classified ad in either your local Sunday newspaper and or your weekly

"Penny Saver" or "Thrifty Nickel." Place an ad like the following in the "real estate wanted" section:

> Active investor seeks real estate agent specializing in handyman houses. Looking for all-cash deals and quick closings. Call Kevin at 222-0011.

Get ready, because you will be getting calls—probably a lot of calls. Now, you're in the driver's seat and you simply interview the agents when they call. Why is this ad so powerful? Let's examine the simple concepts behind this little ad that will get your phone to ring off the hook.

On Sunday morning, the paper is full of real estate ads. The first thing all the agents look at is their own ads to make sure everything is correct. Next, many will glance at the "real estate wanted" section to see if their listings match anything people are looking for. This section typically has ads from other investors that say something to the effect of "I buy houses." You may at some point want to place such an ad yourself. In any event, your ad is in a high-visibility section that many real estate agents look at.

Your ad says that you are active. To an agent, this means either that you are actively looking for property (that's good) or that you are a frequent buyer (also good). It says that you want to be contacted by a specialist in handyman properties. This is an invitation to any agent who has a handyman property to give you a call. But the most exciting verbiage in the ad, from an agent's perspective, is that you say you will pay *all cash* and you want a *quick closing.* This is a no-brainer for an agent. This means that there will be no financing hassles and that the agent will get paid quickly. You're the type of client real estate agents dream about!

The Real Estate Agent Mating Ritual

When the phone starts ringing, you have to get through the screening phase, or the mating ritual if you will. You have to clearly state, "This is what I'm looking for, this is how I operate, this is the volume of business I expect to generate" (if you're planning multiple projects), and so forth. Likewise, you need the prospective real estate agent to send out signals. If you have a match, great—you set up a time to meet. If not, you move on and find another prospect.

It is very important during this initial contact that you clearly communicate your desired criteria. For example, you could describe the type of deals you're looking for as:

- Handyman, fixer-upper single-family houses located in decent neighborhoods, not in any marginal, high-crime areas
- Preferably vacant and institutionally owned houses (bank REOs) in need of a lot of work, not just cosmetic repairs
- Homes priced well below retail market value (after repairs)

You need to communicate that you will be offering all cash for the properties, with few contingency clauses, and therefore you expect substantially lower pricing. Tell the agent that your offers are based on precise market-derived data, and that they are not just random, lowball offers. The agent needs to understand up front that you expect only one out of maybe five of your offers to be initially accepted. However, the agent needs to know that you will want to follow up on each property and will continue to submit offers periodically on the same property until it is sold, either to you or to someone else. Tell the agent you want a buyer's agency agreement applicable to all houses presented to you.

The Buyer's Agent

In recent years, a significant change has come about in the real estate industry that you need to be aware of and must take advantage of—the concept of a "buyer's agent." Traditionally, the real estate agent has always been legally obligated to represent the best interests of the seller. This means that the agent is required to secure the highest price possible for the house, even if he or she is not the listing agent. In this typical situation, both the listing agent from company A and the selling agent from company B legally work first and foremost for the seller. This is still true today, under the normal agency agreement. However, what you want is a buyer's agent—or a buyer's agency agreement that results in someone who works exclusively for *your* best interests.

Are buyer's agents hard to find? Fortunately, not any more. This arrangement is becoming very common in most parts of the country. In fact, in a recent survey conducted by the National Association of REALTORS,® 41 percent of all buyers nationwide said they used a buyer's agent when purchasing their last home. To locate a buyer's agent in your area, contact the Real Estate Buyer's Agent Council at 800-648-6224. They can provide you with a nationwide directory of member agents or provide you a referral over the phone. Alternatively, look at agent listings in your local Yellow Pages—buyer's agents usually identify themselves as such in their advertisements.

Buyer's agents come in two basic varieties—either a nonexclusive or exclusive buyer's agent. Nonexclusive agents work at a full-service realty office, in some cases representing buyers and in others representing sellers who've listed their properties with the firm. An exclusive buyer's agent doesn't take any seller listing and doesn't work for a real estate office that does take listings—they work solely for buyers. In either case, you and the real estate agent sign a buyer's agency agreement, the result of which is that the agent works exclusively on your behalf in any deal presented to you. Is there any big advantage of one over the other? Probably not, but just beware of any in-house listings presented to you in a nonexclusive agent situation—this could be a conflict of interest, in which you may not get the best possible deal. On the other hand, working with an exclusive buyer's agent will eliminate virtually all potential conflicts. It's really a matter of personal preference.

There is one important aspect of the buyer's agency agreement to be aware of—you, the buyer, are responsible for paying your agent's commission (typically 3 percent of purchase price). You can tackle this issue in one of two ways. You can just lower your offer price by 3 percent and pay your agent the money at closing, or you can specify in the purchase agreement that the seller is to pay the fee. Because listing agents usually split commissions with selling agents anyway, there's no extra cost to the seller, and the listing agent usually will accept this split commission arrangement.

In my experience, and in that of many others in the business, real estate agents can account for a large percentage of the properties you end up buying. They have access to critical information that you need and they provide the expert services you cannot function without. Start building long-term business relationships with several of them. Don't forget to take them out to lunch every once in a while and send them a thank-you card when appropriate. If you get the chance to refer a client to them, do it! This is how good business relationships are built.

Diamonds in Your Own Backyard

Characteristics of Neighborhoods and Target Fixer-Uppers

*B*efore you and your real estate agent hit the bricks and start looking at properties, you need to have a good idea of what your target property looks like and where it is likely to be located. In pursuing the real estate rehab investment opportunity, it really doesn't matter where you live—in the big city, the suburbs, or the country—you can make money in any of these areas if you adhere to a couple of basic business principles. In particular, you must produce a house that appeals to a large number of people (sell what people want to buy), and it must be located in an area or neighborhood that people who can qualify for a loan want to live (location, location, location). Of course, the implementation of these concepts can become a little tricky without further details.

You can learn about two elements of the search strategy in this chapter:

1. Where to focus your attention and efforts in terms of neighborhood selection.
2. The characteristics of the properties you should consider buying within the selected neighborhood or neighborhoods

The Number-One Criterion for Selecting Profitable Neighborhoods

In any city, large or small, there are neighborhoods that will produce profitable investments and neighborhoods that are unprofitable using the quick-turnaround, rehab-and-sell technique described in this book. Because tremendous variety in neighborhood characteristics can be found throughout the country, it is difficult to definitively describe the good versus the bad neighborhoods from an investment perspective. Let me offer some general guidance, because this is an important investment consideration.

Profitable neighborhoods always have this characteristic: People who have saved enough money for a down payment and can qualify for conventional bank financing want to live in this neighborhood. This, above all else, is the best indicator of a potentially profitable neighborhood.

The question is, "How can I tell if a particular neighborhood meets this criterion?" The only way to do this is to take a look at the sales statistics over the past couple of years. The best way to do this is through your real estate agent, who has access to this information on the local MLS database. In general, here's what you are looking for:

- An active real estate market; that is, many closed-sale transactions, coupled with a number of pending sales and current listings.
- A high percentage of the sales (more than 75 percent) are to owner-occupants, not to investors buying rental units.
- The majority of buyers purchase the homes with conventional financing, not with real estate or land contracts from the sellers.

Your real estate agent can easily and quickly pull up this information on any neighborhood by simply running what's known as a comparative market analysis, or CMA, on the MLS computer system. With this step completed, let's take a look at some of the other desirable characteristics of an ideal, target neighborhood.

Older Neighborhoods

This is where you want to be: the solid, clean, older neighborhood where pride of ownership is evident everywhere you look—neat and clean lawns; few junk cars in the streets; no garbage lying around; schools, shopping, and churches are nearby; and a low-to-moderate crime rate. Most of the homes are owner-occupied, a few are rentals, and the occupants are hard-working, law-abiding, moderate-income people who care about their neighborhood. The houses are at minimum 20 to 30 or more years old and are showing signs of age.

Keep in mind though, this neighborhood is not perfect—it has some warts. There is some crime and families have their problems, just like everywhere else. Lifestyle changes can occur suddenly as a result of retirement, job loss, illness, or death. These sudden changes can result in homes that become poorly maintained or that need to be sold quickly if the owner does not have the financial resources to deal with the changes. Foreclosures are not uncommon in these neighborhoods.

Many of the homes are showing signs of age and a few may be vacant or even boarded up. But 15 percent to 20 percent of them have undergone or are currently undergoing renovation. Younger, first-time homebuyers who have down payment money and credit are attracted to the area because of the affordability factor. These young families are slowly fixing up their new homes, often with "sweat equity." Housing prices are in the lower to middle end of range for the community, and values are steady or increasing moderately. As discussed earlier, the real estate market in the neighborhood is active, based on current, pending, and sold listings during the past 12 months.

Every city, town, suburb, village, or rural community has at least one, if not many, areas that fit this description of the ideal older neighborhood. Your agent will be able to help you identify several of these "pockets of opportunity" in your community. This is where you want to focus your attention, because it is in these areas that you will consistently find the fixer-uppers that will meet our investment criteria. Figure 4.1 provides you with a convenient checklist to use in selecting neighborhoods to work in.

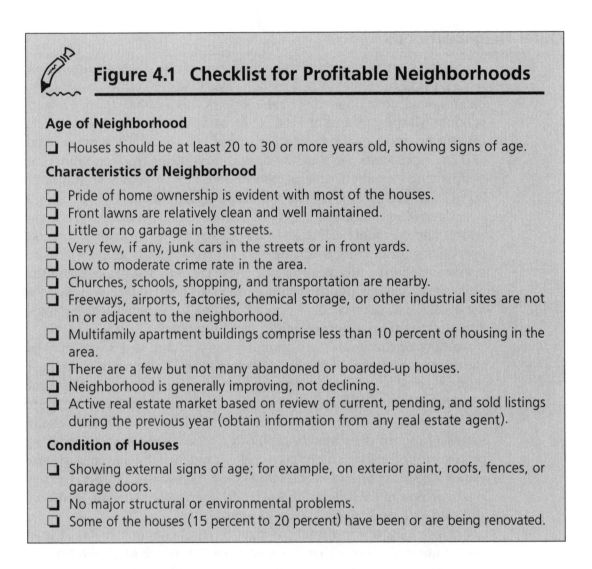

Figure 4.1 Checklist for Profitable Neighborhoods

Age of Neighborhood
❑ Houses should be at least 20 to 30 or more years old, showing signs of age.

Characteristics of Neighborhood
❑ Pride of home ownership is evident with most of the houses.
❑ Front lawns are relatively clean and well maintained.
❑ Little or no garbage in the streets.
❑ Very few, if any, junk cars in the streets or in front yards.
❑ Low to moderate crime rate in the area.
❑ Churches, schools, shopping, and transportation are nearby.
❑ Freeways, airports, factories, chemical storage, or other industrial sites are not in or adjacent to the neighborhood.
❑ Multifamily apartment buildings comprise less than 10 percent of housing in the area.
❑ There are a few but not many abandoned or boarded-up houses.
❑ Neighborhood is generally improving, not declining.
❑ Active real estate market based on review of current, pending, and sold listings during the previous year (obtain information from any real estate agent).

Condition of Houses
❑ Showing external signs of age; for example, on exterior paint, roofs, fences, or garage doors.
❑ No major structural or environmental problems.
❑ Some of the houses (15 percent to 20 percent) have been or are being renovated.

Just Say No to Expensive Neighborhoods

As a general rule of thumb, just say no to more expensive neighborhoods. On occasion, you can find opportunities here, but I would suggest that your time is better spent elsewhere. Let's take a look at the downsides associated with these areas:

- Very few houses ever become fixer-uppers in these neighborhoods, therefore your time and effort versus potential reward ratio is not attractive.

- Costs to purchase and renovate can be huge. You are better off spreading your risk capital out over two or three smaller deals rather than one big deal.
- The pool of potential buyers is very small compared to the lower-priced homes. The marketing period can be much longer, resulting in significantly higher holding costs (loan payments, utilities, insurance).
- Higher-priced homes are subject to very volatile price fluctuations in both directions. Your risk is in a downtrending market, where these homes will typically decrease in value at a much higher rate than the lower-end houses.

The bottom line is that low-risk business opportunities are just not found in these neighborhoods. If you happen to stumble on to a potential candidate there and you happen to have a good source of money at your disposal, you might consider a more expensive house in an upscale neighborhood. Just make sure the external economic factors are on your side—strong housing demand, growing economy, and downtrending interest rates. Otherwise, you are just shaking the dice!

Fixer-Upper Candidates: The Good, the Bad, and the Ugly

This is the part where you get to meet your business partner, so to speak, the fixer-upper. To set the stage for this introduction, you have to get rid of some of your preconceived notions about the type (physical condition) of house you're interested in.

The movie title *The Good, The Bad, and The Ugly* provides excellent adjectives for the range of fixer-uppers that you might consider. *The good* would be the house that needs a little touch-up paint here and there and maybe some new carpet and fresh front landscaping. *The bad* is a total wreck that basically needs to be bulldozed! *The ugly* needs extensive plastic surgery. Let's discuss each one of these in more detail so that you have a good mental picture of each type.

The Good Fixer-Upper

Your instincts and preconceived notions probably tell you that this is the type of house you should be looking for. It's basically a nice house that just needs a little cosmetic touch-up work here and there to make it shine. In the rehab business, nothing could be further from the truth—you will not make money buying the cosmetic fixer-upper! Now, I know that this is contrary to your instincts and contrary to what you've read or been told. So let me explain.

The problem, from a business standpoint, is that you can rarely buy a house that just needs some minor repairs at a price sufficiently below retail market value for you to make a reasonable profit on the time and money invested. For example, let's say the house needs fresh paint inside and out and new carpet—everything else is fine. We'll estimate the cost for these items at $5,000. If the full retail market value for the house is $125,000 in this neighborhood, the homeowner typically will list the house for that amount. The most that he will come off the price is usually the $5,000 needed to make the repairs. He is not a motivated seller, because he knows that someone who is willing to invest a little sweat equity and wants to live in the house will come along and pay between $120,000 and $125,000.

Where is your profit in a deal like this? It makes absolutely no sense to invest $120,000 plus $5,000 in repairs and get $125,000 in return. In fact, you would probably lose money on this deal when you factor in holding and selling costs.

This is the type of house that may make sense for a long-term investor looking for good rental property or an owner-occupant who wants to earn a little sweat equity. It is not the type of house that fits the rehab investment criteria. So don't waste your time or your real estate agent's time looking at these properties.

The Bad Fixer-Upper

This house is the one you want to stay away from—it has the wrong things wrong. It has major structural or environmental problems that cannot be economically solved. Examples of structural problems could include serious defects in the concrete slab or concrete block foundation, or no permanent foundation (e.g., it is built on wooden timbers); it may be sitting on ground that has subsided or is subject to flooding or mudslides; it might have extensive wood rot or termite damage throughout the house; the subfloor could be extensively damaged; a two-story house might have no bathrooms on the upper level; its rooms could be too small and impossible to enlarge because one or more walls contain load-bearing support beams; it might be a one-bathroom house in a neighborhood that has all two-bath homes; wiring, heating, and plumbing could be inoperable or need to be completely replaced.

Major environmental problems would be things like extensive presence of exposed asbestos insulation (in ceiling, walls, and pipes), lead-based paint that is chipped and peeling and must be removed from the entire structure, heavy chemical contamination of soil, contaminated drinking-water supply, and high-level indoor radon contamination.

Keep in mind that the mere presence of asbestos insulation or lead-based paint are not deal killers—it is only in those instances where the exposed areas cannot be easily patched and where the entire structure needs to be "treated" that the cost to fix would likely be prohibitive. The same is true of minor radon contamination that frequently can be corrected at a modest expense (Chapter 13).

These major structural and environmental problems are deal-killers—*Never ever buy a house with these problems.* You cannot throw enough money at these houses to ever satisfactorily fix the problems, and some of the problems are not fixable, period. In addition, houses with a history of serious contamination problems will always carry with them the potential for long-term liability. You don't need these headaches. The bulldozer is the only solution and that's not the business you're in.

The Ugly Fixer-Upper

Okay, you're finally ready to meet your future business partner and the object of your quest. The only problem is that this house is indeed, ugly. Get over it though, because this is the house that will make you money. Your job is to turn lemons into lemonade.

Let's take a look at the characteristics of the typical, ugly fixer-upper.

Exterior of house
- Curb appeal is at or near zero.
- There is little, if any, front landscaping.
- Exterior paint is faded and chipped; stucco is cracked; or siding is falling apart.
- Roof shingles are curled up or missing.
- Front door is battered and beaten; screen door is ripped.

- Windows are cracked, broken, or boarded up.
- Driveway and walkways are in poor condition.

Interior of house
- Strong odors are present.
- Rooms are dark, with poor lighting.
- Carpeting and flooring are worn out.
- The ceiling has water stains, holes, or cracks.
- There are holes in the drywall or plaster walls.
- The bathroom has soft, water-damaged flooring.
- There is mold around tiles in shower or tub.
- Kitchen cabinets are falling apart and missing hardware.
- Light fixtures are broken or missing.
- Furnace is not operating properly.

Is this really the house you're looking for? You bet it is! This is exactly the house you're looking for. It's a real mess all right, but it appears that the key structural components are sound (this will later be verified by a professional inspector). The repairs will cost a pile of money but all can be fixed with no long-term liability issues. The challenge will be in negotiating a good price, based on the cost of repairs, desired profit margin, and after-repaired value (retail market value).

Is this the type of house you imagined as your target property? Probably not, but let me assure you that this is exactly the type of house that will make you the big bucks, if you can purchase it at the right price. This is the classic "dirty dog" property. Obviously, there is not going to be a lot of competition for this house (there will probably be some), because most people would never even get out of their car to look inside. The trick in this business is to develop a knack for seeing the possibilities, not just the problems.

What is it about this type of property that makes it attractive? Why is this house better than the cosmetic fixer-upper? The primary difference is not the magnitude of the problems—it is the motivation and flexibility of the seller. The seller is likely to be either an individual who couldn't care less about the house, as evidenced by its current condition, or a bank that took the property back in a foreclosure and wants to get it off the books. In either case, the seller knows the house is in junky condition and realizes that it will only sell at a large discount and well below retail value for the neighborhood. The seller will eventually come to realize the need for some flexibility in price, financing terms, or both, in order to get the property sold.

If the house is boarded up or just vacant, so much the better. Just imagine what the owner of a boarded-up or vacant property is asking. "Will someone please take this junker off my hands?" Flexibility in financing terms also is an important characteristic of this seller. He or she knows that traditional, conventional financing is not going to be an option for a buyer of the house in its as-is condition, so the seller likely will need to provide some owner financing. This set of circumstances and a motivated seller who is receptive to flexible terms will create the opportunity for you to purchase at a bargain price that will make you money.

How do you find these junker properties, in decent neighborhoods, with motivated sellers? You get your real estate agent to do it for you.

Working with Your Agent to Find Bargain Properties

*N*ow you are ready to begin your search for that bargain handyman property that will make you a pile of money. You know it's out there, just waiting for you and your real estate agent to find it.

At this point, many people take the path of least resistance—they simply tell their agent to call them when they have found a candidate property to look at. I am suggesting that you be a little more proactive in the process. Some agents know exactly what to do and how to do it; others may need a little prompting from you. Following are some ways to search the MLS database to pinpoint neighborhoods and specific target properties. Make sure to ask your agent to do these searches and show you the results.

Goldmining for Properties in the MLS

Let's say you're in Denver and you have your eye on a neighborhood called Snow Heights. You've done a preliminary review using the neighborhood checklist in Figure 4.1, and everything looks good so far. As you drive around, you notice some For Sale signs from both FSBOs and real estate agents. At this point, you don't know much about the prices in the neighborhood or how active the market has been, so you call up or go visit your real estate agent and say, "I'd like to get a comparative market analysis for the Snow Heights addition, using all active, pending, and closed sales that have occurred within the past year."

Within two to three minutes maximum, your real estate agent will have a nice printout of all the information you requested, plus some very interesting statistics. Figure 5.1 shows you an example of the type of information this kind of search reveals.

This data will give you an excellent snapshot of the current real estate market and activity in the neighborhood over the past year. You will gain a good feel for the price range and average prices of houses sold, the level of activity, currently active listings, and some idea of cost per square foot. Armed with this basic information, you can intelligently begin your search for bargains in the neighborhood and just as importantly, you have an idea of the maximum retail value you could sell a house for in the area.

Using the sample MLS printout in Figure 5.2, let's look at the active listings in the neighborhood. Listing #52610, located at 1816 Field Dr. NE, particularly attracts our attention because of the low dollar-per-square-foot value at $54.81. Figure 5.3 gives the detailed MLS listing information on this property.

Deciphering the MLS lingo is a little difficult at first, but see if you can follow along as I pick out some of the important information: The house is listed at $99,000 and is a 1,806-square-foot, three-bedroom, 1¾ bath, pueblo style (flat roof) home with a two-car attached garage. The house is about 35 years old and is on a lockbox (LBCF). The house is being sold "as is" at the listing price, and is touted as a "great deal for a handyman." For an additional $15,000, the owner or agent will arrange to install a new roof, new ceilings, carpet, and vinyl, and will warrant heating system and appliances. There is a $74,000 first mortgage (non-qualifying, assumable), and owner will consider all financing options.

After reading this, do you get the impression that this property is a good fixer-upper candidate, with a flexible, motivated seller? Yes, indeed. Here are some things that the listing reveals, without your even seeing the property or talking to the listing agent. The house is listed at a price well under retail market value. The house is a handyman special that, at a minimum, has a leaky roof, damage to the ceilings, has junky

Figure 5.1   Neighborhood Comparative Market Analysis Data from MLS

Active Listings (Ten Found)

	List Price	Sales Price	$/Square Feet
High	$164,900	N/A	$90.17
Low	85,900	N/A	54.81
Median	96,950	N/A	68.80
Average	106,890	N/A	69.98

Pending Sales (Nine Found)

	List Price	Sales Price	$/Square Feet
High	$134,900	N/A	$83.99
Low	84,900	N/A	45.42
Median	114,900	N/A	70.07
Average	110,350	N/A	70.86

Closed Sales (50 Found)

	List Price	Sales Price	$/Square Feet
High	$164,900	N/A	$94.35
Low	85,900	N/A	42.59
Median	96,950	N/A	70.65
Average	106,890	N/A	69.46

carpet and vinyl, and a heating system and appliances that may need repair. The existing $74,000 loan is nonqualifying and assumable (this means that you could take over this mortgage without any credit checks or income verifications). Because all financing options will be considered by the seller, including perhaps an owner carry-back second mortgage (where the seller agrees to loan you a portion of his equity in the form of a mortgage in second position, behind the existing $74,000 first

Figure 5.2   Active Listings Data from MLS

Summary of Active Listings

ML#	Address	List Date	List Price
#45816 SF* 2582	8907 Los Arboles NE $/SF 63.86	6/6/02 Bd† 3 Bt‡ 2	$164,900 Gar 2§
#49033 SF 2158	1829 Somervell St. NE $/SF 59.54	7/23/02 Bd 3 Bt 2	$128,500 Gar 1
#49288 SF 1374	2611 Gen. Chenault NE $/SF 90.17	7/18/02 Bd 3 Bt 2	$123,900 Gar 1
#52488 SF 1670	9401 Cordova NE $/SF 61.61	9/10/02 Bd 3 Bt 1	$102,900 Gar 1
#52610 **SF 1806**	**1816 Field Dr. NE** **$/SF 54.81**	**9/10/02** **Bd 3 Bt 2**	**$99,000** **Gar 2**
#49124 SF 1675	2509 Glorieta St. NE $/SF 56.65	7/23/02 Bd 3 Bt 2	$94,900 Gar 0
#54783 SF 1108	9505 Woodland Ave. NE $/SF 84.38	10/17/02 Bd 3 Bt 1	$93,500 Gar 0
#47246 SF 1108	9018 Claremont NE $/SF 79.37	6/20/02 Bd 3 Bt 1	$87,950 Gar 0
#55162 SF 1155	9204 Claremont NE $/SF 75.71	10/25/02 Bd 2 Bt 1	$87,450 Gar 1
#52985 SF 1165	9524 Woodland NE $/SF 73.73	9/18/02 Bd 4 Bt 1	$85,900 Gar 0

*SF = Square Feet
†Bd = Bedrooms
‡Bt = Bathrooms
§Gar = Garage

Figure 5.3   Listing, 1816 Field Drive

ML# 52610 Stat A AD   1816/ FIELD DR./NE LP$ 99000 Area 5/NEHTS
LOMETRO1 LS 60×110 +/–   SF 1806+/–   Age 35+/–   ZA H20
OwnAgt N Lgl LOT 17 BLK 138 SNOW HEIGHTS ADD

——————————————— LISTING OFFICE INFORMATION ———————————————

HowShown: LBCF
Agent: Name
Office   Name
Owner   Name
Tenant   Name

————————————————— GENERAL INFORMATION —————————————————

Style TRACT/   Type SINGLE Gar 2/AG/OTHER #Bdrm 3 #Bth 1.75
Floor CARPET/   Bldr UNKNOWN GarOpen N   MBrBth 1
Roof FLAT/TAR-GVL FldZn N Face WS PavStr Y   MBth SHONLY
OthRm FAMILY/SERVICE/   View Ext Feat OTHER /
Const FRAME/STUCCO/   LandScap F&B / / /

———————————— APPROX ROOM SIZES AND DESCRIPTIONS ————————————

Living   25×13/MCA/OTHER   Fam-Den   19×15/MCA/FIREPLC
DiningRm   11×10/MCA   Kitchen   12×11/MVA/GASELEC/
MstrBdrm   12×11/MCA/CEILFAN   2ndBdrm   12×10/MCA
Dir FROM WYOMING EAST ON INDIAN SCHOOL TO FIELD AND NORTH TO HSE.
*** "AS IS" AT LIST PRICE*** GREAT DEAL FOR HANDYMAN***
FOR $114,900 EVERYTHING NEW! ROOF, CEILINGS, CARPET, VINYL, INSPECTED AND REPAIRED
HEATING AND APPLIANCES W/1 YEAR WARRANTY. ALL UPDATES WILL BE DONE PRIOR TO CLOSING.
BUYER WILL HAVE CHOICE OF COLORS. FOR MORE INFO, CALL L/A @263-XXXX

————————————————— UTILITIES INFORMATION —————————————————

Heating   GAS   /2+UTS   /   /   Cooling   EVAP /
Water   CITY /   /   /   /   Sewer   CITY /

————————————————— ADDITIONAL FEATURES —————————————————

Oven/Range   OTHER   INTERIOR   /   /   /   /
Dishw N   Disp   N   Comp N   Wind METAL/SASH   Yard /
Refrg Y   Wash   N   Dryer N   Misc OTHER   Rent /
Micro N   Intrcm N   Hndcp N   PL   N   Tenant Pays
             Skylit N   Cable Y   FP   Y   Laundry   SER/

————————————————— FINANCIAL INFORMATION —————————————————

1Bal$ 74000/NOQUAL/RECDOT/   IR 11.000% 1P $720 PI$ 726 1H
2Bal$ 0/NONE
3Bal$ 0/NONE
TE $ 74000
Finance Considered   ALL /

mortgage), there is the possibility of a low down payment or no-down deal. Do you think you could get the repairs that are listed done for less than $15,000? Of course you could! This property is definitely one you would want to go out and inspect.

Like any good database of information, the MLS can be searched for key words or phrases that are contained within the listings. Here are some good ones to have your agent use in searching active listings: *handyman, handyman special, as is, TLC, needs work,* and *motivated seller.* Another favorite one that I like to search is *VLB,* which indicates the house is "vacant on lockbox." Anytime you have a vacant house, chances are you have an owner who is making double house payments and is motivated to sell quickly. Ask your real estate agent to do some searches using these words and phrases—you may be surprised at what pops up. I recently did a search in the Albuquerque MLS and came up with 27 active listings in the handyman category. You just don't have access to this information unless you're working with a good agent.

Most MLS systems are tied in with the local county tax assessor records. With this capability, another powerful tool is available—you can find out the name and address of the owner of any property. Let's say you're out and about one day, and you see a really "nice" junker property. There's no For Sale sign and the house looks vacant. You jot down the address, give your real estate agent a call, and within minutes, you can have the name and address of the owner. Your agent could then contact the owner and see if he or she might be interested in selling. This is a simple yet powerful technique that you and your agent can work on together. You scout the neighborhoods to locate prospects and the agent does the research and contacts the owners. A good team effort in this regard has the potential to uncover that bargain before anyone else even knows it's for sale.

Let me share with you another little "secret" MLS goldmining technique. Ask your real estate agent to search the MLS for all handyman listings that have expired or have been canceled over the past year or two. You can get a complete printout of the listing, with all the details, just like an active listing. This can be an incredibly successful technique for finding highly motivated sellers. In the case of expired listings, you have a seller who wanted to sell, but a buyer was not found during the listing period (usually a period of at least 90 days). Regardless of the reason the house did not sell, you have an excellent lead and little or no competition.

The same is true of canceled handyman listings. People cancel listings for many reasons. Again, it doesn't really matter why—what matters is that you have another good source of leads for finding potentially motivated sellers. With both expired and canceled listings, you have your agent look up the owner's name and address via the MLS tax records, and then simply contact the owner to see if he or she is still interested in selling. This technique can be very productive, but is often overlooked. Make sure your agent researches these listings for you.

Dialing for Dollars with FSBOs

For sale by owners (FSBOs) are an important segment of the marketplace that you cannot afford to ignore as you search for your handyman property. Many times, I have found excellent fixer-upper properties from this source. However, because you are conducting your search primarily through your real estate agent, you have to make a decision on how to handle FSBOs: either entirely on your own or through your real estate agent. Understand the situation—a FSBO has no obligation to any real estate agent. No commission will be paid to an agent, unless that agent can get the owner to agree to either list the property or agree to a one-time showing with a negotiated commission if the property is sold. In many cases, FSBO owners have no interest in dealing with agents. In other cases, they are more than happy to agree to a one-time showing. You just never know.

In fairness to your agent, here's how I recommend dealing with the situation. Take the lead in contacting FSBOs over the telephone. If you find a hot prospect, tell your agent about it to give him or her an opportunity to get a listing or a one-time showing agreement. If the agent strikes out, you can move on it with a free conscience and your agent will appreciate your looking out for his or her interests.

Plan to spend a couple of hours each and every week calling FSBOs. Sit down with the Sunday classifieds section of your local daily newspaper, the weekly papers, Help-U-Sell listings, or *For-Sale-By-Owner* magazine (not available in all areas), and begin your initial screening of properties. You're looking for some indication that the property may be a fixer-upper. The smart owner who wants to attract attention to an ad will include the usual key words: *handyman special, needs TLC, selling as is,* and so forth. If not, you can sometimes get some clues based on area or neighborhood. Go through and circle every one that looks interesting and then start calling.

You know what your criteria are, so your job is to find out if the particular house meets those criteria. If the house is not advertised as a handyman, you need to find out what the condition is, over the phone. Just say something like this, "I couldn't tell from your ad, but what I'm looking for is a house that needs a little work. Is your house already fixed up?" You'll be able to tell immediately if you have a prospect or not. If not, and before you hang up, always ask this question, "Do you know of any other houses for sale in the neighborhood that might fit the handyman category?" I've gotten several goods leads just by asking this simple question. The point is, never pass up the opportunity to prospect.

I suggest keeping a dedicated notebook for this activity. Just jot down the phone number and address of each property you call on. You can write down other information as well, but the main reason for the notebook is to keep track of who you've called. Next week, you'll never remember if you already called on a house. If you're handy with the computer, set up a telephone number database and sort by ascending or descending numbers and keep it updated. You can then instantly see if you've called before.

Does all this calling every week seem like a lot of wasted effort? Well, if you do it for a week or two and then quit, it is indeed a wasted effort. Calling FSBOs is much like many other marketing techniques—it's a numbers game. Each call you make that is a bust gets you that much closer to the one where you hit the jackpot. Look at it like this: Let's say you diligently spend two hours each week on this for 50 weeks. That's 100 hours of your time. And let's say, as a result of all your effort, you find only one deal. On this one deal, let's assume you net only $10,000 (this should be a minimum profit target). That means that you made $100 per hour of effort. Are you making that much now in your present job?

The techniques discussed in this chapter are more or less the traditional paths for finding target properties. You and your agent should be able to identify many good prospects using these methods. But there is another whole world of real estate bargains out there that you should know about—the world of foreclosures. I call it the real estate underground. Let's find out more about it in the next chapter.

The Real Estate Underground

Foreclosures and Bank REOs

*E*very day all across America, people lose their homes because they can't make their mortgage payments. Without a doubt, it is a devastating tragedy for the families who face this dark reality. Why does this happen? The most common reasons are job loss, divorce, medical problems, or death of the breadwinner. Foreclosures are the "dirty little secret" of the real estate world, where properties quietly and involuntarily change hands, often at bargain-basement prices. The general public is generally unaware of these opportunities. If they do know of their existence, they will shy away because the deal is too complicated (lack of knowledge) or they just don't want to be involved in a transaction where somebody loses their property (it's not your fault).

But for the real estate rehab investor, these properties offer the potential for significant profits because they often are in bad shape and need renovation. The skilled foreclosure investor will buy properties at discounts of 20 percent to 50 percent of market value. This pool of acquisition prospects simply cannot be overlooked if you're serious about the rehab business.

In spite of the potential rewards, you need to understand that profitably purchasing properties before or at foreclosure sales requires you to have a good understanding of the laws and procedures that regulate this legal process. State and local laws regarding foreclosure differ widely from state to state, and it's in your best interest to acquaint yourself with the regulations for your area if you choose to pursue these opportunities.

Purchasing properties after the foreclosure, from the bank or other lending institution (referred to as REOs or real estate owned) is essentially the same as buying from any other seller in a normal transaction. And, as you will see, REOs are perhaps the best all around source of rehab properties.

Mortgage or Deed of Trust?

Before getting too far along in looking at opportunities in your local foreclosure markets, you need to know about how real estate loans are secured in your area—either through a mortgage or a deed of trust. As a practical matter, there is not a huge difference from an investor's viewpoint. In states where a mortgage is the most common instrument, the foreclosure process is usually referred to as a *judicial foreclosure,* because it is handled through a court process. In contrast, in states with trust deeds or deed-of-trust loan documents, the foreclosure is nonjudicial and is handled by the trustee who has been granted a power of sale in the event of default (note that some mortgage states provide for a nonjudicial process).

Most states use a mortgage as the preferred document. This is simply a two-party agreement between the borrower (the mortgagor) and the lender (the mortgagee), which establishes a special interest in the property known as a lien. In the event of default on the loan, the lender must file a lawsuit against the borrower, seeking to foreclose and obtain the right to sell the asset to recover the loan balance. The courts typically direct the local sheriff to handle this sale. This is a cumbersome, expensive, and often lengthy process that can last more than a year in some jurisdictions.

The other important issue with a mortgage is the borrower's right of redemption. All states give a borrower a certain amount of time to bring the loan current and avoid losing the property through foreclosure. However, many mortgage states (and some deed-of-trust states) give borrowers the right of redemption *after the sale of the property at auction.* This period could be short (one month) or it could last as long as one year, as is the case in Alabama and Kansas. In some mortgage states, the statutory redemption period precedes the sale.

Deed-of-trust states provide the lender with rights similar to those of a property owner, which has the effect of putting the lender in a much stronger position in the event of default. With a deed of trust, title to a property is actually transferred to a third-party trustee as security for the loan. The borrower is referred to as the trustor and the lender is called the beneficiary. In the event of default, the lender directs the trustee to hold a trustee's sale (after proper public notice) and auction off the property to recover the loan balance and associated costs.

If this is all a little confusing, the message should be clear—get help in understanding the laws and procedures in your area before you venture into the foreclosure markets. Your local county recorder's or sheriff's office is likely to have information on the foreclosure laws and procedures in your area. You should also check with a local attorney who is well versed in this segment of real estate law. I've included a summary tabulation of mortgage and deed-of-trust information, by state, in Appendix B. Be sure to check with your local authorities for the most recent information.

The Three Foreclosure Markets

The foreclosure cycle has three distinct phases, each of which offers a unique market in which the investor can participate. The preforeclosure phase is that period (which varies by state but typically is 120 days) between which the lender files a notice of default and the property is sold at a public auction (trustee's or sheriff's sale). During this period an investor can purchase the property directly from the seller. The second phase is the public auction or trustee's/sheriff's sale, where the investor has the opportunity to bid on the house at an auction usually held at the county courthouse. If the house is not purchased by an investor at the auction, the lender will take back or otherwise acquire the property and it becomes part of the bank REO inventory (third phase). Investors can then purchase the property either directly from the lending institution or through a local real estate agent.

Some investors specialize in one particular phase of the cycle, while others pursue all three. Figure 6.1 provides a summary of the advantages and disadvantages of each phase.

For the remainder of this chapter, attention is focused on the third phase of the foreclosure market—bank or government REO properties. This market is the most appropriate for the novice investor and many of the opportunities can be easily accessed with the help of your real estate agent. Those interested in more information on the preforeclosure and public auction markets are referred to Chapter 17, where some of the more advanced techniques are discussed.

Bank REO Market—Superstore for the Rehab Investor

This is the marketplace of choice for the rehab investor. It has all the advantages of the "traditional" market, plus some advantages you won't find anywhere else. Of the three foreclosure markets, be sure to get plugged into and participate in this one.

After the trustee's/sheriff's sale, if nobody bids on the property, ownership reverts to the lender. All lenders have an REO group or department that is responsible for getting rid of their inventory of REOs. It's kind of a backwater area of the bank, clearly out of the mainstream. Most banks don't like to advertise that they even have such a department—after all, it represents failure and a money-losing operation. As a group, REO departments are highly motivated sellers. To use the phrase made popular by Robert Allen in his famous book *Nothing Down,* they are the classic "don't-wanter" sellers. Banks are in the lending business, not the real estate business, and whenever they foreclose on a property, they are motivated to get rid of it as soon as possible.

Now, understand that the banks are not necessarily going to give their property away at any price. REO officials have bosses, boards of directors, and stockholders to worry about. However, if the particular bank has a large inventory of REOs, they often are anxious to work out a deal with any interested buyer.

Figure 6.1   Investments in the Three Phases of Foreclosure

	Preforeclosure	Public Auction	Bank REO
Required Cash	Low	High	High
Interact with Homeowner	Yes	No	No
Financing Risk	Yes	No	No
Ability to Inspect House	Yes	No	Yes
Clear Title Issues	Maybe	No	No
Homeowner Right of Redemption	No	Yes	No
Profit Potential	High	Medium to High	Low to High

Bank REO Departments

There are virtually hundreds of different brands of lending institutions throughout the country: banks, mortgage companies, finance companies, credit unions, and savings-and-loan companies, all of which will have REO properties for sale from time to time. The problem is, some of the lenders handle the sale of REO properties directly through in-house staff while others list their properties through local real estate brokers.

How do you find out what's available in your area? You'll have to contact all the lenders who are active in your area to find out how they handle sales of REO properties. Be forewarned that this is going to require some effort and persistence on your part. This is because it is not unusual to be bounced around on the telephone from one department to another, and in many cases you will need to make out-of-state calls to plug into the right office. Some lenders will put you on their mailing list while others require you to send a self-addressed stamped envelope each month to obtain a nationwide listing of their REO properties.

In recent years, there has been a proliferation of online foreclosure list companies who want to sell you subscription services. For a fee, they provide a list of bank and government (HUD/VA) REO properties and who to contact locally for more information. Sounds good, right? The problem is that many of the subscription services sell you useless and outdated information. Some try to sell you an annual subscription for $250 or more, while others offer a monthly subscription from about $15 to $30 per month. There are a few very good list providers, but you need to be able to spot and avoid those that hype ridiculous promises of deep discounts and fabulous wealth. Visit my Web site <www.rehabwiz .com> for current recommendations.

While you're busy making these contacts, start checking around with the local real estate offices to see who may be handling REOs for lenders in the area. Many realty offices maintain lists of bank REOs as well as government foreclosure properties (HUD/FHA/VA) that are currently available. Many offices advertise "free listings" of these properties as a way to attract you, the REO buyer, to visit their office. Take advantage of these promotions as a way to learn the players in the local market. Your real estate agent will be able to help you research this market.

The most important thing to know about lender REO properties is that everything—and I mean everything—is negotiable. Price, financing, and closing costs are obviously the key elements of any deal, and all are negotiable in any lender REO deal.

Financing deserves special mention here because it is one of the few times that I might suggest you consider borrowing money from a bank to acquire property. Many lenders offer financing on their REO properties as an incentive in order to get them out of the "nonperforming asset" category. They want to move the property and get it off their books. It is not at all unusual for these lenders to allow 10 percent or even 5 percent down payment on nonowner-occupied houses. In many cases their credit and loan approval criteria are much less stringent, as the lender is motivated to keep the loan in-house rather than to sell it on the secondary market. Some aggressive lenders will even kick in loan money for repairs, particularly if you show them a carefully constructed market analysis and renovation plan. The point is, there are few "rules" here, so don't be afraid to make an offer with some creative terms.

You need to understand an important point of psychology as you approach the process of submitting bids on REO properties. Oftentimes, when we prepare an offer on a house owned by an individual, we mentally include our knowledge or perception of the owner's financial situation. How much equity does the seller have? Can the seller afford to reduce the price? These factors shouldn't influence your calculations but let's face it, they sometimes do. When it comes to REO properties—forget it! The lender has no "equity" because it is free and clear of any loans. In almost all cases, the lender is going to lose money on any given property on which they foreclose because of the costs involved in the legal process, holding costs, and selling costs. It's just a matter of how much money they are willing to lose. Do you really care how much the lender loses? Of course not, so don't even think about this issue when you prepare your bids!

In the next chapter, you will learn how to calculate your offer or bid price. For now, just realize that your price may differ significantly from what the lender has published as the list price. Do not let this influence you one way or the other. Just prepare your offer, based on what the property is worth to you, and let it fly.

One of the most frustrating aspects of dealing with REO properties is the total unpredictability of how lenders make decisions on offers they receive. Don't even try to figure it out because I'm convinced it's a random process that cannot be predicted. Each lender has its own procedures. These are changed constantly, as economic conditions change both within and outside the walls of the institution.

The Secret of Buying Bank REO Properties

In a word, the secret to buying bank REO properties is *repetition.* You must be prepared to submit your offer over and over and over again until it is accepted or the property is sold to someone else. Because the process of offer acceptance is totally random, an offer that was rejected last month has a good, if not better chance of being accepted this month. I can't explain it—I don't know why, but I do know that it happens all the time.

One of my friends makes a game out of it. He sets up a three-week schedule for each property he's interested in, and diligently submits offers like clockwork, until the property sells (to him or someone else). He has even gotten offers accepted that were lower than his earlier offers! Use this as a model in your own investment activities—keep after it with frequent offers until the property sells. Without a doubt, you will end up with your fair share of successful deals, and at a price that allows you to earn a good profit. See Chapter 18 on success stories for one of the great REO tales of all time!

Government REOs—Steals and Deals from the Bureaucracy

The Department of Housing and Urban Development (HUD) is the federal agency that provides insurance to lenders against the risk of loan default through its FHA loan program. When a default occurs, the lender forecloses, files a claim with FHA, and the property is conveyed to HUD. HUD then sells these homes on the open market through local real estate brokers, on a competitive bid basis or through open-cry auctions. Nationwide, HUD takes title to 70,000 to 100,000 foreclosed homes each year. Some areas of the country are more active than others due to population density and local economic conditions.

Current economic conditions (2003) are such that foreclosures are at record levels in some communities. You would think that with this significant increase in inventory of HUD homes, bargains galore could be found. In fact, just the opposite is true. HUD bargains are much more difficult to find these days, particularly when compared to prior years. The reason is a unique confluence of unlikely events—record high foreclosures and record low interest rates. The economy has suffered a painful, multiyear recession, while at the same time experiencing a very strong housing market due to increasingly lower interest rates. As more and more buyers enter the market, competition has increased for affordable homes offered by HUD.

HUD homes can still be purchased at below market values (after-repaired value) if the home needs repairs. Remember, HUD homes are sold *as is*. For the most part, the cost of making repairs has been considered by HUD when setting the offer price on a particular home. The homes you want to focus on are the uninsured houses that need a minimum of $5,000 in repairs.

Uninsured HUD homes are the ones that do not meet minimum FHA housing standards and cannot be financed through an FHA mortgage. These homes by definition exclude almost all of the general public who would buy HUD homes on an owner-occupied basis as a primary residence. The only exception is the rare owner-occupant buyer willing and able to buy the home through the FHA 203(k) program, which provides financing for both purchase and repairs. This leaves other investors as your competition for these homes. And this competition can be fierce and very competitive in many areas of the country.

To get an idea of the HUD homes market in your area, go to the HUD homes Web site <www.hud.gov/homes>, select your state, click on Bid Statistics, and then choose the cities that are of interest to you. From this link, you will be able to see all of the HUD homes sold within the past 60 days, the asking prices, the number of bids received on each property, and the bid amount, as well as the winning bid amount. This will show you the level of competition in the HUD marketplace and the extent to which homes are being bought below, at, or above the HUD asking price.

In researching the update for this section of the book, I was struck by overwhelming number of HUD homes that are being sold at prices well above the HUD asking price. In cities all across the country, people are willing to pay more than the asking price, which is based on the *as is* appraised value. I noticed one home in Brooklyn, New York, that was offered at $275,000 and sold for $420,000–a whopping 52.7 percent increase over asking price. Obviously, this was a very desirable home in an area of high demand. But I am seeing the same thing (selling price higher than asking price) in almost all the cities I looked at during my research. This represents a big change from five years ago when I first published this book. At that time, many if not most HUD homes were selling at prices of 5 percent to 25 percent *below* asking price on a routine basis. The message is that times change and as a real estate entrepreneur, you have to adapt to the changes.

Does this mean that you can no longer find bargains in HUD homes? Not at all. It just means that they are harder to come by in most market areas. In my own city of Albuquerque, New Mexico, most of the HUD homes are currently selling at or above the asking price, just like most other cities across the country. However, according to the last 60 days statistics, six homes sold at prices ranging from 9.7 percent to 26.3 percent *below* asking price. I see this same pattern in other cities. Digging a little deeper, it appears that the less desirable "junker" homes are the ones that typically sell at below asking price. These are exactly the ones we want to go after.

Remember, the extent to which you can purchase a HUD home below asking price does not indicate whether you are getting a bargain. To me, a bargain simply means you are buying it at a price that can make you money. In some instances, you can buy a HUD home at or above asking price and still make money—sometimes a lot of money, if you know your market. That of course, is the key to success—knowing your market inside and out.

This gets back to the basic premise introduced in Chapter 2, using the Maximum Purchase Price formula. You must be able to figure out *with a high degree of certainty* what the house will sell for after the appropriate repairs have been completed. I discuss this in much more detail in Chapter 8. For now, the basic concept when working on HUD homes is this: calculate the maximum purchase price just like you would on any other property, and submit your bid accordingly.

In the current climate, you may not get the winning bid very often. That is okay. The last thing you want to do is get caught up in *auction fever* and overpay for a property. If you pay too much, your profit evaporates very quickly, which is not the purpose of the exercise! Keep your head and keep submitting those offers that are designed to make you money. That's what it's all about.

HUD's Infamous 203(k) Program

This was one of the all-time great financing programs for the rehab investor. Started in 1978, this program allowed investors to finance both the acquisition and the rehab costs of any single-family home (HUD home or non-HUD home), all in one long-term, assumable mortgage. Down payment for investors (nonowner occupant) was 15 percent of the after-repaired value. Investors could be an individual, sole proprietorship, or a group of individuals (corporations or partnerships were not allowed). In spite of all the red tape associated with this program, it was a pretty good deal for the aggressive investor who could figure out how to profit working in the system.

This was such a great program that I was going to devote an entire chapter to it in this book. Effective November 14, 1996, however, the 203(k) program was suspended to all investors, including investors desiring to use the program with HUD-owned properties. The moratorium remains in effect today.

What the heck happened? Apparently, some investors (along with lenders and nonprofit organizations) have been extensively abusing the program. According to HUD's Office of the Inspector General in its interim report issued on July 15, 1996, "The 203(k) program, as currently designed, is too risky because it permits investors, nonprofits, and lenders to walk away with big profits leaving HUD liable for the mortgages. The rehabilitation work is far from satisfactory. High claims and defaults are occurring on loans to investors and nonprofits and seem likely to increase."

For a long time after this program was suspended, it was thought that it would be reinstated for investors after some reforms were developed. However, it hasn't happened and there is no indication that it will ever again be available to investors. But you never know. Things could change tomorrow, so it's a good idea keep tabs on the program through your nearest HUD office or on the Web at <www.hud.gov> for the latest updates.

More Government Giveaways

HUD is not the only game in town—just one of the most popular! You can find bargain REO properties through a lot of other government agencies. Check out these potential sources: the IRS, the Department of Veterans Affairs (VA), the Federal National Mortgage Insurance Association (Fannie Mae), and county tax sales.

Internal Revenue Service

The IRS will sometimes seize the home of an individual who couldn't come up with the money the IRS claims is owed. The agency will then auction the property to the highest bidder, but for no less than what is owed to the IRS. Properties are sold as is, but inspection before the sale is allowed. All IRS properties are sold with a six-month right of redemption. Check with the local office on listings and bid procedures.

The Department of Veterans Affairs

The VA forecloses on loans just like HUD does and sells them to the public through local real estate brokers. You don't have to be a veteran to buy a VA repo. Check your local papers for VA listings. In some areas, the VA will auction properties.

Federal National Mortgage Association

Fannie Mae, or FNMA, is a good source of REO properties. After all, they are responsible for 25 percent of all home loans in the United States. The REOs are marketed through local real estate brokers or sometimes directly. Financing is available for many properties. To obtain a list of FNMA's REO properties in your area, go to the FNMA Web site <www .fanniemae.com>, click on the Resources link under the Home Buyers and Homeowners section, and then select the Fannie Mae-Owned Property Search link. Just enter the city and state of interest and you will see all of the FNMA REO properties currently available through any local real estate office.

County Tax Sales

Failure to pay your local county real estate taxes can ultimately result in foreclosure. This is particularly common with raw land or developed lots, but single-family homes are available in some jurisdictions. After a lengthy process, the county will auction the properties to the public. Check with your local tax collector's office for listings and procedures. This is an excellent source of bargain properties in some areas.

Bargain properties are out there in great numbers and with a little bit of luck and a lot of effort, you and your real estate agent can locate your fair share. Select several of the techniques that are most appealing to you, considering your local circumstances, and aggressively get after it—these techniques will become your niche in the market.

Probably the most fundamental question in the entire realm of the rehab business is, "How much should I pay for a house?" Let's go on to the next chapter and find out.

Count Your Chickens before They Hatch

Figure Your Profits before You Buy

*T*his chapter, although short, is perhaps the most important in the book. This is because it speaks to one of the most fundamental concepts of the rehab business—how to calculate your maximum purchase price before you make an offer on a house.

Knowing that you make your profit in this business when you buy, the technique of calculating how much to pay for a property is significant to your future success with this investment.

Start at the End

The biggest mistake in the buying decision process is the starting point. Novice investors have an overwhelming tendency to start their thinking process at the listing price. The thinking goes something like this: "Gee, if I can buy this house at a discount of 15 percent below the listing price, it would be a bargain." I'm sure this approach comes from the experience of buying a normal house, not a fixer-upper, where the listing price usually is fairly close to the true market value of the property. In this case, a 15 percent discount may in fact be a bargain;

however, this thinking process is dead wrong in the world of real estate rehab because it starts at the wrong place. Listing price is irrelevant.

The listing price of a fixer-upper house frequently represents a fantasy. It is the culmination of a dream on the part of the owner with the real estate agent directing the script. It is an attempt to capitalize on the "greater fool theory" wherein an unsuspecting buyer comes along and overpays for a property because of ignorance or deceit on the part of the owner or agent. Use of the greater fool theory has been very successful because of the lack of sophistication of the buying public. This concept is responsible for producing the famous real estate phrase *caveat emptor,* meaning *buyer beware.*

Maximum Retail Value

The correct starting point in any buying decision that involves a rehab property is maximum retail value (MRV). This is defined as the maximum price a knowledgeable buyer would pay for a property, after it has been completely renovated, considering recent comparable sales in the immediate neighborhood. It answers the basic question, "How much could I sell it for after I fix it up?" This is always the starting point in figuring out how much to offer on a rehab house. Unless or until you know this number, don't even think about a purchase offer. *Never buy a property unless you know how much it will be worth after it's fixed up!*

How do you determine maximum retail value? The easiest and most cost-effective method is to have your real estate agent prepare a comparative market analysis (CMA) for you. Your agent should be able to provide you with this estimate very quickly. Make sure you ask the agent to provide you with a printout of the comparable sales that were used. This will allow you to develop a sense of comfort that the estimate is reasonable. I would also strongly suggest that you go out and drive by these houses to further develop a "comfort zone" with the value estimate.

If you have any uncertainty about the MRV estimate, or if you're not using a real estate agent, you will need either to estimate the value yourself (based on your knowledge of sales in the neighborhood) or to hire a real estate appraiser to help you out. If you don't have a good fix on market values in the neighborhood you're looking at, a local appraiser is your best bet. Because you are not asking for an appraisal for borrowing purposes and you don't need a formal signed report, you should be able to negotiate a good price for such an estimate. In fact, the appraiser doesn't even need to see the house in order to give you a good estimate of what it will be worth after the repairs are made. Just provide the appraiser with all the details as you know them (including the all-important square-feet-of-living-area number), and a detailed list of proposed renovations. The appraiser should be able to give you a good number with no more than about an hour of work. If you want something in writing, ask for a letter of opinion. In the next chapter, I'll get into the details of appraisals so that you will know exactly what questions to ask your agent or appraiser.

Go Figure—Calculating the Purchase Price

The basic formula for calculating your purchase price starts with the MRV and then subtracts all of the various costs associated with the purchase, sale, and rehab, and *subtracts your profit.* By including your target profit in your purchase price calculation, it ensures that you will get one! The formula is shown in Figure 7.1.

Let's take a look at each of the subcomponents to make sure we have a good understanding of what to plug into the formula:

- *Purchase costs* are any costs associated with the initial acquisition. These could include, if applicable, any loan application fees, loan points and loan broker fees, closing costs, appraisal fees, termite inspection report, structural inspection fees, and buyer's broker fees. Do not include earnest money because that money is usually applied to closing costs and is already accounted for in that category. Likewise, do not include your down payment; it doesn't matter if you put 5 percent down or 50 percent down—this money is equity, not an expense, and it will be returned to you when you sell.
- *Rehab costs* are the costs of the repairs and improvements you plan to make on the house. This would include a detailed breakdown of all materials and labor expenditures necessary to get the house in "move-in" condition prior to sale.
- *Holding costs* are expenditures for services during the time between purchase and sale. This usually includes interest expenses for loans, utilities, taxes, and insurance.

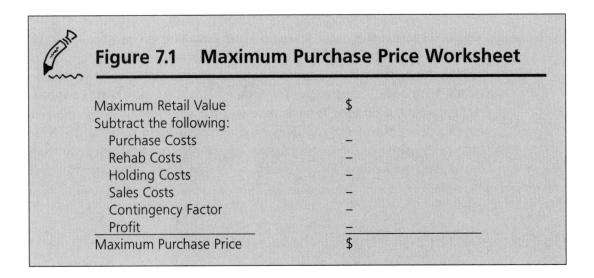

Figure 7.1   Maximum Purchase Price Worksheet

Maximum Retail Value	$
Subtract the following:	
Purchase Costs	–
Rehab Costs	–
Holding Costs	–
Sales Costs	–
Contingency Factor	–
Profit	–
Maximum Purchase Price	$

- *Sales costs* are the costs for selling the property after you complete the rehab. Use a figure of about 3 percent of sales price if you do the selling yourself or 6 percent if you use an agent. Also include your share of anticipated closing costs.
- *Contingency factor* (or "Oops Fund") is included to anticipate that you will overlook something. In the excitement and rush to "get the deal done," you invariably will miss some expenditures up front. Even if you did a thorough job at the inspection stage, something unanticipated always pops up during the rehab phase. If you feel confident in your rehab expense estimate, based on an inspection of every nook and cranny, use a figure of 1 percent of the maximum retail value. Otherwise, use a value of 3 percent to 5 percent, depending on your comfort level with the estimates.
- *Profit* is the amount you expect to net after all expenses. This is a premeditated amount that you establish yourself, based on such factors as risk, time investment, and dollar investment. How much do you want to make on this particular deal? If the property is in very bad shape and is going to require large amounts of time and expenditures for repairs, you should factor in a higher profit, on the basis that high risk equals high reward. For any rehab project wherein you are participating in the funding, I suggest a minimum profit target of $10,000. Anything less is just too much trouble for the effort. On smaller houses in the lower-

priced neighborhoods, $10,000 to $15,000 net profit will be the normal objective. Larger houses in the mid-priced neighborhoods usually will allow for higher profits. Generally, a minimum target of 15 percent net profit is suggested on houses that exceed $100,000 retail value.

- *Maximum purchase price* is the top dollar figure you, as an investor, would pay for the property. It is essentially the wholesale value of the house. Depending on your negotiation strategy with the particular seller, this may or may not be your initial offer price. In most cases, you will offer something less than this amount with your initial offer. The exception would be if you are dealing with a bid situation (public auction, bank REO).

Let's put the formula into practice with an example. We're looking at a house that meets our initial criteria. It's a three-bedroom, two-bath, 1,450-square-foot junker in a decent neighborhood. Maximum retail value, based on recent sales provided by our real estate agent, is $90,000. Rehab costs have been estimated at $9,000. Purchase cost will be about $3,000, which is primarily the points and closing costs from our private money lender. Holding costs will be about $2,500 for interest expenses and utilities during the four-month anticipated holding period. We will use an agent for the sale of the property, so at 6 percent this would be $5,500. We feel fairly confident in our repair estimates so we'll use a contingency of about 2 percent or $2,000. Our desired profit is $15,000. To see what our maximum purchase price should be, refer to Figure 7.2.

To the extent that the listing price on our property is near our maximum purchase price of $53,000, we will have a good shot at making a deal. Even if the listing price is not near our target purchase price, we will want to make an offer and keep making offers every three to four weeks until the property is sold. As we've learned, that's how it's done by the successful rehab investor.

Estimating two components of our maximum purchase price formula, the estimate of maximum retail value and the estimate of repair costs, requires special care. If we get these wrong, with wrong defined as "way off," then our ability to earn our maximum projected profit will diminish. It's important to get these estimates as accurate as possible. In the next chapter, we'll examine the key concepts of the art of real estate appraisal. In Chapters 12 and 14, we'll delve into renovations—which ones to make and how to calculate how much they will cost.

Figure 7.2   Maximum Purchase Price Calculation

Maximum Retail Value	$90,000
Subtract the following:	
Purchase Costs	– 3,000
Rehab Costs	– 9,000
Holding Costs	– 2,500
Sales Costs	– 5,500
Contingency Factor	– 2,000
Profit	–15,000
Maximum Purchase Price	$53,000

The Fine Art of Real Estate Appraisal

Determining Maximum Retail Value after Repairs

*T*he ability to accurately determine the maximum retail value of a house after repairs is one of the key fundamental concepts in the real estate rehab business. As we learned in the last chapter, you never buy a house until you know how much it will be worth after it's fixed up! Maximum retail value (MRV) is essentially the after-repaired value. You need to know this value not only to sell the house after the rehab is done, but, of equal importance, to calculate how much to pay for the house to begin with. Your strategy is to buy it wholesale, rehab it, and sell it retail.

The process of estimating MRV includes having a basic understanding of several fundamental concepts of real estate appraisal. Although I am a licensed real estate appraiser, I want to assure you that the concepts you need to know as a person in the rehab business are quite simple. The goal is to provide you with sufficient information so that you can intelligently discuss with your appraiser or real estate agent how they arrived at the MRV. It is well beyond the scope of this book to teach you precisely how to appraise a house and calculate MRV on your own. However, with the help of a real estate agent or appraiser, a novice investor can accurately calculate MRV.

Appraisal 101—The Basic Concepts

A real estate appraisal is simply an *estimate* of value. Note the emphasis on the word *estimate*. This is not rocket science wherein precise mathematical calculations result in irrefutable facts. Rather, it is more correctly described as an art because it depends heavily on the talent and judgment of the practitioner. The final outcome of the appraisal process is an opinion of value, not a fact of value. This opinion, while based on factual information derived from the marketplace, is always judgmental.

Modern appraisal practice uses three basic approaches to value, or techniques, to arrive at a value conclusion. You will see all three approaches to value discussed, to some extent, on all standard appraisal reports. The cost approach develops the value of a property (house plus land) by estimating how much it would cost to build the structure today, subtracting depreciation due to age and condition, and then adding in the value of the land the house sits on. The income approach estimates value based on the rental income a property produces (based on market derived capitalization rates or gross rent multipliers). Finally, the sales comparison approach estimates value based on the evaluation of recent sales of similar properties.

I will focus exclusively on the sales comparison approach, because it is the most relevant and most accurate technique to use when dealing with the typical single-family house in need of repair. The cost approach is really accurate only when dealing with new construction because of the inherent problems in estimating depreciation on older homes. The income approach is usually more appropriate for larger-income properties, such as apartments or commercial buildings.

The Sales Comparison Approach

The underlying theory behind the sales comparison approach to value is that the subject property, the one being appraised, should be worth about what similar properties have recently sold for. That makes sense, doesn't it? When you go to the supermarket to buy tomatoes, you expect to pay about what you paid last week, assuming the supply (availability) hasn't changed much and the quality (condition) of the tomatoes is the same. It's the same with houses—you would expect to pay (or sell) at about the same price as what similar houses recently sold for.

There are several concepts you need to understand about a "comparable sale." First of all, comparable sales are actual sales of properties where the transaction has closed. Appraisals are never based on pending sales or on active listings. In the realm of real estate appraisal, the term *recent sale* means a sale that closed, preferably within the past six months (up to one year can be used, if absolutely necessary). In a fast-changing market (either up or down), it's even more important to select sales that are truly recent (otherwise you get into the sticky issue of "time adjustments," which we will ignore in this discussion). Your task is to find at least three closed sales with which you can compare to the property under consideration. Once you have narrowed the field to recent closed sales, three primary criteria are used to select the comparable sales to be used in the appraisal.

Three Criteria for Selecting Comparable Sales

The three most important factors in picking out which closed sales to use in the appraisal are proximity; size of house; and age, condition, and amenities.

1. *Proximity.* The comparable must be located close to the house you are evaluating. In other words, it needs to be in the same general neighborhood. This is to make sure that you are comparing apples to apples, in terms of external characteristics that might influence value. What does the "same general neighborhood" mean? Well, there is no magic formula for this. (Remember how judgment plays a big role in the appraisal process?) In some urban or even suburban areas, neighborhood characteristics could easily change within just a few blocks. In rural areas, it could be several miles. Just make sure the comparable is as close as possible and that the neighborhoods are very similar, if not identical.

2. *Size of house.* We all know that a 1,200-square-foot house is going to be less valuable than a 2,000-square-foot house in the same neighborhood, all other factors being equal. So, you want to choose comparables that are as close as possible in square

footage to that of the house you are evaluating (the subject). For example, if the subject is 1,500 square feet (above-ground heated living area—this does not include garages, workshops, basements, or the like), ideally you would like your comparables to be in the range of about 1,400 to 1,600 square feet. If you have comparables right at 1,500 square feet, so much the better.

3. *Age, condition, and amenities.* You would like your comparables to be similar in age, general condition (junker versus doll house), and have similar amenities such as bathroom count, garage, flooring, fireplace, security system, pool, hot tub, landscaping, and so forth.

Adjustments—Correcting for Differences

How in the world can you possibly find comparable sales that meet all of these three criteria? You want them to be in the same neighborhood; you want them to be the same square footage; and you want them to be the same age, same condition, and have the same features and amenities? Impossible!

Well, you're absolutely right. It usually is impossible to find three comparable sales that are identical in every way to the property you are evaluating. Sometimes, appraisers can do it with new, tract homes in an active subdivision. But with the older homes that you are targeting, forget it!

How then do you correct for the fact that you cannot find exact replicas of your subject? The answer is that you must make what are called *adjustments.* These simply are dollar amounts that you add to or subtract from the original selling price of your comparable, to compensate for the presence or absence of a particular feature, when compared to your subject. By making these dollar adjustments to comparables, you attempt to make the properties "equal" in order to determine the value of the subject.

For example, let's say your subject is a 1,500-square-foot house, with one bathroom. You find an excellent comparable that recently sold for $70,000. It is also 1,500 square feet, but it has two bathrooms. Because your comparable has a feature that is better than our subject, you have to correct for this. You do this by taking away from the comparable a dollar amount for the extra bathroom. You do this in order to make the comparable equal to the subject. Let's say that in your local market, the extra full bathroom is worth $2,000. Assuming all other aspects of the two houses are identical, you would subtract the $2,000 from the comparable's sales price of $70,000, and conclude that your subject is worth $68,000. It's that simple!

Now, if the subject has a feature that the comparable does not have, you compensate for this by making a positive adjustment to the comparable. In other words, you add dollars to the comparable's sales price. As an example, let's say your subject is 100 square feet larger than the comparable. In your market, you adjust at $25-per-square-foot difference. So, in this case, you would add $2,500 ($25 × 100 square feet) to the original sales price of the comparable. This then, would make the two houses equal for that feature. See how easy it is?

One very important thing you need to know about adjustments— the dollar value of an adjustment does not equate to how much it would cost to install the feature. Adding a full bathroom to a house may actually cost $4,000 to $7,000 (or more). But you, as a consumer in the marketplace, are not willing to pay an extra $4,000 for this feature. In fact, by comparing many sales of similar houses with and without the extra bath, we find that you are only willing to pay an extra $2,000 for this feature. The point is, for most features, the dollar adjustments are based on market-derived values, not on the actual cost of the feature. Furthermore, these dollar amounts vary with different price range and quality of homes, and certainly vary from city to city and state to state.

What this means, of course, is that I cannot give you a list of features that may differ among comparables, along with the dollar amounts for the adjustments. What is valid in Albuquerque is totally invalid for San Francisco or New Orleans. Adjustments are always derived from local market conditions. You will simply have to work with your local appraisers to find out these values for your particular market.

One final point on features and adjustments: So that you are not in any way misled, I want to emphasize that I have barely scratched the surface on this whole issue. There are many, many potential adjustments that may be appropriate in a particular case. And some of these can get somewhat complicated in terms of specifically how they are mathematically calculated. For example, there is the whole issue of how to adjust for differences in age, condition, and quality of construction.

It's just too complicated for our discussion—besides, it would probably bore you to death! Some other potentially important adjustments could include differences in lot size, location (e.g., adjacent to busy street), financing concessions, view, and landscaping, to name a few. Be aware of these issues and be prepared to discuss them with your appraiser.

Completing the Appraisal

The appraisal process goes something like this. The appraiser receives the assignment from you: "I need a letter of opinion on a house I'm thinking about buying. Right now, it's a junker. What I'd like to know is the current as-is value and how much it will be worth after it's all fixed up. In other words, what the current as-is value is and the maximum value it could sell for 'as repaired,' considering the neighborhood. I'll fax over the details on the house and a list of repairs."

The appraiser, after receiving all the information, goes to work on the computer, dialing into the local MLS system, and calling up all active, pending, and sold listings within about a one-mile radius of the house. Based on a review of this preliminary information, the appraiser will select four or five potential comparable candidates from the sold listings (active and pending listings are reviewed just to get a feel for current market activity in the neighborhood).

Three of the comparables will be selected for the final analysis, based primarily on similarities to the subject, including the subject's future renovated condition. The information will then be entered into the appraiser's software program, with all of the appropriate adjustments. The software program will do the math automatically, making either positive and negative adjustments as appropriate to the original selling price of the comparable. This process is then completed for each of the three comparables. The end result is three usually different values. For example, after all adjustments, the values might be something like $89,000, $86,500, and $88,000. This is normal and is referred to as the *range of value.* Figure 8.1 shows an actual appraisal with adjustments for each comparable resulting in the range of value numbers. The appraiser will then do what's called the *final reconciliation,* which is the somewhat subjective process of selecting the final value. The reconciliation is essentially based on the appraiser's judgment as to which comparable is

Figure 8.1   Sample Appraisal Sales Comparison Analysis

FEATURE	SUBJECT	SALE 1		SALE 2		SALE 3	
Address	1210 Autum Drive	1380 Winter Lane		1401 Spring Court		1222 Summer Drive	
Proximity to Subject		3 Blocks Northeast		2 Blocks West		1 Block West	
Sales Price	$	$	167,800	$	161,400	$	165,900
Price/Gross Liv. Area	$ 0.00 ☑	$ 82.66 ☑		$ 86.22 ☑		$ 86.68 ☑	
Data & Verif. Sources		Exterior, MLS		Exterior, MLS		Exterior, MLS	
VALUE ADJUSTMENTS	DESCRIPTION	DESCRIPTION	+ (-) $ Adjustment	DESCRIPTION	+ (-) $ Adjustment	DESCRIPTION	+ (-) $ Adjustment
Sales or Financing		Convt. DOM 87		Cash DOM 92		Convt. DOM 71	
Concessions		Non Disclosed		Non Disclosed		Non Disclosed	
Date of Sale/Time		Current		Current		Curent	
Location	Seasons Park	Seasons Park		Seasons Park		Seasons Park	
Site	.22 Acre	.22 Acre		.22 Acre		.22 Acre	
View	Average for Dev.	Average for Dev.		Average for Dev.		Average for Dev.	
Design (Style)	Ranch	Ranch		Ranch		Ranch	
Actual Age (Yrs.)	A8/ E4--6	A8/ E4--6		A9/ E4-6		A7/ E4-6	
Condition	Average	Average		Average		Average	
Above Grade Room Count	Total 7 / Bdrms 4 / Baths 2.50	Total 7 / Bdrms 4 / Baths 2.50		Total 6 / Bdrms 3 / Baths 2.00	+1,500	Total 7 / Bdrms 4 / Baths 2.50	
Gross Living Area	1,947 Sq. Ft.	2,030 Sq. Ft.	-2,490	1,872 Sq. Ft.	2,250	1,914 Sq. Ft.	990
Basement and Finished	n/a	n/a		n/a		n/a	
Rooms Below Grade	n/a	n/a		n/a		n/a	
Garage/Carport	2 Garage	2 Garage		2 Garage		2 Garage	
Amenities	Semi-Custom	Semi-Custom		Semi-Custom		Semi-Custom	
	FP,SS,JT	2 FP,SS,JT	-1,000	FP,JT	+1,000	FP,SS,JT	
Net Adj. (total)		☐ + ☒ - $	3,490	☒ + ☐ - $	4,750	☒ + ☐ - $	990
Adjusted Sales Price of Comparables		Gross: 2.1% Net: -2.1% $	164,310	Gross: 2.9% Net: 2.9% $	166,150	Gross: 0.6% Net: 0.6% $	166,890

most likely to be representative of the subject. Once the final value is selected, the appraiser will report the numbers to you verbally or in a letter of opinion, according to your instructions.

You should know that this brief letter of opinion is no longer accepted by lending institutions for purposes of lending under federally insured loan programs. It may, however, be acceptable for loans through private lenders.

As-Repaired versus As-Is

You'll notice that in this example we asked the appraiser for both an as-is value and an as-repaired value of the house. Why? Because you will need both values if you intend to borrow money from a private lender. Ordinarily, you don't really care what the retail value is because if you buy it at all, you will buy it wholesale. However, as you will see in

Chapter 10, private lenders often loan on the basis of MRV, but use the as-is value in setting up an escrow for repairs. Remember that the as-is value is really the current retail value, which is irrelevant to the buying decision. You will take the MRV as-repaired from the appraiser and plug it into the formula in the last chapter and calculate the maximum purchase price. You will then be ready to make your offer on the property.

Once you become active in one or more neighborhoods, you will get to know the retail values of the type of homes you are working with. At that point, you will be knowledgeable enough to calculate the MRVs on your own. Until you reach that point, I would urge you to develop a good relationship with a local appraiser. A good appraiser has a wealth of information on local market conditions and can become a very valuable adviser for your real estate rehab activities. Take advantage of this resource.

Cash Is King in This Business

Even If You Don't Have Any!

*C*ash is king in the real estate business. With it, you can do anything. Without it, you just need to know how to get it! In this chapter, I hope to dispel once and for all the myth that you have to have money to make money. If you have some (or a lot) of money to start with, that's great—you will learn how to make even more money through the conservative use of leverage. If you have no money, you will learn how to attract money like a magnet, using your wits, not your credit.

Nothing Down—Alive and Well, but Different

Robert G. Allen is one of the great influences in my life, and in the lives of many others. He became rich back in the late 1970s and early 1980s by buying real estate with no money down. He became even richer by teaching his techniques to thousands of investors all across the country. His book, *Nothing Down,* was wildly popular and still stands today as one of the all-time best-selling real estate books.

The techniques taught by Robert Allen are just as valid today as they were 25 years ago. In fact, the techniques are timeless and will forever be valid. However, it is the *application* of the techniques that is much different today.

Back in those days, because of the extremely high rate of inflation, the buy (at any price) and hold strategy was a killer concept. Buy anything at full retail value, hold on to it for a few years, and you would make a lot of money. Leverage the deal to the maximum with borrowed money because it maximized your return on invested money (yield). If you paid too much, no problem; inflation would bail you out! Those were exciting times and many people made huge profits. I remember one house I bought retail in 1980 and sold 18 months later for a $50,000 profit!

But times have changed. Inflation is down to 3 percent or so and real estate values are based more on local supply-and-demand factors, as they should be. In some areas, prices continue on a downward slide (parts of southern California, for example). In other areas, prices are increasing. The point is, you can no longer count on price inflation to make you money. Therefore, buying retail and holding on for profits is no longer a viable strategy.

Nothing down has always meant *no*ne of your own *money down.* It doesn't necessarily mean no money changes hands or that the seller receives no money. Sometimes it happens—sellers are so desperate to get rid of a property that they will take notes for 100 percent of their equity—the classic paper-out deal. Realistically, in most cases money changes hands in a nothing-down deal—it just comes from somewhere other than your own pocket.

In Chapter 11 on negotiating, I will show you two scenarios, an all-cash offer and a split-funding offer, both of which result in a no-money-down deal. The seller gets lots of cash, but in this case it comes from a private mortgage lender.

The key difference in the application of no-money-down techniques that I suggest, is their use solely for short-term, quick-turnaround, rehab projects where the property can be bought wholesale. In contrast, I urge you to avoid no-money-down deals where you buy a property at or near full retail value and hold for the long-term appreciation.

What's the difference? The difference is in the period during which you are exposed to high-risk leverage.

Expose Yourself—Briefly—to High Leverage

In the contrasting scenarios just described, you are fully leveraged at the start, at least on paper. By definition, you are fully leveraged because all of your equity in the property is borrowed.

Let's say you bought a $100,000 house at value and you were able to buy with no money down. The outstanding loans on the property equal $100,000. If property values go up 10 percent over the next couple of years, you make $10,000 (notwithstanding cash flow, which would probably be negative). But what if you lived in an area where values went down 10 percent due to a recession or plant closings in the area? You still owe $100,000, but the property is only worth $90,000. You're upside down with negative equity and negative cash flow! This situation happens all the time all across America, and not just to investors. It happens to ordinary homeowners who, through no fault of their own, bought at the wrong time in the economic cycle. High leverage is high risk. When you expose yourself to it for long periods, there is a very good chance that it will eventually gobble you up.

Let's look at a no-money-down rehab situation and use a split-funding deal (for an example of how this works, see Figure 9.1). It's called split funding because the seller receives equity in two pieces—some with the down payment at closing, and the rest with a balloon payment in six months. (I discuss this further in Chapter 11.)

All of the money is borrowed, so I am also fully leveraged. But wait! Because I was able to buy the property wholesale, I had instant equity of $12,500 on the day I signed the deal. How much equity you get will depend on how far below retail value you are able to buy the property. In this case, the retail value was $55,000 and I bought at $42,500. By closing, my equity position was reduced to only $4,500 because I borrowed $15,000 for the down payment and repair costs. Regardless of the amount, I have already built in a small cushion. At this point, I have a loan-to-value ratio of 92 percent ($50,500 in loans divided by $55,000 value), which is a high-leverage situation. Over the next three months, I spent $8,000 on repairs (the original $7,000 estimate was low) and now have a house worth $73,000. I've just increased the value by another $18,000 giving me a total equity of $22,500. The loan-to-value ratio is now only 69 percent ($50,500 divided by $73,000).

Figure 9.1   Split-Funding Deal

Retail Value after Repairs	$73,000
Current Retail Value	$55,000
Repair Cost Estimate	$ 7,000
Purchase Price Wholesale	$42,500
Loan from Private Lender—First Position	$15,000
Loan from Seller—Second Position	$35,500
Cash to Seller at Closing for Down Payment	$ 7,000
Cash to Buyer at Closing for Repairs	$ 8,000

Within three months, I've gone from a high-leverage, high-risk situation to a much lower-leverage, lower-risk position. If the market dropped 20 percent tomorrow, I'd still make money! Remember this: If you use a high-leverage, no-money-down technique, make sure your exposure period is very brief. That's the beauty of the rehab business—the conservative use of leverage.

One final comment about the no-money-down philosophy: While I think it is a great way to do real estate business when used in a conservative manner, I urge you not to make it the centerpiece of your efforts. Too many novice investors get caught up in the terms associated with a deal (e.g., no money down) and don't pay enough attention to the most important aspect—the price! Focus on the price first, and then the terms. If you happen to get it for no money (of your own) down, great. If not, then do the deal anyway if you can get it for the right price!

All Cash, All Cash, All Cash

If you haven't figured it out yet, I like all-cash deals! Why? There are several reasons, but the biggest advantage is the steep discount you can often negotiate on an all-cash purchase. There's an old adage in real estate that the more cash you put in a deal, the lower the purchase price. The opposite is also true—the less cash down and more the seller has to carry, the higher the price. Cash is indeed, king.

You might be thinking, what's the big deal? Every time I've bought a house to live in, the seller always gets cashed out because I get a new loan. Well, you're right. In a traditional home purchase, that is the normal transaction and you will not get a discount for cash.

But are we talking about a traditional home purchase? No way! The houses we deal with are the junkers. These houses couldn't qualify for a bank loan if Bill Gates was the buyer! Unless you're going to be an owner-occupant under the FHA 203(k) program or something similar to it, you will not get a bank to loan you money on a fixer-upper (with rare exceptions). Don't waste your time and effort chasing loans with traditional lending sources, unless you already have a good banking relationship.

Many sellers realize that their house is not financable, particularly if they're working with a real estate agent, but many don't. So it is your job to inform them during your initial contact.

Without bank financing, what does that leave in the mind of the seller? Owner financing or seller carry-back financing. The sellers come to realize that if they are going to sell this junker, they are going to need to carry at least some of the financing. Is this something they want to do? In most cases, no. They are like you or me—they want all the money now!

This situation sets up the perfect scenario for a dual offer—an all-cash offer at a steep discount and an offer where seller financing is involved (more on this in Chapter 11). Put them both on the table and let the sellers choose.

What we're talking about here is cash—cold, hard cash that's needed to do the deal. Cash is needed in a real estate transaction for any or all of the following, depending on how the deal is structured:

- Earnest money deposit
- Cash out existing loans
- Down payment toward all or some of sellers' equity
- Real estate commission (sellers pay but usually need your money)
- Closing costs

No Money? No Problem—Here's Where to Get It!

Where are you going to get the cash to do your deal? If you're willing to work hard and use your brain, not your credit report, you can get the money you need to do the deals. It doesn't matter if you're broke or bankrupt; you can find the money for real estate investments if you find the deals. Find the good deals—and the money will come!

One of the absolute best sources of short-term money for your real estate rehab business is from private mortgage brokers or directly from private lenders. This is particularly true for those deals where you need cash at closing and can't get it from the other sources discussed later. The thing about these lenders is that, for the most part, they couldn't care less about your credit history. What they do care about is the equity in the collateral you are offering. Loans up to 70 percent of value are readily available, although 50 percent to 60 percent is more typical with the lower-priced fixer-uppers. Know anything about private mortgage brokers or private lenders? Most people don't, so I'm going to devote the entire next chapter to this little-known industry. For now, let's look at some other sources you could tap for money.

First, let's look at your own personal resources. The two best possibilities are the equity you may have in your home and money in your IRA account.

Equity in Your Home? A Good Source of Cash!

If you need cash quick, this is as good as it gets from a traditional lender. Any bank, mortgage company, savings and loan, or credit union is dying to loan you money. I don't know about you, but I get three or four solicitations in the mail each and every week from lenders all over the country wanting to loan money on my house! And frankly, there are some pretty good deals out there if you shop around. I got one in the mail today, offering a loan of 125 percent of my equity!

The most attractive deal I've seen is a line-of-credit arrangement. This is where you simply get approved up to a certain amount and then write a check for how much you need, when you need it. Interest rates seem fairly reasonable and several of the lenders are offering an interest-only payment plan.

Remember, your rehab deals are very short-term. You're going to be in and out in one to six months. Take your proceeds, pay off your loans, and keep the profits. Then you're ready to do the next one, perhaps without any loans!

The Secret Banks Don't Want You to Know about Your IRA!

The banks and the big brokerage houses like Schwab or Merrill Lynch don't let you invest your IRA (individual retirement account) money directly in real estate—they get commissions on stock, bond, and mutual fund transactions. And banks love to have your money tied up in certificates of deposit paying you 1.5 percent, while they loan out your money at 7 percent and pocket the difference! But did you know that if you have a self-directed individual IRA or an employer-based self-directed plan (Keogh, 401(k), SEP, or profit-sharing plan) you can legally invest money from it directly in real estate? Most people don't know that, but it's perfectly legal and specifically authorized by the IRS.

How do I know this is true? I recently transferred a portion (more than $100,000) of my IRA at Schwab into a self-directed third-party IRA administrator and have it invested in private mortgages yielding 15 percent to 26 percent per year, tax free. With respect to real estate, here's a sampling of IRS-permitted investments:

- Leveraged or unleveraged real estate
- Single- and multi-family rental properties
- Commercial real estate
- Trust deeds or mortgages: first, second, or third position
- Tax lien certificates
- Discounted notes
- Streams of payments from existing notes

Some of the third-party IRA administrators (TPAs) have a "certified draft" program that allows immediate access to uninvested funds for the purpose of purchasing real estate at an auction. Several such administrators are scattered around the country. If you have problems locating one, visit my Web site <www.rehabwiz.com> for current information and recommendations.

One thing to keep in mind about using your IRA for real estate investments is that you can't touch or spend the money until you retire. Well, you can, but you will pay income taxes on the distribution plus a 10 percent penalty. This is not the answer to generating spendable income, but it is a great way to build a healthy retirement fund, tax-deferred!

Let me guess, you're thinking, "Well that's great but I don't have an IRA and I need to make money that I can spend right now!" Am I right? Well, I do have a *possible* solution for you that involves the same technique of using IRA funds for real estate deals. The only difference is that you tap into *someone else's IRA.*

It works like this: You find a friend, family member, business acquaintance (anyone with some bucks in a retirement plan) and sell them on the idea of earning a great return on investment by lending you funds for a rehab deal. In other words, they become your private banker! Their funds are secured by real estate in the form of a mortgage or deed of trust, and you offer them a great interest rate—how about 12 percent or even 15 percent? I would set it up on a no-payment basis such that all accumulated interest and principle is due and payable upon your sale of the property. It's tax-free (or tax-deferred, depending on the type of IRA they have) income paid right back to their IRA account. It's certainly a heck of a lot better than what they've been making (or losing) in the stock market lately!

Another variation of this concept is to have two or more IRA investors buy shares of a limited partnership that you form for a specific project. This allows multiple investors to participate, but at a lower dollar amount of risk per individual.

Of course, to make any of this work your private banker(s) must have some or all of their funds with a third party administrator (custodian) that allows and is experienced in real estate investments (as discussed above).

One last point about using your own retirement funds for real estate investing: There are certain restrictions, including the following:

- You may not personally own property that you intend to purchase with your IRA funds.
- The purchase must be for investment purposes only.
- Neither you, your spouse, nor any of your family members (other than siblings) may have owned the property prior to its purchase by your IRA.
- Neither you nor your family members (other than siblings) may live in or lease the property while it's owned by your IRA.
- Your business may not lease or be located in or on any part of the property while it's owned by your IRA.

These IRS restrictions are related to "prohibited transactions" that are designed to keep you and your immediate family from personally benefiting from the use of your IRA funds. You own the IRA and your IRA is making money, but you don't get to "double-dip" by also getting to use the property while it's owned by your IRA.

Jump-Start Your Investing with Partners

Many successful investors got their start by working with partners. You can do the same. Do you have any family, friends, relatives, or acquaintances who have a little cash they might want to invest with you?

The basic philosophy of the arrangement is this—that you do all the work in finding the bargain property, getting it rehabbed, and sold. Your partner can be silent (nonparticipating) or active, but puts up some or all of the cash required. The two of you then split the profits in an equitable fashion.

If you have absolutely no money in the deal yourself, here's what I suggest as a fair split. In compensation for your efforts and expertise in finding the deal and managing the rehab and sale process, you receive a project manager bonus of $2,000, if the net profits exceed $12,000. The remaining profits after the sale would be split equally (if the net does not exceed $12,000, you do not receive the bonus but would equally split the proceeds). That's a fair deal, don't you think? You just need to convince your partner!

This type of arrangement is similar to what is commonly known as equity sharing. The difference is that most equity-sharing scenarios are in the context of a long-term, buy-and-hold situation. In contrast, this is basically just a short-term partnership arrangement (actually, the correct term is a *joint venture* if it's a one-project deal). Let me suggest that you make any such arrangement just that—short-term. Don't get yourself entangled in any long-term partnership. It may sound appealing on the front end, but it almost always breaks down somewhere along the way. Just do it one deal at a time, for as long as you need or want outside financial participation.

You don't need long-term partners. After you do one or two deals, you should have plenty of money to go it alone. Let me share with you the words of Henry David Thoreau: "The man who goes alone can start today; but he who travels with another must wait till that other is ready."

How to Attract Money like a Magnet

Okay, you're flat broke or you have very little money but you want to get started in the rehab business. You want to bring in a partner, an investor, or even a private mortgage lender. What do you need to do?

I've mentioned it before, but here it is again: Find the good deals—and the money will come. As simple as it sounds, that is absolutely the secret to attracting money like a magnet! If you use your brains, skills, and wits to go out and find the good deals, you won't have any trouble finding people to kick in their money.

In this situation, what you're bringing to the table is the opportunity for someone else to make money. What they're bringing to the table is the money to do the deal. It's the classic win-win situation, where both parties benefit. You get paid for doing all the hard work and they get paid for financing the project. And for you, it's a none-of-your-own-money-down deal!

The concept is good, right? The trick is in implementing the idea. The secret is in the packaging. In order to sell your deal to a partner or investor, you have to package it and put a bow around it!

It's one thing to approach a friend (with money) and talk, talk, talk in generalities about doing a real estate deal. What you have to do is be organized, be professional, and have the specifics written down. The best approach to attract partners or investors (or even private mortgage brokers) is actually a two-step approach: present your proposed venture and present the details of actual investment opportunities.

Present Your Proposed Venture

In the first meeting, you give them a copy and review your rehab project plan, as presented in Chapter 2. This gives them a clear overview of your investment objective, how you intend to conduct business, and a general approach to profit sharing. It's kind of a prospectus on your proposed venture that you review and discuss in a comfortable, no-pressure atmosphere. There is no deal on the table, so there is no pressure to make a decision today. However, you do want them to make a decision soon as to whether they are interested in looking at deals as they become available. People will judge you on how well you present your ideas and how clearly you have thought things through. People won't put money in the deal if they think you don't know what you're doing! Do your homework and put together the best presentation you can. You will need to decide whom you are willing to approach, but the key to success will be the presentation. You must present yourself as a go-getter, someone who has the skills and ambition to get the job done. Sell yourself, discuss risks and how they will be minimized, and then focus the rest of the discussion on how the other party will benefit from the relationship. Answer the question, "What's in it for me?" and you will succeed in getting people to participate in your venture. If they are interested, it's a good time (before an actual deal becomes available) to see your attorney and get a partnership or joint venture agreement worked out, including the profit-split arrangement.

You can obtain a suggested joint venture agreement from my Web site <www.rehabwiz.com>. You can adapt this to your specific situation and then have your attorney review it for you.

Present the Details on Actual Rehab Investment Opportunities

Some partners will have given you the green light to start making offers on properties that meet your investment criteria. This is the best approach, because it eliminates the step of having your partner review each deal before you make an offer. Some partners, however, will want to do just that—review each deal before the offer is made. That's not a big problem. Let's put together a worksheet that summarizes the key aspects of a deal so that you can present the information in a clear, crisp, and consistent manner. Figure 9.2, Investment Opportunity Worksheet, has been developed for this purpose. Note that some of the details of this worksheet, such as development of the rehab plan costs and private mortgages, are discussed further in subsequent chapters. Additionally, see Appendix A for an example of a worksheet that has been filled out for presentation of an actual deal.

Other Sources of Money for Deals

I hesitate to mention the use of credit cards as a source of cash to do deals, but many people successfully got their start this way. I hesitate because I know consumer debt is already at an all-time high. But, if you get your hands on five or six (or more?) cards with a $1,000 to $5,000 line of credit, you can generate a lot of cash quickly. I know you won't

Figure 9.2 Investment Opportunity Worksheet

Date: _____

Property Address: _____ City: _____ State: _____

Listing Type: ❑ REALTOR® ❑ FSBO ❑ REO ❑ HUD ❑ VA ❑ Other _____

Property Description: _____ Bedrooms _____ Bath _____ Style

_____ Sq.Ft. Age: _____ yrs. Garage: _____ car ❑ None

Other Information: _____

_____

Listing/Asking Price $ _____

Rehab Plan Cost Summary

Repair Category	Cost Estimate
Roof	
Foundation	
Site Drainage	
Electrical System	
Heating and Cooling	
Hot Water Heater	
Concrete	
Fireplace	
Termite Damage	
Exterior Wood	
Stucco or Siding	
Landscaping	
Junk Removal	
Exterior Paint	
Interior Paint	
Flooring	
Kitchen Rehab	

Figure 9.2 Investment Opportunity Worksheet

Bathroom(s) Rehab	
Interior Walls	
Windows	
Skylights	
Light Fixtures	
Doors	
Security System	
Sizzle Features	
Other	
Subtotal	
Contingency	
Total Estimated Cost	

After-Repaired Maximum Retail Value: $ _____
   Based on Neighborhood Comparable Sales

Maximum Retail Value	$
Subtract the following:	
Purchase Costs	–
Rehab Costs	–
Holding Costs	–
Sales Costs	–
Contingency Factor	–
Profit	–
	_____
Maximum Purchase Price	$

General Structure of Offer (check all that apply):
❏ All Cash   ❏ Split Funding   ❏ Seller Financing
❏ Assumption   ❏ Private Mortgage   ❏ Bank/Mortgage Co.

Figure 9.2 Investment Opportunity Worksheet

Financing Options and Profit Projections

1. All Cash—Assumes Private Mortgage and Investor/Partner

Purchase Price $ _____

Private Mortgage Net Amount
@_____% LTV (broker fees subtracted) $ _____

Additional Cash Required
- For Purchase _____
- Closing Costs _____
- For Rehab _____
- For Holding _____

Total Additional Cash (from Partner/Investor) $ _____

Profit Projection (Assumes cash-out)

Expected Resale Value $ _____

Private Mortgage Payoff $(_____)

Return Partner/Investor Cash $(_____)

Real Estate Commission @ _____ % $(_____)

Net Profit $ _____

Project Manager Bonus (if applicable) $(_____)

Adjusted Net Profit to Be Split $ _____

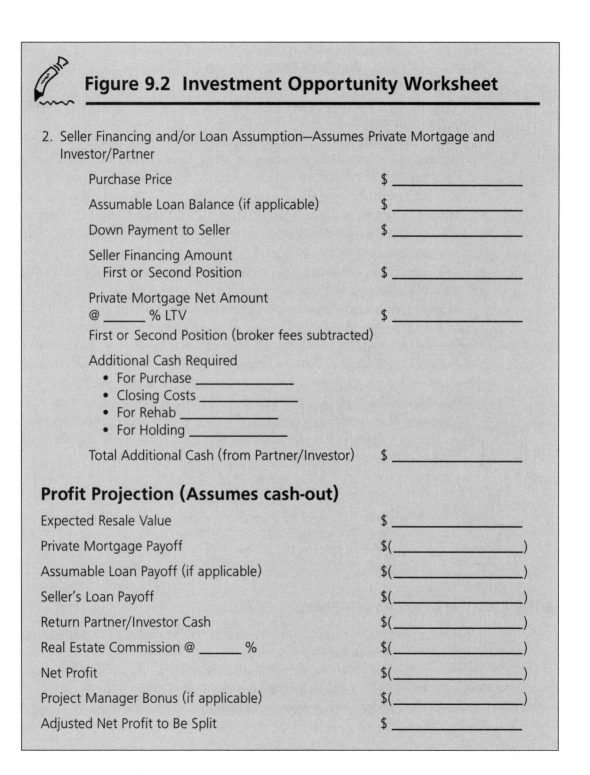

Figure 9.2 Investment Opportunity Worksheet

2. Seller Financing and/or Loan Assumption—Assumes Private Mortgage and Investor/Partner

Purchase Price $ _____

Assumable Loan Balance (if applicable) $ _____

Down Payment to Seller $ _____

Seller Financing Amount
First or Second Position $ _____

Private Mortgage Net Amount
@ _____ % LTV $ _____
First or Second Position (broker fees subtracted)

Additional Cash Required
- For Purchase _____
- Closing Costs _____
- For Rehab _____
- For Holding _____

Total Additional Cash (from Partner/Investor) $ _____

Profit Projection (Assumes cash-out)

Expected Resale Value $ _____

Private Mortgage Payoff $(_____)

Assumable Loan Payoff (if applicable) $(_____)

Seller's Loan Payoff $(_____)

Return Partner/Investor Cash $(_____)

Real Estate Commission @ _____ % $(_____)

Net Profit $(_____)

Project Manager Bonus (if applicable) $(_____)

Adjusted Net Profit to Be Split $ _____

have any trouble getting the cards, if you don't already have them. The typical American adult already has nine credit cards and receives about 15 solicitations each year! If you go this route, write it in blood that you will pay off the balances immediately on the sale of your first rehab investment property.

Are you worried about the high interest rates with credit cards? Have you done the math? Let's say you borrowed $10,000 at 18 percent on your credit cards. That would be $1,800 for a full year's use of the money. But, because you are only going to use it short-term, maybe six months on a rehab project, your cost would be about $900. Compare that to a 10 percent interest rate you could possibly get somewhere else. Your six-month cost would be about $500. Are you going to quibble over a $400 difference when the deal is going to make you at least $10,000? It's the cost of doing business!

Do you own anything of value that you could use for part or all of a seller's equity? A real estate note on another property is always a good possibility. It's a stream of monthly income that has value. If you offer this to a seller, always try to get credit for full face value of the current balance. Be aware, however, that a smart seller will discount the value depending on the duration of payments. The time value of money concept dictates that money received farther out in the future is not as valuable as money received today. Make your offer based on the current balance and see what happens.

Another favorite is trading your recreational vehicle (RV) for equity. I've never done this, but I know people who have. In fact, just today I saw an ad in the paper from some guy selling his house and wanting an RV for his equity. These deals are out there—people willing to accept RVs, land, cars, whatever. Get creative and make an offer!

Is the Existing Loan Assumable?

Remember, the cash requirements in a deal may just mean paying all or a portion of the seller's equity (and applicable closing costs identified previously). If there is an assumable loan from a private lender, FHA, or VA, then your actual cash requirement will be considerably less because the existing financing remains intact. This is a huge advantage to you as a buyer (or a seller).

Private lenders may or may not put a due on sale clause in their loans. Many do not, so their loans are assumable without qualifying. On the private mortgages that I make, I provide for a *qualifying assumption,* so that I can have the option to extend the loan to a new buyer and otherwise have some level of control in the sale. Also, I usually have an assumption fee or transfer fee that the new owner will need to pay at closing. This increases my yield on the loan, but it is also fair. An assumable loan is an extremely valuable piece of paper! Wouldn't you be willing to pay an assumption fee for the privilege?

The only other nonqualifying, assumable loans out there are certain VA and FHA loans. VA loans closed before March 1, 1988, and FHA loans closed before December 15, 1989, do not contain the dreaded due on sale clause and are freely assumable by anyone. Loans closed after these dates also can be assumed, but you have to qualify. If you run across one of these, check it out—it might be worth the paperwork hassle to qualify. Even though you intend to keep the house only long enough to fix it up, having a qualifying, assumable loan may be very helpful when you sell.

Structuring the Deal—Putting It All Together

With so many options and possibilities to choose from—all cash, split funding, private lenders, no money down, IRAs, owner financing, assumable loans, credit cards, notes, RVs—it's kind of confusing, isn't it? How do you decide what options to pursue?

Unfortunately, I can't give you a cookie cutter answer and tell you how to do it. All of the options I have identified thus far (there are many, many others) are simply intended to stimulate your thinking about possibilities. On any given deal, many of the options may not be available. And really, that's the point—you need to evaluate each deal independently and see what options fit the circumstances.

One of the most important considerations in any deal is the sellers' motivation and flexibility. The seller's situation and needs for cash will oftentimes self-select the solution. For example, if the sellers are starting a new business and need all of their cash now, then obviously an offer with owner financing is not going to fly. You absolutely must find out about the sellers' circumstances and needs in order to structure a deal that makes sense. This step is crucial. In the chapter on negotiating, I'll cover this in some detail. If you think the sellers might be flexible, use the dual-offer technique.

The other variable that will narrow the choices is your own situation. Maybe you haven't had or taken the time to develop partners to participate in financing projects, or you simply decide that you would rather go it alone. If you already have the financial resources, then you're off and running. If not, you will likely need the expertise of a mortgage broker who deals in private lending. As you will see in the next chapter, access to capital through this resource can make or break many a deal. The wise use of these funds can skyrocket you to success in the rehab business.

Another consideration is the endpoint of the process—how you intend to sell the property when the rehab is completed and you collect your profits. In many cases, you will want to be totally cashed out, and so you will want to sell to someone who can get conventional bank financing. This probably will be your goal in most cases—but there are alternatives.

During the normal economic cycle, there are periods when mortgage interest rates are sky-high and buyers are scarce—not necessarily because of the lack of demand but because they can't qualify for the payments with a conventional mortgage. To keep going in this market environment, you need to think ahead and create a situation where you can offer financing with the sale of your property.

For example, let's take another look at the split-funding deal shown in Figure 9.1. When the rehab work is finished, the property is valued at $73,000. There is a $15,000 first mortgage and a $35,500 second mortgage due to the seller in three months (as you recall, it had a six-month balloon and it took three months to finish the rehab). The total of outstanding loans, then, is $50,500.

In a tough market, I could have gone back to a private lender and gotten a 70 percent loan on the new value of $73,000. A 70 percent loan would have given me $51,100, enough to pay off all existing loans. Additionally, I could have negotiated with the private lender to get an assumable loan, probably with a five-year balloon. Then, I could offer the house for sale with assumable financing, a huge advantage in a tight market. I probably would not get all of my remaining equity ($21,900) with a down payment and would likely need to carry a second mortgage. But

I would have gotten a good portion of my profits up front, and I'd be off and running on the next deal (in real life, I sold the property to a buyer who cashed me out with a new loan).

So how do I prioritize the options? First of all, if there is assumable existing financing, I always grab it. The next issue is the seller's equity. I have a very strong bias toward paying off the seller with all cash—and of course, at a steep discount.

If the seller owns the house free and clear or has a very large equity position, I like the short-term, split-funding option. This often is an easy sell to an owner if you present it right. He gets a small but sufficient down payment up front, and the rest of his equity within a short time frame (6 to 12 months). You explain your plan to rehab the property and show him how the value will increase in just a couple of months. This provides him with an added sense of security, assuming he doesn't think you're a flake!

The strategy to buy low, rehab, refinance, and sell with an assumable loan is an excellent tool to have in your arsenal. I've used it several times in difficult markets. Unless you're in a slow market though, you don't need to use the technique on a routine basis, unless you want to use it as an investment tool for your profits—an excellent choice!

Of all the things that you may have learned in this chapter, there is one point I very much hope you get—you don't need to have money of your own to get started and be a success in the rehab business. All you have to do is be very good at finding the bargain properties. Find the good deals, and the money will come!

As I've emphasized all along, the key to success with this investment strategy is to be a talented finder of bargain property that has potential. Indeed, with this strategy you will be able to attract money like a magnet! One of the best sources of that money is someone you may not have met: the private mortgage lender. Let's move on and find out about these mysterious characters!

Spotlight on the Private Mortgage Industry

Show Me the Money!

Guard thy treasure from loss by investing only where
thy principal is safe, where it may be reclaimed if desirable,
and where thou will not fail to collect a fair rental.

—Money Lender's Credo,
    as explained by Arkadin in
    The Richest Man in Babylon (G.S. Clason)

*T*he credo of the ancient money lenders is still the guiding principle of the loan business today. Money is available at a "fair rental" if it is secured by an asset that can be reclaimed if the payments are not made. This is a sound business theory that makes sense to all the participants—the lender, the broker, and the borrower.

In practice, however, problems arise when investors and brokers (and government agencies) begin to erect barriers to the access of capital. Just because you offer a valuable asset as security for a loan and have the ability to repay it doesn't necessarily mean your loan request will be approved. In fact, did you know that about 33 percent of applicants who prequalify for Fannie Mae conventional home loans end up being rejected?

The Games Bankers Play

Many of us have run the gauntlet with banks to obtain loans for the houses we live in. For me, it's been a series of okay experiences because my credit and income have always been good. But I've seen the torture and pain inflicted by the banks in the faces of friends and family as they have attempted the run. Many fail because of the games bankers play: debt ratio too high, slow payment history, previous bankruptcy, credit dispute, period of unemployment, self-employed, and the list goes on and on.

From the perspective of a person pursuing a short-term rehab investment, bankers simply are not needed. They are entities of no direct significance or importance when buying the property. Harsh words? Perhaps, but for good reason—most of them will not loan you money on houses that need significant repairs, period. As I've mentioned before, there are a few exceptions, like the 203(k) program for owner-occupants, but we're investors and we're not interested in moving from house to house to get federal financing! Besides, who wants to waste the 40 to 60 days of time it takes these conventional lenders to make up their minds? It's just not worth the hassle and aggravation.

The Little-Known World of Private Mortgage Lending

Private money lending has been around since the birth of civilization. People with money will lend it, if they feel their loan is secure and they receive a fair rent. Somewhere along the line though, these private lenders have been overshadowed by the mainstream institutional lenders. Most people know little, if anything, about the world of private mortgage lending. Let me assure you, these private lenders are still out there in droves, anxious to lend their hard-earned cash on the right real estate investment.

One of my very first ventures was a fixer-upper located in a small town in Northern California, back in the late 1970s. The house wasn't in terrible shape but it needed painting, carpeting, and general cleanup. The best thing about it was that it had a nonqualifying, assumable FHA loan. I could buy the house for $40,000 and assume the $25,000 existing loan. The problem was, I didn't have the $15,000 to pay the seller's equity.

My real estate agent took me aside and told me he knew of an "investor" who might be willing to loan me some of the money. He could possibly arrange a $10,000 loan if I could come up with a $5,000 down payment. The loan would be secured by a second mortgage on the house, payable in monthly installments over a seven-year period. I said to the agent, "Great! When can I meet this guy?"

To make a long story short, I did the deal but, of course, never met the guy who loaned me the money. The real estate agent was acting in the capacity of a private loan broker, in essence, he was an intermediary between the private lender and myself, the borrower.

This simple beginning would lead to many other such deals over the years. As I further developed my rehab strategy, private lenders and private mortgage brokers became ever more important to my ability to do deals. The reason was simple—they could provide the money when nobody else would! That, my friends, is the essence of the private mortgage industry—they can provide the money for rehab projects when nobody else will. If you can bring them the right deal, the money will become available. Find the good deals—and the money will come.

Private Lenders—Who Are These People Anyway?

Believe it or not, private lenders are people just like you and me. They come from all walks of life and span the spectrum of social and economic status. Indeed, some are very rich and belong to the social elite. The vast majority of private lenders are middle-class people who have accumulated cash savings over the years that they want to invest. Many have active business careers, working for some company or have their own company, while others are retired. Some are active in the real estate industry, but many are not. I guess the only common thread is that these are all people who want to earn a good safe return on their investments without taking enormous risks.

People with excess cash in the bank or money in their IRAs want to see their savings grow over time. In order to accomplish this, they must invest the money in something, even something as simple as certificates of deposit (CDs) or money market funds, which are "guaranteed" in that your principal is not at risk. Currently, they are paying 1 percent to 2 percent interest. In reality, they are guaranteed to lose money, because such investments barely keep up with inflation! So most people are willing to put at least some, if not all, of their money into more profitable investments.

The stock market is a popular alternative, and for good reason. Historically, the market has provided an average annual return of about 10 percent over the past 100 years. But the bull market of the 1990s has been replaced by a crushing bear market that has virtually wiped out many aggressive investors. Many more conservative investors have seen their retirement portfolios shrink in value by 25 percent or more during this bear market.

In the previous edition of this book, I waxed poetic about the great bull market we were experiencing at the time (late 1997). But I was also smart enough to predict that a correction of some sort was almost guaranteed. That prediction turned out to be correct, unfortunately. In that earlier edition, I also mentioned a prediction by noted economists John Campbell of Harvard and Robert Shiller of Yale that appeared in the January 13, 1997 edition of *The Wall Street Journal,* wherein they predicted that the stock market would not crash but instead meander sideways for the next five to ten years. Well, they were wrong about the crash, but the jury is still out on the sideways prediction. In any event, it is quite evident that the stock market version of the buy-and-hold strategy is as risky as the real estate version!

The point of this discussion of the stock market is that many investors are now, more than ever, seeking to diversify their savings and retirement funds into other assets that offer a more certain outcome. Investing in real estate or real estate mortgages meets the desired criteria for many people—safety, income, and the potential for extraordinary capital appreciation. Whether you are looking to invest your own IRA funds or putting together a joint venture or partnership deal with other people's IRA funds, the economic cycle could not be better than right now for convincing people to at least dabble with some of their funds in real estate.

Let's look in a little more detail at such an investment from the lender's perspective.

Take My Money, Please! Why Private Lenders Lend

The most fundamental concept in the world of investing is the concept of yield. To keep it simple, yield is basically just the amount of profit returned on an investment, usually expressed as an annual percentage. For example, an investment yielding 10 percent means your invested capital would grow by 10 percent each year. If these profits are reinvested and they also earn 10 percent, then the yield is said to be compounding at 10 percent. In other words, you are earning interest on the interest.

Let's say you have $25,000 in savings and you're considering a couple of different investment alternatives. One is a bond mutual fund that offers a yield of 4 percent. The other is a private real estate mortgage with a yield of 12 percent. Obviously, you're going to make more money at 12 percent, but how much more? Take a look at Figure 10.1, and you will be astonished. Over a five-year compounding period, you will make $13,643 more, simply by increasing your investment yield from 4 percent up to 12 percent. Notice what else happens during the five-year period at 12 percent—your investment has almost doubled! And look what happens over a ten-year period—your $25,000 initial investment grows to over $$77,000 which is $40,640 more than you would make at 4 percent! Pretty much of a no-brainer, wouldn't you say? Bottom line, that is why private lenders lend. Particularly today, when alternative investments offer such low returns.

The Mechanics of a Typical Private Mortgage

On the surface, the mechanics of a private mortgage appear to be the same as a conventional bank mortgage. The mortgage or deed of trust documents look the same and the closing ceremony at the escrow company is the same. One obvious difference is that, instead of a bank or institutional investor, the funds are provided by a private individual—hence the name *private mortgage.* To the borrower, however, this would be transparent because the lender does not sit at the closing table. What are the other differences?

Private lenders demand and get much more security for their loans. There is a significant difference in the amount of money loaned relative to the value of the property—otherwise known as the loan-to-value ratio (LTV). The LTV is calculated by dividing the loan amount by the current (or after-repaired) retail value of the property. Loans arranged through private lenders rarely exceed an LTV of 75 percent and the typical LTV is in the 50 percent to 60 percent range. Compare that to conventional bank loans, which for owner-occupants are in the 90 percent to 97 percent LTV range.

Private lenders demand and get higher interest rates for their loans. Although regulated by state usury laws (some states, such as New Mexico, do not have usury limits), private lenders normally charge

Figure 10.1 Savings Growth at 12% Compared to 4%

5-Year Period

Amount Invested	4%	12%	How Much More?
$ 10,000	$ 12,167	$ 17,623	$ 5,456
25,000	30,416	44,059	13,643
50,000	60,833	88,117	27,284
100,000	121,665	176,234	54,569

10-Year Period

Amount Invested	4%	12%	How Much More?
$ 10,000	$ 14,802	$ 31,058	$ 16,256
25,000	37,006	77,646	40,640
50,000	74,012	155,292	81,280
100,000	148,024	310,585	162,561

20-Year Period

Amount Invested	4%	12%	How Much More?
$ 10,000	$ 21,911	$ 96,463	$ 54,569
25,000	54,778	241,157	186,379
50,000	109,556	482,315	372,759
100,000	219,112	964,629	745,517

in the 9 percent to 18 percent range, with 12 percent to 15 percent being more typical on residential property.

Private lenders demand and get short duration terms for their loans. Private mortgages are normally written for relatively short durations. For a rehab investor, it is common to write an interest-only note with a balloon due in one or two years. For an owner-occupant homeowner, a 15-year amortization loan with a balloon in five years is common.

There is relatively little hassle. A private loan application is usually one to two pages in length and the loan can be closed within a week to ten days, depending on the circumstances. None of this 40- to 60-day torture chamber routine the banks put you through! You will know within a couple of days max whether you will get the loan.

Default

What happens if the borrower defaults on the loan? This feature is basically the same with a private loan or a conventional loan—the lender has several options from which to choose. For example, if the borrower's problem is temporary (layoff or short-term medical problem) and appears solvable, the lender can restructure the loan. If the money is insufficient to bring the loan current in one lump sum, extra payments could be allowed or the arrears could simply be added to the principal balance.

Another option lenders, particularly private lenders, have in this situation is to buy the house from the borrower at a steeply discounted price. The borrower then has the option of accepting some money and avoiding foreclosure or being foreclosed on and getting little or nothing.

And finally, there is foreclosure. This, however, is usually rare in private lending because the borrower has so much equity at stake. For example, with a 50 percent LTV loan on a $100,000 house, the borrower stands to lose $50,000 in equity if it goes to foreclosure! People in this situation almost always find a friend or relative to bail them out or they find another lender to refinance the house.

As a prospective borrower, you're probably thinking, "Hey! These guys have got the deck stacked in their favor!" The truth is, private lending is a safe and profitable investment. But you have to also look at it from the other side of the coin. If you want to borrow money to buy a junker to rehab and bankers won't loan you any money, or you're a homeowner and can't qualify for a bank loan, who are you gonna call? You're going to call the private mortgage broker.

The Private Mortgage Broker—The Person Who Knows Angels!

In the business world, *angels* are people or companies who are willing to loan money for company start-ups or expansions. They are also known as *venture capitalists.* I like to think of private mortgage lenders in the same way—as angels. They have certainly been angels to me when I've needed money to do a rehab deal. The question is, how do you find them?

The best way to do this is through a private mortgage broker—the person who indeed knows angels. The private mortgage broker is in the business of matching up private lenders with borrowers and handling all of the details on both ends. This broker is the go-between, so to speak, and a lot more.

First, the broker has gone to the trouble and expense of developing a clientele of private lenders and, through a variety of means, has educated them in the rewards of private mortgage lending and has developed business practices to ensure the success of their investments. Although these private lenders may come from anywhere around the country or even from overseas, the broker is responsible for placing their money in profitable investments.

The private mortgage broker must possess an intimate knowledge of the real estate markets in which he or she is working. The broker must know, for example, if a rehab property is located in a neighborhood that has desirable characteristics or is in a marginal area with limited potential. The same is true if the loan is made to a homeowner. The broker must use his or her professional knowledge and experience in evaluating potential deals, including evaluation of the worst-case scenario—is the value really there if we have to foreclose?

Following the placement of a loan, the broker must be ready to spring into action if the loan ever goes into default. The broker needs to be there to help in the collection of back payments and assist the private lenders in making decisions on whether to allow a borrower to reinstate the loan or to foreclose. A good loan broker also will assist in coordinating any foreclosure action with a local attorney and coordinate the sale of the property to maximize the lender's profits. The good loan broker protects lenders and makes their investments as hassle-free as possible.

How do you find private mortgage brokers? Well, right up front, you need to know that they are not physically available in every little community around the country. They do, however, make up a small but growing percentage of all mortgage loan brokers, even in the larger cities.

First, dig into the Yellow Pages under Loans, Mortgage Loans, or Real Estate Mortgages. Look for ads that use these terms: *nonqualifying, bad credit OK, self-employed or no job OK, specialize in difficult loans, nonconforming loans, hard-money loans,* or *investor loans available.* The use of these words indicates that the mortgage broker may be working with private lenders and thus may be making low LTV loans. The next step is just getting on the phone and asking, "Do you offer private mortgage loans or loans for rehab properties?" Sooner or later, someone will refer you to the right person.

In the event you discover that no one in your area handles these loans, don't give up. Just get the phone directory of the nearest big city and start the process all over again. Many private loan brokers will place loans in smaller communities because they can perform their due diligence through local real estate appraisers and real estate brokers. Keep networking—it will pay off eventually. As in any endeavor, persistence wins the day.

Another good place to look for private mortgage brokers is in the classified ads of your local paper or the paper of the nearest big city. Again, look under the Loans or Real Estate Loans classification. As an example, see Figure 10.2, extracted from newspapers around the country. The brokers offering private loans are easy to spot.

If all else fails, it's time for you to get proactive and place your own ad in the newspaper, something along these lines:

> Rehab specialist seeking short-term private mortgage funds for SFH projects. Call Kevin 222-4444.

It's hard to predict in advance, but you will likely get some interesting calls. Curiosity seekers, real estate agents, and hopefully, individuals or mortgage brokers with money to lend. Unless you're really savvy about the mortgage process, I suggest you deal with mortgage brokers and not with private lenders directly.

After years of working with private mortgage brokers on many rehab deals, I came to appreciate the valuable services they provide to the real estate community and to investors. Imagine being in a situation where you've gone out and hunted down the deal of a lifetime. When all's said and done, you're going to make a $30,000 profit on this rehab

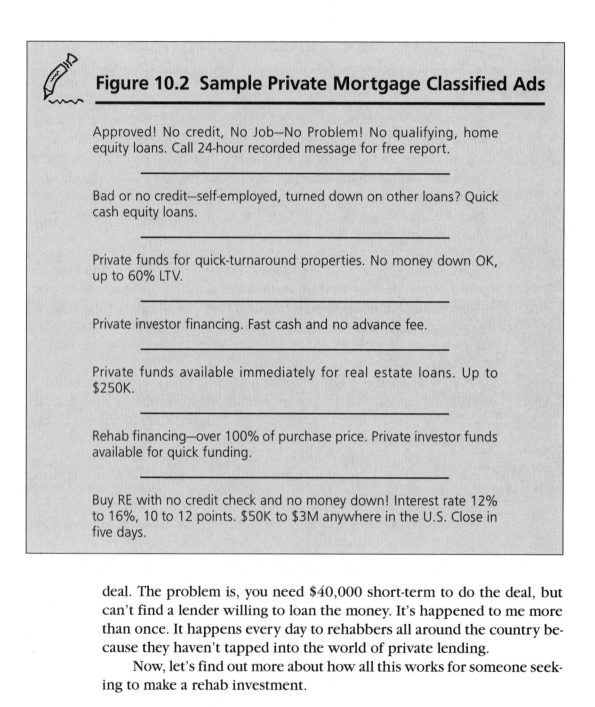

Figure 10.2 Sample Private Mortgage Classified Ads

Approved! No credit, No Job—No Problem! No qualifying, home equity loans. Call 24-hour recorded message for free report.

Bad or no credit—self-employed, turned down on other loans? Quick cash equity loans.

Private funds for quick-turnaround properties. No money down OK, up to 60% LTV.

Private investor financing. Fast cash and no advance fee.

Private funds available immediately for real estate loans. Up to $250K.

Rehab financing—over 100% of purchase price. Private investor funds available for quick funding.

Buy RE with no credit check and no money down! Interest rate 12% to 16%, 10 to 12 points. $50K to $3M anywhere in the U.S. Close in five days.

deal. The problem is, you need $40,000 short-term to do the deal, but can't find a lender willing to loan the money. It's happened to me more than once. It happens every day to rehabbers all around the country because they haven't tapped into the world of private lending.

Now, let's find out more about how all this works for someone seeking to make a rehab investment.

Private Mortgage Loan Criteria for Rehab Projects

Right off, you should know that there are no hard-and-fast rules in the private mortgage arena. I have talked to brokers all around the country, and the criteria are all over the map. I'll describe a synthesis of that information. And keep in mind that these criteria are applicable to the rehab investor. Most brokers also loan to the owner-occupant homeowner and the lending criteria for them usually is a little different.

Equity

Universally, the number-one lending criterion is existing equity in the house. In other words, LTV. As I've mentioned before, most brokers require LTVs in the range of 50 percent to 70 percent.

Many brokers do not exceed a 65 percent LTV on loans involving a rehab project. Period. Nonnegotiable. The reason for this seemingly stringent standard is simple—risk. From the lender's viewpoint, funding a rehab involves a lot of uncertainty. Does this guy really know what he's doing? What is the quality of his work? What is the quality of his subcontractor's work? Will he perform according to his rehab plan? Will he be able to sell the house for as much as the appraisal predicts? How fast will he be able to sell it? Can he make the mortgage payments? And so on and so forth.

Now, I will share one little secret with you: After you've established yourself with a private mortgage broker and have demonstrated your abilities to perform as planned, there is a good chance that you can start getting higher LTV loans—maybe up to 70 percent or even 75 percent once you establish a good track record.

For now, let's work with the 65 percent LTV and see how you can do deals on that basis. First, it's important to understand what is meant by *value* when using the term *loan to value.* Generally, this means the after-repaired value or maximum retail value after repairs. This is great news! You mean I'll get 65 percent of what the house will sell for *after* the rehab is done?

Yes, but here's how it typically works in practice. Let's say the house, after repairs, will be worth $100,000 according to the appraisal. The appraiser also estimates the as-is retail value at $80,000. But you don't buy retail—you buy wholesale and were able to get it at $50,000.

Your repairs are estimated at $15,000. Based on this information, you will be able to get a total loan of $65,000 because that is 65 percent of the after-repaired value of $100,000. However, at closing, you will only get 65 percent of the as-is value, which would be 65 percent of $80,000, or $52,000. The remaining $13,000 of the loan would be placed in escrow and made available as repairs are completed. Note that you were able to buy this house with none of your own money down plus you were able to get all the money needed for repairs.

Do you see why the $13,000 is kept in escrow? There really are two reasons for this. First, it is to make sure that the repairs are indeed completed and completed in a satisfactory manner. If the repairs are not done right, no money is released. With a $13,000 escrow, the money probably would be released in two increments, as work progresses, as kind of a carrot and stick approach: Do the work and get the money.

The second reason is to keep the LTV at 65 percent at all times during the rehab process. This provides the needed security for the private lender. If the entire $65,000 was released at closing, the lender would be exposed to an 81 percent LTV situation, way too risky on a rehab project. What's to prevent the borrower from just taking the $15,000 and running off to Tahiti? Hey, it's happened!

Can the private mortgage loan be in second position? Yes it can, as long as the total of the first and second loan does not exceed the 65 percent LTV criteria. For example, let's say you have a house valued at $50,000 as is, and $80,000 after repairs. It has an assumable first loan on it with a principal balance of $10,000. To keep the 65 percent LTV criteria, you could get a $42,000 second mortgage (65 percent of $80,000 or $10,000), but would receive only $22,500 at closing. The remaining $19,500 would be released as repairs were completed. See how that works?

The bottom line is the 65 percent LTV. If there's 65 percent equity in the house, there is a good chance your loan will be approved. This is absolutely the most important lending criterion for any loan broker dealing with private money—security in the event something goes wrong.

Here's one other point about the LTV: The total loan is based on the value after repairs and the money available at closing is based on the as-is value. How many banks lend on that basis? None. If you could ever get a bank loan, it would always be based on what you *paid* for the house, even if you bought it up to two years ago! In that case, you are being penalized for finding a bargain and being a good negotiator. Under the private lending scenario, what you paid for the house is not a factor, but current market value is. To the extent you can buy the house at a price below current market value, you will be rewarded. I hope you see this distinction. It all comes down to one thing: Find the good deals and the money will come!

The loan-to-value ratio is one criterion, albeit the most important one. With a rehab loan, the loan broker will consider other factors, such as location. The property must be located in an area that is showing improvement and otherwise has potential. The neighborhood needs to be a place where people with the money for a down payment want to live. There has to be a demand for property in the neighborhood, as reflected by recent sales in the area.

Aside from the appraisal, the next most important document to the loan broker will be the rehab plan. The broker will want to know exactly what repairs are planned and how much the rehab is going to cost. Be professional and work out a detailed plan that demonstrates your knowledge and foresight. If the broker thinks you don't know what you're doing, there's a good chance you won't get the money. Many brokers will work with newcomers by sharing knowledge and offering advice, but others will not. I know one broker in California who works only with highly experienced rehabbers.

How about the borrower's credit history? Usually this is not a big factor, although some brokers make a bigger deal out of this than others. Usually they check to see if a borrower has any judgments pending, but that's about it as far as credit history goes. Bankruptcy? This usually is not an issue unless it's currently pending and hasn't been resolved. Previous foreclosures? This could be a problem. If you have this on your record, be prepared to fully explain the circumstances. It could be a deal-stopper.

Current income is obviously an important consideration. A borrower needs to be able to demonstrate sufficient income to cover living expenses and payments on the proposed mortgage. Where's the money coming from to cover the payments? If there is no regular income, can you show money in the bank? Alternatively, you might propose that six months' worth of payments be withheld at closing from the loan proceeds. This will take the pressure off of you and provide a sense of security for the lender.

Do you already own the property or are you getting the loan as part of a purchase? It doesn't really matter to the loan broker, as long as a clear title can be produced. This is one of the first things a loan broker will check before proceeding too far with the loan application. As the borrower, it's up to you to make sure there are no problems with the title.

I've mentioned the appraisal and want to emphasize that it is one of the most important documents in the loan process. The amount of money you receive will be based on the value report the broker receives from the appraiser. As the borrower, you will be paying for this, so you want to have a pretty good notion that your value estimates are realistic. Remember, the loan broker usually needs an as-is and an as-repaired appraisal. Some brokers allow you to order the appraisal but most will bring in an appraiser they know and trust.

Private Mortgage Terms—
Don't Step over Dollars to Pick Up Pennies!

Gulp! You want to charge how much interest? 15 percent? That's outrageous! The banks are only charging 6 percent for the 30-year fixed-rate loan!

Get it together! If you could get 6 percent money for rehab projects, there wouldn't be any need for private mortgage lenders. But banks are banks, and as I've said many times, they will not loan money on junkers. Bank money is not available—but private money is!

The cost of money is based on two factors: availability (supply and demand) and risk factors. We've already discussed the risk factors associated with lending on rehab properties. Regarding availability, we also know the answer—it's not available through traditional lending sources. Therefore, as Economics 101 tells us, if the supply is low and the demand is high, the price is going to be high.

After having said all that, let me put this point in perspective. In the rehab business, we have an immediate need for the money to buy the property and pay for repairs. If we have done our homework in the process, we will be selling the house within six months, and will be receiving a nice profit of between $10,000 and upwards of $30,000. Does it really matter what the cost of the money is over a six-month period?

Let's quickly do the math. If we have a $50,000 loan at 15 percent, interest only, we will pay $3,750 in interest over a six-month period; if we had the same loan at 11 percent from some other source (it won't be a bank!), we would pay $2,750, a difference of $1,000. One thousand dollars is nothing to sneeze at, but let's be realistic. I either pay the money, do the deal, and collect my profits, or I walk away, do nothing, and earn nothing! Don't step over dollars to pick up pennies!

The cost of borrowing money is a cost of doing business. It should be included in your buying and holding costs, and therefore already accounted for in your maximum purchase price calculation. In other words, it's not really costing you anything if you've deducted it in calculating the purchase price. It's all a matter of perspective.

Private Mortgages Aren't Free—How Much Will It Cost?

Interest payments are not the only costs you will incur in borrowing the money. Just like with a conventional bank loan, there are fees and other closing costs that need to be paid by someone—either you as the borrower or the seller. If you already own the house, then you will be responsible for all of it. Here's a list of typical closing costs:

- Mortgage broker fee
- Loan origination fee (points)
- Title abstract
- Title insurance
- Credit report
- Appraisal
- Prepaid fire insurance and taxes
- Termite inspection
- Recording fees
- Survey
- Attorney fee or escrow company fee

Some of these items are optional and are not always included, depending on the broker or area of the country. For example, many brokers do not have a survey performed, pull a credit report, or charge a loan origination fee (points). Also, in some parts of the country a termite inspection would not be necessary. Most of the other items are going to be present in any loan. Of course, the charges for each item will vary according to local market conditions.

Without a doubt, the largest cost of obtaining a loan will be the mortgage broker fee. This fee is regulated in most states and ranges from a low of about 5 percent up to 10 percent (maybe more in states without a regulated fee). This percentage is calculated on the loan amount. For example, in New Mexico brokers can charge up to 6 percent, so the fee on a $75,000 loan would be $4,500.

The normal practice is to deduct all of the necessary fees from the loan amount and disburse them to the appropriate parties at closing. The exceptions to this are the appraisal fee, which normally will need to be paid by the borrower when the work is done, and any loan origination fees, which usually are added on to the principal amount.

At the time you sit down with your loan broker to apply for a loan, he or she will provide you with a good-faith estimate, showing you all of the costs and how much you will net from the loan proceeds. In the earlier example using the $75,000 loan, you might net approximately $69,000 (depending on the circumstances). However, you will owe $75,000, and your payments and interest charges will be calculated based on that amount.

Indeed, the cost of borrowing money, be it through conventional financing or private financing, is not free. But, like all of the other costs associated with doing a rehab project, it is the cost of doing business. Include it in your purchase price calculation and it won't cost you a thing. It's all a matter of perspective.

Private Lending Is out of the Closet!

It's all out in the open now. The spotlight has been placed on the private mortgage industry. It's out of the closet and on its way to becoming a mainstream entity. Now that you know about it, take advantage of all that it has to offer. Use the availability of private mortgage money to supercharge your investment career. Forget the constraints placed on you by the conventional banking community. Now that you know where the money is and how to get it, it's time for you to get out there and go after it!

Street-Smart Negotiating

Getting Your Offers Accepted

*I*n the real estate game, there is nothing worse than making a bad deal. With this in mind, you must always be prepared to walk away from any deal, without reservation. If the numbers don't work or the terms can't be worked out satisfactorily, move on to the next deal. But don't make the mistake of just mechanically submitting an offer and forgetting about it if it's not accepted. It's one thing to be out there submitting offers, and it's another thing to get those offers accepted. This is accomplished only through your ability to successfully negotiate with your sellers.

Skillful negotiating is an art form that can be learned. Some will be more successful than others, just because of practice and natural ability. But we can all learn some of the basic concepts.

Ugly Houses and Motivated Sellers

In the rehab investment field, you are dealing with ugly houses and motivated sellers, period. If the house is not ugly, you won't be looking at it; if the seller is not motivated, you won't be buying it. It really is that simple.

The sellers that you will deal with, for the most part, will be either private owners or institutions (bank or government REOs). Private owners may or may not be motivated to sell. Part of your job is to find that out as soon as possible. Institutions are always motivated to sell, but their level of motivation varies with time and market conditions.

In working on a deal involving a private owner, virtually every aspect is potentially negotiable: price, terms, closing costs, inspections. With institutions, it's the same thing but you typically will be offering all cash. An exception to this may be when the institution is willing to provide funding to the REO investor (or owner-occupant) or when you are working a preforeclosure deal and negotiating with a lender to assume a mortgage or obtain a short payoff (mortgage amount reduction).

As we discussed previously, the secret to success in dealing with institutional owners is persistence and follow-up. Figure out your maximum purchase price, submit your offer, and keep submitting your offer until you get the property or it's sold to someone else. Unless you have the time and ability to build relationships (schmooze) with REO officials, this is about all you can do.

Private owners are another story; this is where your street-smart skills and savvy can make you a bundle.

Meet Your Adversary—The Private Owner

Does the word *adversary* bother you? Most of us don't like the whole idea of an adversarial situation. We like to get along and to be liked by people we come in contact with. In a real estate transaction, however, you truly have an adversary. Whether you're a buyer or a seller, the other party is the opposition, trying to stack the deck in his or her favor, and you're trying to do the same thing. With each and every deal, the financial stakes are huge, so you need to put on your game face and play to win.

Now that you're in the right frame of mind, you're ready to meet the private owner, face to face. The initial face-to-face meeting is really important. Regardless of whether real estate agents are involved, you need to meet and interact with the owner. There are several reasons for this, which I discuss later, but think about this: Is it realistic to expect an owner to agree to a significant price reduction or to offer carry-back financing to an unknown, faceless person? I don't think so.

One of the most important reasons for this face-to-face meeting is so that you can ask questions—lots of questions. How old is the house? How long have you owned it? When was the roof replaced? Does the heating system work? Do you have a permit for the addition? Are you planning to get rid of that junk car in the front yard? How long has the house been on the market? You're doing your due diligence, learning everything you can about the house and, equally important, you're starting to establish some rapport with the owner. Make eye contact, smile when appropriate, and show the person you're honest—not some sleazy character out trying to steal property!

The Two Most Critical Questions to Ask Every Seller

As I mentioned before, you are not going to be buying a particular house unless the seller is motivated. Why? Because unless the seller is highly motivated to get rid of the property, you will not be able to negotiate a profitable deal. The two questions that follow are designed to find out just how motivated the seller is.

1. *Why are you selling the property?* There are an infinite number of answers a seller could respond with, and all of them will give you an idea of motivation. If the answer is, "I'm selling my rentals so I can put a large down payment on the new house I'm building," then you know the seller is motivated to get a deal done quickly. On the other hand, if the answer is, "Well, I'm thinking about retiring to Florida next year and I just wanted to see what I could get for this place. I'm not in any big hurry to sell," then you have a problem. The seller is not feeling any pressure to sell quickly or to even sell at all. You may still want to make an offer, but you are unlikely to get any significant concessions.

2. *How much would you take if I offered you all cash?* This is a must-ask question, even if you don't intend to offer all cash. Its primary intent at this point is to merely gauge the seller's flexibility and motivation. But promise yourself that when you ask this question, you will remain silent. No matter what the seller responds with, you remain silent.

"Well, I'm asking $125,000. I've got to have that price."
Silence!
"But, if you were willing to pay me all cash, well, I could consider an offer of maybe say, $110,000."
Silence!
"You know, if you were willing to close in two weeks, well, maybe I would be willing to take about $105,000."
Silence!

Now obviously, this exact scenario does not play out every time you ask the question. Sometimes, the response will be, "Hey, the price is $125,000, take it or leave it!" You've accomplished your goal—you found out the seller is not particularly motivated. But you will be surprised and amazed at the responses you get when dealing with a motivated seller! The combination of an all-cash offer (verbal) coupled with silence is extremely powerful!

As Robert Allen said in his book *Nothing Down,* "The first person to mention a number loses." Indeed, silence is golden—and devastating! Make eye contact, ask the question, and then shut up!

Negotiating from a Position of Strength

The absolute worst negotiating position to be in is a situation where you really, really want the property. Have you ever bought a house to live in? Remember the emotions you went through, hoping and praying your offer would be accepted, worrying about someone else coming in with a better offer? This is the situation you want to avoid, always and forever. Not only on your next house to live in, but with any house you buy as a rehab investment. You know that if you can't get your price or terms, there are many other deals out there waiting for you to discover.

Negotiating from a position of strength is at the outset a mental attitude. First and foremost, it is the attitude of being prepared to walk away at the end if you can't get the deal you need to make the numbers work. Making a deal in which you lose is just unacceptable.

Let me be clear on this point—this is an internal mind-set, not one you want to display to the seller, at least not initially. The worst thing you can do is to begin your negotiations with an attitude of arrogance or self-righteousness. If you offend the seller to the point of disliking you, your deal is going south, no matter how desperate the seller is. Even if your offer is accepted, there are an endless number of ways the seller can get back at you before the deal is closed.

Negotiating from a position of strength requires you to arm yourself with the right tools and knowledge before you venture into the marketplace. Here is what you need to know before you make an offer:

- *Know where your money will come from.* Having cash in the bank or a private mortgage broker lined up in advance gives you a special advantage in negotiations. You know and your sellers will know that you can perform. If you have to depend on a traditional bank loan, you are in a weak position, but at least get prequalified before you go out and start making offers. If you plan to include seller financing, you also are in a somewhat weaker position, so be prepared to offer attractive terms.
- *Know the sellers' reason for selling.* This allows you to know how to structure an acceptable offer. Do they need all their money now, or would they be receptive to receiving payments over time at a good interest rate?
- *Know your maximum purchase price.* This requires that you know the retail market values in the neighborhood, develop a solid cost estimate for repairs, and know your buying cost, holding cost, selling cost, and projected profit.
- *Know your local market conditions.* What's happening, right now, in the market? Is the market so hot that you have a lot of competition for fixer-uppers? What's going on with the retail side? Are houses selling?
- *Know your exit plan.* Presumably, you are going to buy, fix up, and sell. That's your basic business plan. But maybe you've decided to flip this deal wholesale to another investor. Do you have investors lined up?
- *Know that you are prepared to walk away.* Adopting this mindset in advance gives you the needed confidence to enter the arena, knowing that you will make a profitable deal or the deal won't be made!

You are now in a position of strength that you have created for yourself. You've met the owner and know his or her motivation and needs; you've inspected the house and know what your maximum purchase price is going to be; you know where the money is going to come from (except for any seller financing you may propose); you know what you're going to do after you buy it; you know what's going on in the marketplace; and you know that there are plenty of deals out there and that if this one doesn't work out, you're going to walk away. You are now ready to prepare a written offer and start the final round of negotiations. Are real estate agents involved?

Real Estate Agents as Potential Roadblocks

I like real estate agents—some of my good friends are real estate agents. But the truth is, sometimes they can be a royal pain in the neck! When it comes to presenting offers and negotiating with sellers, many would rather you be as far away as possible; they are fearful you may butt heads with the seller or otherwise mess up the deal and their commission. I can understand their concerns but, if possible, you need to be present when the purchase offer is presented. Alternatively, you can try to arrange a private meeting with the seller before the offer is made. The point is, you and the seller need to meet face to face.

Legally, nothing that I know of should prevent you from meeting privately with the seller. You will need to overcome the roadblocks put up by your real estate agent, the listing agent, and sometimes, the seller. Simply put, you need to let them know that you insist on meeting with the seller and assure the agent that you are not trying to circumvent his or her position or ability to earn a commission. If push comes to shove, just tell the agent, no meeting, no offer! Or put it right in your offer: Buyer reserves the right to be present when offer is presented to seller.

Now, are you prepared to go this far? Really, it depends on your confidence in yourself and your real estate agent. If you know or sense that your agent is a good negotiator, then give him or her the opportunity to prove it. If it doesn't work out, take control on the next deal.

As Agatha Christie said, "Where large sums of money are concerned, it is advisable to trust nobody."

Five Strategies to Get Your Offers Accepted

What I am about to share with you now are the five key strategies that I have successfully used over the years to get my offers accepted. There are many more ideas that could be incorporated into your game plan and I would encourage you to seek out other books on this subject. Of course, each deal is unique, but here are the commonsense strategies that I have found to be the most powerful.

Never offend the seller. This was mentioned earlier and is presented here again for emphasis. If the seller does not like you or does not trust you, a satisfactory deal will not happen. It's easy, in the heat of the battle, to fall into the trap of making personal remarks, particularly if this is initiated by the seller in reaction to your offer! But with everything you have, resist the temptation. It will sour the deal quicker than any other factor. Know going into your meeting that this may happen and visualize ahead of time your cool and calm nonreaction. Be polite and look for ways to ease the tension.

Save price for last. In almost all of the deals I have done with private owners, price is the major sticking point. Mention your offer price up front and get the owner's initial reaction (usually negative). Then agree to "come back and discuss price later." Try first to find an issue you can agree on, such as closing date, or inspection, or trash removal. Talk it out and try to reach an agreement. Do the same with every other negotiable issue, such as closing cost split, personal property (appliances), financing. Now you've shown each other that you can work together and it's time to deal with the price issue.

Offer all cash if possible. Nothing is more powerful in a real estate negotiation, particularly in a slow market on a rehab property that a bank won't touch, than an all-cash offer. An all-cash offer is powerful because it is final. There is no seller financing to haggle over, no future payments to worry about, and no concern about the buyer getting turned down for a loan at the bank (assuming a bank would loan on the house). Go to closing, pick up your check, and you're on your way. It's over and done with forever! Make sure (if it's true) that the seller understands that there are only two financing choices—all cash or some combination of cash and seller financing. Because of the condition of the house, banks will not lend money unless all the repairs are made, in advance, by the seller. Is the seller willing and able to make these repairs? You advise the seller that you are in a position to offer all cash, and spend a lot more money on repairs, but only if you can make a profit on the deal. Show the seller the list of repairs you plan to make and your cost estimate. If the seller questions your profits, you should just point out, "What's the point of me making all these repairs if all I get back is the cost of the repairs?"

Be more flexible on price if seller financing is involved. If you're asking the seller to carry back some or all of the financing, even for a relatively short time, as in a split-funding deal, ease up a little on your bottom-line price. After all, you are saving some big bucks compared to what a bank or loan broker would be charging you in points. For example, if a loan broker is charging you ten points on a $50,000 loan amount, that's $5,000. If you're saving that much through seller financing, you can afford to give some or all of that up in your final price negotiation. Don't step over dollars to pick up pennies, or worse yet, lose the whole deal!

Hold back your best offer. With private sellers, don't make your best offer with your first offer (a government-bid situation is different). Sellers expect to do some haggling and view your first offer as a trial balloon. Don't disappoint them! Plan on one or more counteroffers. These give you the opportunity to show good faith and movement toward a resolution. Just don't give up your chips too soon, and don't give them up without receiving something in return.

Purchase Agreement Forms

Be aware that there are literally hundreds of "official" or "standard" purchase agreement contract forms. The truth is, there really is no such thing! To be sure, your real estate agent will have forms that "everyone uses" in your community. That doesn't mean you have to use that particular form.

The best advice I can give you on this is twofold:

1. Read and understand every word in any contract you are using.
2. Seek professional legal advice if you don't understand the contract fully or if you intend to use a nonstandard agreement. (One excellent source for many types of real estate contracts is the Professional Publishing Corporation, 122 Paul Drive, San Rafael, CA 94903; 415-472-1964; <www.profpub.com>)

Using the "Subject to Inspection" Contingency

In general, when you're making lowball offers on houses, you want to avoid using "subject to" clauses. Any such clause weakens the offer. Why? Because a "subject to" clause in essence says to the seller, "I will buy your house at this price, except if this happens or doesn't happen, the deal is off." Compare that to an offer with no contingency clauses. Which is more powerful and attractive to the seller?

The exception to this is the "subject to" inspection contingency clause. Even though it does weaken the offer somewhat, I urge you to include it in all of your offers. It is a cheap insurance policy for you, in case you missed something during your walk-through.

A couple of days ago, I heard from my friend Debbie in Texas. She was the successful bidder at a government auction. Although she had been able to inspect the property beforehand, she did not hire a professional inspector. Because she was financing the property with the 203(k) program, an FHA inspector came to see the house. The inspector discovered severe foundation settling at one end of the house and a totally nonfunctional septic system. Debbie had not been aware of either problem at the time of purchase. These newly discovered problems have added an additional $32,000 in repair costs! Ouch! At this point, she is thinking about forfeiting her $5,000 earnest money and walking away because there is no provision for renegotiation—bids are final. This, indeed, was a very expensive mistake.

The lesson here is that you must anticipate the unexpected and provide yourself an out. That is why "subject to" language in a contract is often referred to as a *weasel clause* or *escape clause,* and for good reason. If you are smart enough to include it in your purchase offer, then you deserve the right to walk away or renegotiate the deal if new information becomes available.

Because the whole concept of a home inspection has become popular around the country, many of the "standard" purchase agreements already have a check box to indicate your intent to make the offer subject to inspection. If this is not the case with the contract you are using, you will need to put it in, perhaps as an addendum. Check with your attorney, but something along the lines of the following should be acceptable:

> This offer is subject to and contingent upon a property inspection which, in the sole judgment of Purchaser, is deemed "satisfactory." Such inspection shall be arranged and paid for by Purchaser. If the Purchaser or Purchaser's agent notifies Seller or Seller's agent that the inspection is "unsatisfactory," then this offer shall be null and void and any deposit made by Purchaser shall be returned. However, this does not preclude the negotiation of a new purchase offer, should the parties so desire.

Use of this clause gives you the power and control in the deal, and otherwise stacks the deck in your favor. Quite frankly, this is the position you want to be in. But let me caution you about abusing this power.

Some people use the inspection report to extract another pound of flesh from each and every deal. They get the results, get contractor friends to give them bogus high repair estimates, and then beat the sellers over the head with demands for more price reductions. Don't play this game; it's unethical and dishonest. Eventually, the word is going to get out to the real estate community about your shady business practices and people will not want to deal with you.

The purpose of the inspection clause is to protect you from the unexpected. Use it solely for that purpose. Certainly, if a major defect is discovered of which you were not aware, renegotiate the deal in good faith or walk away. That's your right and prerogative. But don't use the process as a gambit to manipulate a lower price. In the long run, you will pay the price.

Make Two Offers to Close More Deals

This is one of the most powerful negotiating techniques ever invented! Once I discovered how to use this method effectively, the percentage of my offers getting accepted skyrocketed.

The essence of the method is this—you bring to the negotiating table two signed offers. One for all cash, with a heavy price discount, and one with some form of owner financing, with less of a price discount.

As an example, I recently made two simultaneous offers on an older three-bedroom, two-bath pueblo-style house in poor condition—one offer was all cash and the other a split funding with owner carry-back financing. This was a FSBO that was free and clear of financing, but the owner knew he had to sell at a discount because the house was in such bad shape. He was asking $55,000. I estimated repairs at $7,000 and estimated the after-repaired value at $73,000, based on recent sales in the neighborhood. I sat down with him and presented the following two offers:

1. $32,000 all cash
2. $38,500 split funding; $5,000 down payment with the $33,500 balance due within nine months with no payments or interest. A first mortgage in favor of the seller would be recorded on the property with these terms.

I already had a private lender who would loan $36,000 net at closing if the cash offer was accepted. This would also give me $4,000 to use for repairs. I was hoping he would go for the all-cash offer because it would be a no-money-down (none of my money!) with cash at closing deal for me.

The owner really struggled with the two choices. First, he wanted more money. He had some pressing medical bills and was recently divorced. He also wanted to move to Colorado and start a new business. We talked for about two hours. He hemmed and hawed and couldn't make a decision. Finally, I said, "Look, the offer gives you 24 hours to decide. Think about it tonight, and we'll get together tomorrow and wrap this up."

We got together the next day and finalized the deal. He went for the split-funding deal, but I had to make some changes to make it fly. I would give him $42,500 with $7,000 down and the $35,500 due in six months.

He had to agree to put his $35,500 mortgage in second position, behind a $15,000 first mortgage from my private lender. It was a done deal–he was happy and I was happy! And I still got a no-money-down, cash-at-closing deal!

The psychology behind the two-offer technique is awesome. It eliminates the "Here's my offer, take it or leave it" approach by stimulating an atmosphere of choices. It presumes that an offer will be accepted and focuses attention on alternatives. It's kind of like the new car salesperson who says, "We have this model with either standard or automatic transmission. Which would you prefer? Do you like the red or the green?"

Playing the Numbers Game for Fun and Profit

Did you hear about the guy in California who sat down with the MLS book and made 1,500 offers on houses in his area? As the story goes, he actually got 40 offers accepted. This is the ultimate numbers game, one I would never suggest you play.

Making an offer on a house is a serious business. People's financial lives are at stake, so it's nothing to be frivolous with. Submitting 20 offers at one time, over the fax, is a good way to become a persona non grata! It's another good way to get the real estate community upset with you and your broker!

A realistic goal would be to get about one in every five to seven offers accepted. This, of course, will depend on whom you are dealing with (private owners or institutions) and how well you do your homework. And it will depend on your ability to get in front of the owners to personally negotiate the deal.

You are now armed and dangerous! You have the knowledge and skills to go out and negotiate the deal of a lifetime–you know, the one that will come along every few days or so!

CHAPTER 12

Open Your Eyes and Sharpen Your Pencil

Home Inspections and Estimating Repairs

*I*dentifying what needs to be fixed and how much it will cost is what this chapter is all about. Now I know this whole subject can be a little intimidating. After all, there are few among us, including myself, who are experts at all aspects of home repairs. But the truth is, we don't have to be a home repair expert to succeed in this business. We simply need to be observant and cultivate the ability to develop ballpark repair cost estimates in our local market. Remember, professional help is always available, which we will learn to utilize in all of our transactions.

The Two-Step Inspection Technique

The process I like to use and teach is a two-step approach. First, you inspect the house on your own and develop a checklist of repair items and estimated costs, which are used in your purchase price calculations. You submit an offer based on this estimate but include a "subject to inspection" clause (discussed in the previous chapter). After the offer is accepted, you bring in a professional home inspector to check out the house. If any surprises are discovered, you renegotiate the offer, bring in another engineering or construction specialist, or walk away.

Using this two-step approach gives you several powerful advantages:

- It minimizes the expenditure of funds on inspection services until after an offer is accepted.
- It allows you to efficiently evaluate properties and get your offers submitted without a lot of time spent (wasted) getting estimates or otherwise getting trapped in the "paralysis of analysis" syndrome.
- It provides you with a level of confidence—if you missed something of importance during your own inspection, it likely will be detected when the professional inspector is brought into the picture.
- When dealing with FSBOs or REALTOR®-listed property in particular, it can provide you with significant leverage in negotiating a lower price, even with a less motivated seller.

Two instances when this approach cannot be used is when bidding on a foreclosure property at sheriff's auction and, similarly, when bidding on a HUD home at their open-cry auctions. With these types of properties, "subject to" contingency clauses are not allowed. With these properties, you have to make some assumptions, pay your money, and take your chances.

Spend the Time Doing Your Due Diligence Walk-Through

Doing your due diligence simply means doing your homework. This is when you are out by yourself or with your real estate agent looking at property. And when doing homework, what's the difference between getting an A or getting a C or D? It's usually the difference in time and effort spent.

It's easy to get caught up in the rush to go out and inspect three, four, or five properties in an afternoon. Your real estate agent may be in a hurry to get back to the office and start writing up offers for you. Or you may be in a hurry to do the same, so you breeze through the house, make a few quick notes, and move on to the next one. Big mistake. That's worth repeating: *Big mistake!*

You need to spend some quality time at each house you plan to submit an offer on. How can you possibly do a good job estimating repair costs if you don't spend the time looking for the skeletons in each house?

I typically spend 45 minutes to an hour at each house, sometimes more. Let me suggest you do the same, particularly if you're just starting out in this business. Successful investors are cautious and patient—you should be the same. Keep in mind that if you do overlook something, it's not the end of the world. Anything serious will get picked up by the professional inspector that you'll bring in after your offer is accepted.

Tools of the Trade

Here are just a few of basic tools you need to take out with you on your inspection trips:

- A clipboard and inspection sheets to record information
- A camera to photograph the front and back of the house (and perhaps other items of interest)
- A flashlight to inspect the attic, crawl space, furnace, and other dark corners
- A little ice pick to probe areas of suspected wood rot or termite damage
- A small level to check for sloping floors
- An inexpensive electric current meter to check if power is present in all of the electrical outlets

You should carry these basic tools with you and use them at each house inspection. They easily fit into a fanny pack or small backpack. I also bring file folders if I'm inspecting more than one house to keep the inspection sheets organized.

Are the Wrong Things Wrong with the House? The Deal-Killers

Theoretically, anything wrong with a house can be fixed, if you throw enough money at it (excluding location or other external factors). To some extent, this is true. But if certain problems are present, it is just better to walk away. In my opinion, here are the "wrong things wrong" that you should always avoid:

- Severe foundation settling or poured slab failure
- Extensive roof truss damage
- Hillside instability, landsliding

- Obsolete floor plan requiring a room addition (e.g., four-bed-room, one-bath)
- Illegal room additions or garage conversions, zoning violations
- Severe drainage problems
- Property line encroachments (minor issues are correctable)
- Extensive lead abatement or radon mitigation required
- Contaminated water well

All of these items may be correctable, given sufficient time and money, but my advice is to just walk away if any of these conditions are present. These are the deal-killers that you should look for and, without exception, avoid. There are plenty of houses out there for you to make money with—you don't need to solve these types of problems.

Environmental contamination problems including asbestos, lead-based paint, radon, mold, wet basements, and water well contamination are particularly important issues that you must be familiar with as a real estate entrepreneur. I go into a lot more detail on these problems in the next chapter.

Tune Your Antenna to Look for These Red Flags

If the house doesn't have the deal-killer items, you then look for serious but correctable defects that are candidates for your problem-solving efforts: problems with the foundation or roof, wood rot, electrical rewiring, and drainage, to name a few. What you need to look for are the symptoms of problems that have the potential to cost a lot of money to fix and therefore should raise a red flag if observed. They are the big-ticket items that you need to be aware of so that you can incorporate the "cost to cure" in developing an offer price.

Figure 12.1 provides a checklist that can be used to identify these potential problem areas and to record your observations. As noted on the form, these are not necessarily deal-killers—just problems or symptoms of problems that will need to be investigated and corrected if you choose to buy the property. It also will be useful to use in your discussions with the professional home inspector, if your offer is accepted and you hire someone for this service.

Use of the term *red flag* should not intimidate you. It is intended as a means to alert you to serious and costly problems so that you can in-

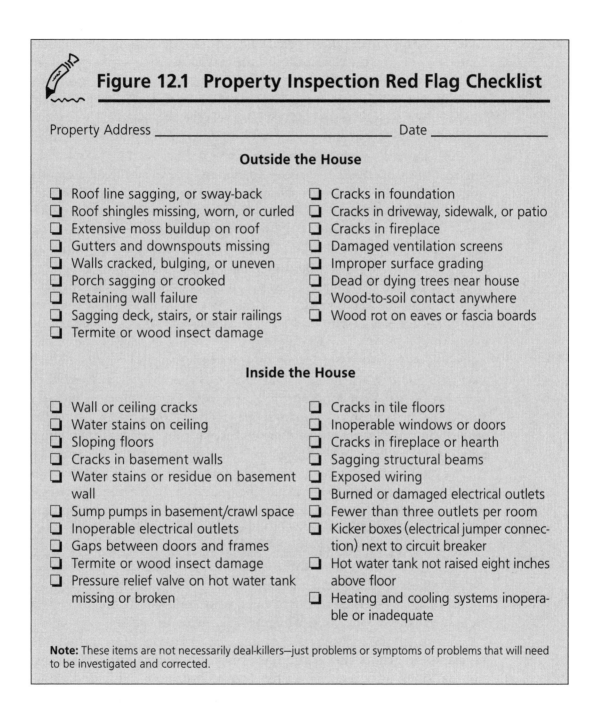

Figure 12.1 Property Inspection Red Flag Checklist

Property Address _____ Date _____

Outside the House

- ❏ Roof line sagging, or sway-back
- ❏ Roof shingles missing, worn, or curled
- ❏ Extensive moss buildup on roof
- ❏ Gutters and downspouts missing
- ❏ Walls cracked, bulging, or uneven
- ❏ Porch sagging or crooked
- ❏ Retaining wall failure
- ❏ Sagging deck, stairs, or stair railings
- ❏ Termite or wood insect damage

- ❏ Cracks in foundation
- ❏ Cracks in driveway, sidewalk, or patio
- ❏ Cracks in fireplace
- ❏ Damaged ventilation screens
- ❏ Improper surface grading
- ❏ Dead or dying trees near house
- ❏ Wood-to-soil contact anywhere
- ❏ Wood rot on eaves or fascia boards

Inside the House

- ❏ Wall or ceiling cracks
- ❏ Water stains on ceiling
- ❏ Sloping floors
- ❏ Cracks in basement walls
- ❏ Water stains or residue on basement wall
- ❏ Sump pumps in basement/crawl space
- ❏ Inoperable electrical outlets
- ❏ Gaps between doors and frames
- ❏ Termite or wood insect damage
- ❏ Pressure relief valve on hot water tank missing or broken

- ❏ Cracks in tile floors
- ❏ Inoperable windows or doors
- ❏ Cracks in fireplace or hearth
- ❏ Sagging structural beams
- ❏ Exposed wiring
- ❏ Burned or damaged electrical outlets
- ❏ Fewer than three outlets per room
- ❏ Kicker boxes (electrical jumper connection) next to circuit breaker
- ❏ Hot water tank not raised eight inches above floor
- ❏ Heating and cooling systems inoperable or inadequate

Note: These items are not necessarily deal-killers—just problems or symptoms of problems that will need to be investigated and corrected.

clude them in your purchase price calculation. These items are the deficiencies you expect and want to be present, at least to some extent, in all of your properties. Why? Because they will make you—the problem-solver—money. The trick is to identify them up front and include the cost to repair them in your rehab plan. Where you get into trouble is when you don't see the problem and therefore don't account for the costs to fix it.

Are you really saying you want a house to have termite problems, a sagging foundation, or a bad roof? Absolutely! For example, if a sagging foundation can be fixed with a simple jack post or two, why shouldn't you be willing to tackle it and be rewarded for solving this problem? Remember, you are looking for houses with solvable problems, not cosmetic flaws. The more problems there are, the cheaper the purchase price and the more profit potential for you, the problem-solver.

How do you distinguish between, for example, a foundation problem that is fixable and one that is a deal-killer? It's simple—after your initial offer is accepted (with the "subject to inspection" clause) you bring a structural engineer into the picture who has the expertise to evaluate the problem. It costs money to do this, but the cost can be split or otherwise negotiated with the seller. The same is true for termite, roof, or other problems. Your job and the home inspector's job is to identify problems. The next step, evaluating the feasibility and cost to correct the problem, is done by an expert that you hire (for the smaller, less complicated issues, you and or the inspector can reasonably estimate costs).

As you wander slowly through the house, taking notes and perhaps pictures, you will want to check out the operation of certain mechanical and electrical devices. If any of the appliances are going to stay and are salvageable, turn them on to see if they work. Make a note if they don't work, because you can use that in your price negotiations.

Run the water in all of the faucets and tubs, and flush the toilets—you're looking for leaks under the sinks and looking for evidence of slow drains. Will any of the plumbing need to be upgraded? Are there soft spots in the bathroom floor or on the tub enclosure walls?

Check out the heating and cooling systems to the best of your ability—are there grunts and groans? Are there any recent inspection tags? Can you smell gas or see oil drips? Can you see soot marks indicating combustion problems? Should the house have a central heating and air system? The answer is yes, particularly if the neighborhood comparable sales have it!

Look at the electrical panel—is it the modern circuit-breaker type or the older fuse box? A circuit-breaker system in an older home indicates the electrical system has been upgraded. The breaker panel should have a number on it indicating the amperage delivered to the house. With all the modern appliances and computers, the house should have 150–200 amps. Does the house have 220-volt service for a stove and clothes dryer? Use your electrical circuit tester on all of the outlet plugs to see if you have power. Do-it-yourself homeowner wiring is very common and very dangerous. Do you see any electrical cables hanging in the basement, lamp-cord wiring in closets or bedrooms, open metal junction boxes with covers missing and wire nut connectors hanging out of the box, or missing electric switch and outlet plate covers? These are signs of the do-it-yourselfer and they spell trouble!

Check out the attic if the house has one. What is the condition of the insulation? Can you see any evidence of water leakage or rotten wood? Get up there with your flashlight and crawl around for five or ten minutes.

If the house has a crawl space underneath, jump down there with your flashlight and at least look around a little (your termite inspector and house inspector will do a complete inspection). Do you see any vertical wooden supports in contact with the soil? Does the crawl space provide access to all areas of the house? Do you see any large cracks or water stains on the foundation walls? Has the owner installed sump pumps, indicating seepage or drainage problems?

Inspecting for Routine Repair Items

At this point, you've looked for the presence of potential deal-killers and potential big-ticket items (foundation, roof, etc.); now we're ready to note the more routine repairs that are typically present and readily observable in any fixer-upper property. It is also the time to note any upgrades and sizzle features you would want to incorporate into your overall rehab plan to address the marketability issue.

These are the things like kitchen rehab items, bath rehab items, carpeting, painting, lighting, drywall and plaster repair, and landscaping (to name a few). The best way to make notes about these items is, you guessed it, a form! The form in Figure 12.2 is intended to be used in the

Figure 12.2 Rehab Plan Checklist

Repair Items and Cost Estimate

Property Address _____   Date _____

Inspection Item	Comments	Repair Cost
Roof ❑ Repair ❑ Replace ❑ OK		
Foundation ❑ Repair ❑ OK		
Site Drainage ❑ Repair/Upgrade ❑ OK		
Electrical System ❑ Repair ❑ Upgrade ❑ OK		
Heating and Cooling ❑ Repair ❑ Upgrade ❑ OK		
Hot Water Heater ❑ Repair ❑ Replace ❑ OK		
Concrete: Patio/ Driveway and Sidewalks ❑ Repair/Refinish ❑ Replace ❑ OK		

Figure 12.2 Rehab Plan Checklist

Inspection Item	Comments	Repair Cost
Fireplace ❏ Repair ❏ Replace ❏ Install ❏ OK		
Termite Damage ❏ Treat ❏ Repair ❏ OK		
Decks and Stairs ❏ Repair ❏ Replace ❏ OK		
Exterior Wood ❏ Repair ❏ Replace ❏ OK		
Stucco or Siding ❏ Repair ❏ Replace ❏ OK		
Landscaping ❏ Upgrade ❏ Replace ❏ OK		
Junk Removal ❏ Exterior of house ❏ Interior of house ❏ OK		

Figure 12.2 Rehab Plan Checklist

Inspection Item	Comments	Repair Cost
Paint ❑ Touch up ❑ New Paint ❑ OK		
Flooring ❑ New Carpet ❑ New Vinyl ❑ New Tile ❑ Refinish Hardwood ❑ Repair Subfloor		
Kitchen ❑ Repair and Paint Cabinets ❑ Replace Cabinets ❑ New Countertops ❑ New Sink and Fixtures ❑ Replace Appliances ❑ Plumbing or Electrical Upgrade ❑ New Window or Skylight ❑ Install New Microwave ❑ Other		
Bathroom #1 ❑ New Sink and Vanity ❑ New Medicine Cabinet ❑ Replace Toilet ❑ New Mirror ❑ Bathtub Enclosure ❑ Repair or Replace Wall Tile ❑ Replace Bathtub		

Figure 12.2 Rehab Plan Checklist

Inspection Item	Comments	Repair Cost
Bathroom #1 (cont.) ❑ Refinish Bathtub ❑ New Window ❑ Repair Subfloor ❑ Plumbing Repair/ Replace ❑ Accessories (towel racks, etc.)		
Bathroom #2 ❑ New Sink and Vanity ❑ New Medicine Cabinet ❑ Replace Toilet ❑ New Mirror ❑ Bathtub Enclosure ❑ Repair or Replace Wall Tile ❑ Replace Bathtub ❑ Refinish Bathtub ❑ Repair Subfloor ❑ Accessories (towel racks, etc.)		
Interior Walls ❑ Repair Sheet Rock or Plaster ❑ Remove Paneling and Resurface ❑ OK		
Wallpaper/Borders ❑ Bathrooms ❑ Kitchen ❑ Other		

Figure 12.2 Rehab Plan Checklist

Inspection Item	Comments	Repair Cost
Windows ❑ Repair ❑ Replace ❑ OK		
Skylights ❑ Repair ❑ Install ❑ OK		
Light Fixtures ❑ Repair ❑ Replace ❑ Install Ceiling Fans ❑ OK		
Doors ❑ Repair ❑ Replace Front Entry Door ❑ Replace Interior Doors ❑ New Doorknobs		
Security System ❑ Repair ❑ Install ❑ OK		
Sizzle Features ❑ Hot Tub ❑ Tiled Entry ❑ Deck ❑ Garage Door Opener ❑ Attic Drop Stair Scuttle ❑ Mailbox		

Figure 12.2 Rehab Plan Checklist

Inspection Item	Comments	Repair Cost
Sizzle Features (cont.) ❑ Closet Organizer ❑ House Numbers ❑ Laundry Chute ❑ Workshop ❑ Miniblinds ❑ Other _____ ❑ Other _____		

Cost Summary

Repair Category	Cost Estimate
Roof	
Foundation	
Site Drainage	
Electrical System	
Heating and Cooling	
Hot Water Heater	
Concrete	
Fireplace	
Termite Damage	
Decks and Stairs	
Exterior Wood	
Stucco or Siding	
Landscaping	
Junk Removal	
Exterior Paint	

Figure 12.2 Rehab Plan Checklist

Repair Category	Cost Estimate
Interior Paint	
Flooring	
Kitchen Rehab	
Bathroom(s) Rehab	
Interior Walls	
Windows	
Skylights	
Light Fixtures	
Doors	
Security System	
Sizzle Features	
Other	
Subtotal	
Contingency	
Total Estimated Cost	

field to capture your initial thoughts about what repairs, big and small, will be needed to put the house in tip-top shape. Later, we will add the cost estimate for each item to complete the overall rehab plan.

Seller Disclosure and the "As Is" Ploy

Today, in almost every state in the country, sellers, and in some cases real estate brokers, are required to disclose any known problems and defects with the property. This includes environmental problems such as radon or lead paint and structural problems such as a leaky roof or foundation settlement. California started this trend, which has since swept the nation. Some areas are more stringent than others, so you will need to check on the local requirements. A seller or broker who fails to disclose problems may be liable if a subsequent lawsuit is filed.

Typically, these disclosures are made to the buyer in writing after the buyer submits a purchase offer. I always try to obtain this information before I submit the offer, if possible. Some owners will cooperate, some won't. If the property is listed with an agent, see what information he or she has available before you submit an offer. Even if the disclosure is made after you submit your offer, you can renegotiate if something unexpected turns up. Even with these new disclosure laws, some owners and agents will try to sell the property "as is." In the old days, selling "as is" meant that the owner would not warrant anything in the house and that it was up to you to find any problems. If problems were discovered after the sale, it was your problem, not the sellers'. Today, selling "as is" usually has a different connotation. If it is made when full disclosure is required by state law, it simply means that current owners will not accept offers that require them to make any repairs before closing. In this case, owners are still required to disclose any known defects.

In some jurisdictions such as Virginia, however, all existing homes must be sold with either a standard disclosure statement or specifically listed "as is." In this case, a listing "as is" truly means the owner will disclose nothing and will warrant nothing after the sale. Naturally, most people in Virginia know what this means, so the homes listed "as is" will be less desirable than competing homes with full disclosure. Thus, there is a built-in pressure for an owner to disclose.

Wherever you are, be alert when a property is listed "as is." This is a red flag that could mean, "There's something wrong with this house and it's up to you to find it!" Make sure you have a clear understanding of your state's disclosure requirements.

Should you rely on what a seller discloses? Get real! Never rely on anything a seller tells you! Sellers, like everybody else, can range from being shrewd liars trying to deceive you to just plain ignorant and "dumb as a box of rocks." Take whatever they say or disclose with a grain of salt. Even full seller disclosure is never to be used as a substitute for your own observations or for that of a professional inspector.

Finding the Right Home Inspection Professional

The home inspection industry has blossomed nationwide in the past few years, primarily in response to consumer demand. People have become more sophisticated and knowledgeable in their buying decisions. They have come to realize that a home inspection at the time of purchase is actually cheap insurance against a major error in relying on their own judgment. And for the rehab buyer, this service is indispensable.

The primary benefit for the rehab investor is the ability to bring in a skilled professional, acting in a neutral third-party role, to systematically evaluate and diagnose building defects. Unlike you or the seller, this person has no emotional involvement in the outcome of the inspection. The facts are simply observed and reported.

The scope of an inspection varies from company to company and can be tailored, to some extent, by the consumer. According to the American Society of Home Inspectors (ASHI), the typical inspection using their Standards of Practice will include the items in Figure 12.3.

Pretty comprehensive list, eh? Although not required by the ASHI Standards, most inspectors will also provide a ballpark guesstimate on repair costs. Other services could include a radon survey, lead paint testing, termite inspection, and appliance warranties. Of course, all will provide a written report of the findings, usually within two to four days. It will take the inspector anywhere from one to three hours, depending on scope and thoroughness of the inspector.

The cost of the inspection service varies around the country and also varies by the scope of the services requested. Some companies adjust cost based on such factors as listing price, square footage, and age of the house. In our local Albuquerque market, fees range from about $175 for a structural inspection only, up to about $315 for a full inspection including termites. Radon is another $95 and lead paint $150.

The challenge you have is to select the right inspector for your work. It's somewhat like finding a good auto mechanic or handyman—some are better than others and none of them, including the home inspector, needs to be licensed! The proliferation of national franchise operations has increased your options, but you need to be really careful—anybody can buy a franchise! You'll need to check out the background and qualifications of the inspector and ask for references. I use a company that is

Figure 12.3 Home Inspection Criteria

Home Inspection Criteria
American Society of Home Inspectors

- *Structural*—foundation; floors; walls; columns; ceilings; and roof
- *Exterior*—wall cladding; flashings and trim; entryway doors; windows; garage door operation; decks; balconies; stoops; steps; porches and railings; eaves; soffits; fascias; vegetation; grading; drainage; driveways; patios; walkways; and retaining walls
- *Roofing*—roof coverage; roof drainage systems; flashings; skylights; chimneys and roof penetrations; and signs of leaks or abnormal condensation
- *Plumbing*—interior water supply and distribution system, including piping materials, supports and insulation, fixtures, faucets, functional flow, leaks, and cross-connections; interior drain, waste, and vent systems; hot water systems including operating controls, safety controls, and chimneys, flues, and vents; fuel storage and distribution systems; and sump pumps
- *Electrical*—service entrance conductors including service equipment, grounding equipment, main overcurrent device, and main and distribution panels, amperage and voltage ratings; branch circuit conductors, overcurrent devices, and compatibility of ampacities and voltages; operation of lighting fixtures, switches, and receptacles inside the house, garage, and exterior walls; polarity and grounding of all receptacles within six feet of interior plumbing fixtures and all receptacles in garage or carport, and on exterior of structures; and operation of ground fault circuit interrupters (GFIs)
- *Heating*—heating equipment, including normal operating controls, automatic safety controls, chimneys, flues, and vents; solid fuel heating devices; heat distribution systems, including fans, pumps, ducts, piping, dampers, insulation, air filters, registers, radiators, fan-coil units, and convectors; and the presence of an installed heat source in each room
- *Central Air-Conditioning*—cooling and air-handling equipment; normal operating controls; distribution system including fans, pumps, ducts, and piping, air filters, registers, and fan-coil units; and presence of an installed cooling source in each room
- *Interiors*—walls, ceilings, and floors; steps, stairways, balconies, and railings; counters and cabinets; doors and windows; and separation walls, ceilings, and doors between dwelling and attached garage or adjacent dwelling
- *Insulation and Ventilation*—insulation and vapor retarders in unfinished spaces; and absence of same in unfinished spaces

staffed by registered professional engineers. They are thorough and extremely knowledgeable, particularly when it comes to structural issues, such as the foundation. Like anything else, you get what you pay for. Don't just go for the lowest price!

I highly recommend that you accompany the inspector to each and every house. It is the best two- or three-hour education you can get for the money! Tag along and ask questions—lots of questions. You'll be amazed at what you can learn from an experienced home inspection professional. This not only will help you in your future inspections that you will do on your own, it also will give you specific details to use in finalizing the rehab plan on the house in question. As I mentioned before, if something unexpected turns up, you'll have the option either to renegotiate the deal or just walk away from it. I've done both, and you'll be able to do the same with the right language in your purchase offer contract.

One additional note on the termite inspection: In many areas of the country, it is the local custom for the seller to pay for this inspection. Similar to the title inspection, the owner has the obligation to prove clear title and to prove that the house is clear of any infestation. Put it in your contract!

The Art and Science of Estimating Repairs

It took me a long time and a lot of trial and error to get good at this. But you have to master this area in order to be successful in the rehab game. If your rehab cost estimates are consistently too high, resulting in a lower offer price, you will consistently land fewer deals. On the other hand, if your cost estimates are consistently too low, you will consistently lose money! Your goal is to learn how to make good-quality ballpark estimates. If you're off a couple thousand dollars in either direction, it shouldn't matter on the typical deal. If you're off by more than that, you could be in trouble, depending on how much fluff or contingency you built in to the offer price.

What's the secret to success? Well, it really boils down to the time and effort you spend in developing your list of planned renovations and knowing the cost of materials and labor in your local market. There really is no shortcut here. You have to take it upon yourself to get out there in the local marketplace and learn and learn and learn. It takes time and effort and it's an ongoing process.

Some of the real estate gurus teach you to go out to a house and within ten minutes develop your checklist of renovations and your total rehab cost. Gulp! I hate to hear that kind of superficial treatment given to what essentially is the heart and soul of this business. If that's all the effort you give to this critical task, then you're asking for big trouble! Granted, I tend to be more thoughtful and cautious in my approach, but I would rather be more conservative than just blunder ahead and hope for the best—and I would hope that you will do the same.

Now, if you've been working in your local market for a couple of years and you've rehabbed a half-dozen houses, then I would say that you've probably gained enough experience to quickly estimate repair costs. Until you're at this point, do your due diligence, do your home-work, and adopt a healthy sense of caution and patience. Pay your dues through study and effort—not by making big mistakes!

You already have the rehab plan checklist, so you have a mechanism to identify the tasks you plan to accomplish. I can't emphasize enough that you need to carefully record, as precisely as possible, the nature and extent of each rehab project. Go through each room in your mind and look at the pictures you took and visualize exactly what needs to be done to put the house in top condition. Don't gloss over the little stuff—towel racks, miniblinds, wall plugs, trim, garage door opener—these things add up fast! You're now ready to sharpen your pencil and begin the process of estimating the cost of these repairs.

For each job, there are two components—materials and labor—and you will be paying for both. Now, I'm going to give you a couple of ways to get a handle on repair cost estimating. But please, don't rely on just one method. This is an evolutionary process that needs to be refined over time, so don't get lazy.

First, go out, with pencil and notebook, and spend time hanging around your nearest Home Depot or Lowe's or whatever your big home improvement center is. These are the stores where you and your con-tractors are going to get the best prices on materials. The local mom-and-pop stores just can't match the variety and prices of the big chain stores. Spend a morning or afternoon just wandering around, jotting down prices of everything you see you will likely need at some point—toilets, vinyl flooring, bathroom vanities, sinks, fixtures, cabinets, paint, drywall, windows, lumber—you get the idea. You're just compiling a laundry list, so to speak, to get a good feel for prices and price ranges. The best advice I can give you on this is to shop 'til you drop! But this isn't just a one-time venture. You need to do this all the time and at different stores—kind of make a hobby out of it! Watch all the sale ads each week in the paper. The more time you spend looking at materials and qualities of various items, the better you will be at estimating costs.

There are going to be some items such as roof replacement and foundation leveling that you obviously can't price at Home Depot. For roof jobs, you can usually call around to your roofing contractors and get some ballpark estimates over the phone, based on type of roof and size of house. If you don't have a specific house to discuss, then just make one up—say a 1,200-square-foot house with asphalt shingles. If you belong to a local real estate investor's group (and you should!), ask around—they will be able to give you some ideas on prices (and a lot of other good advice too!).

Foundation estimating is a lot more difficult because it is so job-specific. Talk to your home inspector, your investor's group, and call around to some structural engineering companies to get an idea on local price ranges. It's going to depend on the extent of the problem and the type of foundation (slab or block wall). Easy fixes like jack post and shims (block foundation) or drilling concrete pillars every eight feet around one end of a slab are one thing (typically in the $4,000 to $8,000 range). If you have serious soil stability or compaction problems, look out! You could be spending anywhere from $25,000 to $50,000 and on up—these are the foundation problems you walk away from.

Labor cost is such an important topic that I'm devoting an entire chapter to it (see Chapter 15). For now, just keep this in mind—if you want to pay top dollar for your labor, call the company with the big Yellow Pages ad! The person you're looking for to do most of the work is the handyman who has no overhead but is reasonably skilled at many things. For the big jobs like foundation or roofing, yeah, you want the general contractor who can guarantee the work. For the rest, find yourself one of the most underappreciated people in America—the handyman!

The method I've just described, coupled with actually bidding the work out, is by far the best method of developing information for cost estimating. It takes the most work, but it is the most accurate because it is based on local market prices.

The next method of cost estimating is usually less accurate, but still very useful. It is based on the concept of national averages, adjusted for local economic conditions. The resource for this is an excellent publication from Marshall & Swift (a division of McGraw-Hill) called the *Home Repair and Remodel Cost Guide.* It is published annually (late January or early February) and can be obtained by calling the publisher toll-free at 800-526-2756.

It works like this: Marshall & Swift obtains material cost data from building product manufacturers, dealers, supply houses, and the like, from around the country. Labor rates are gathered from 22 trades in each of the researched cities. Local multipliers are developed for each of the cities, based on the local prevailing wages. For each type of repair, a national average is developed along with categories such as "economy," "standard," and "custom." You simply look up the price under the desired category and then apply your local multiplier (listed by ZIP code) and bingo, you have a cost estimate! Just about everything you would want to do (except foundation repairs!) can be found in this book: bathrooms, kitchens, flooring, roofing, electrical, windows, heating and air-conditioning. Some items are priced based on room size, linear foot, square foot, or component. Figures 12.4 through 12.7 give you an example from Marshall & Swift on costs for bathroom replacement, using both the room method and the unit (component) method.

Do you suppose the values would vary much around the country? Let's take a look at an example. The national average for an asphalt shingle roof of economy grade is $1 per square foot. So, a 1,500-square-foot roof would cost $1,500 with materials and labor included. Now, if you live in the New York metropolitan area, you would apply a 1.48 multiplier so the cost would be $2,220. If you live in Brookhaven, Mississippi, you would apply a 0.84 multiplier so the cost would be $1,260. Quite a spread!

Figure 12.4 Bathrooms—Room Method

Costs include replacing the bathroom complete. (New: fixtures, faucets, floor, ceiling, and wall finishes.) Note: If additional fixtures per room are required, add from the Unit Method.

HALF BATH (1 toilet, 1 bathroom sink)

Room Size (Square Foot Area)	Quality Levels		
	Economy	Standard	Custom
25 Square Feet	$1,950	$3,430	$5,240
30 Square Feet	2,010	3,530	5,470
35 Square Feet	2,070	3,660	5,680
40 Square Feet	2,120	3,780	5,860
45 Square Feet	2,180	3,930	6,070
50 Square Feet	2,230	4,050	6,280
Over 50 Square Feet	2,280	4,200	6,510

FULL BATH
(1 toilet, 1 bathroom sink, 1 bathtub w/shower)

Room Size (Square Foot Area)	Quality Levels		
	Economy	Standard	Custom
50 Square Feet	$3,320	$5,570	$8,010
60 Square Feet	3,430	5,820	8,440
70 Square Feet	3,480	6,000	8,660
80 Square Feet	3,550	6,160	8,930
90 Square Feet	3,620	6,320	9,130
100 Square Feet	3,690	6,470	9,350
Over 100 Square Feet	3,750	6,620	9,640

Source: Reprinted by permission of the copyright owner, Marshall & Swift
© 2003 by Marshall & Swift, L.P.

Figure 12.5 Bathrooms—Unit Method

To replace individual items, use the costs below.

Component (Price Each)	Economy	Quality Levels Standard	Custom
Accessories Set (paper and toothbrush holders, soap dish, etc.)	$135	$ 190	$ 275
Bathtub	380	660	1,150
Bathtub enclosure	275	335	410
Bathtub/Shower Combination	915	1,010	1,125
Bidet	480	640	870
Caulking—Bathtub	55	60	70
Faucet	130	185	265
Medicine Cabinet	110	155	220
Mirror	130	205	320
Shower Door	200	285	355
Showerhead	75	100	105
Shower (over the tub)	190	270	330
Shower Rod	25	31	36
Shower Stall	780	955	1,180
Sink—Built-in	275	335	425
Sink—Wall-mounted	320	395	510
Toilet Seat	55	65	90
Toilet—Floor-mounted	460	600	795
Toilet—Wall-mounted	660	855	1,095
Vanity—Metal	285	335	410
Vanity—Wood	320	375	440

Source: Reprinted by permission of the copyright owner, Marshall & Swift
© 2003 by Marshall & Swift, L.P.

Figure 12.6 Typical Bathroom Layout

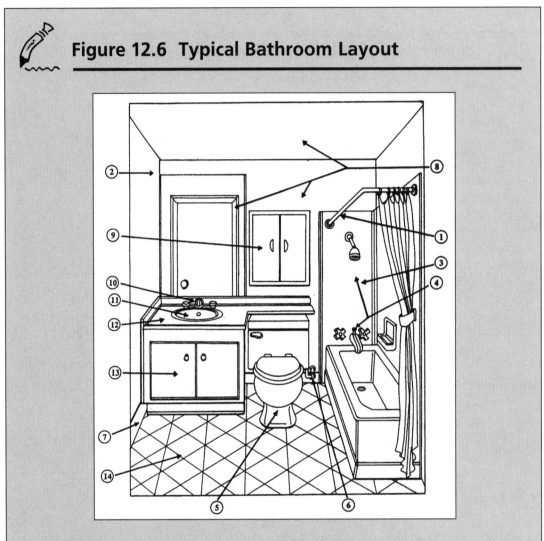

1. Curtain Rod
2. Drywall
3. Fiberglass Tub and Surround
4. Tub and Shower Fittings
5. Tank-Type Toilet, 2-Piece
6. Toilet Fittings
7. Baseboard
8. Paint
9. Medicine Cabinet
10. Bathroom Sink Fittings
11. Bathroom Sink
12. Vanity Top
13. Vanity Base Cabinet
14. Vinyl Flooring

Source: Reprinted by permission of the copyright owner, Marshall & Swift
© 2003 by Marshall & Swift, L.P.

Figure 12.7 Bathroom Component Descriptions

ACCESSORIES SET	Minor bathroom attachments, such as paper holder, toothbrush holder, soap dish.
BATHTUB	Costs include the bathtub, connection to supply piping, and the drain and overflow.
BATHTUB ENCLOSURE	A metal-framed enclosure made with glass or plastic material.
BATHTUB/SHOWER COMBINATION	A one-piece bathtub/shower made of fiberglass. Costs also include the connection to the supply piping and the drain and overflow.
BIDET	Costs include the bidet, faucets, and the connection to the supply piping.
CAULKING (BATHTUB)	A resilient mastic compound between a bathtub and wall or floor surfaces used for waterproofing.
FAUCET	A plumbing valve that combines hot and cold water through one outlet.
MEDICINE CABINET	A bathroom storage cabinet for medical supplies and toilet articles.
MIRROR	A wall-mounted bathroom mirror.
SHOWER DOOR	A shower door made of aluminum-framed glass that operates by sliding on a track or swinging on hinges.
SHOWERHEAD	A pipe and nozzle through which water is sprayed.
SHOWER (OVER TUB)	Piping, controls, and nozzle used to provide water for an over-the-tub shower.
SHOWER ROD	A steel tube on which shower curtains are hung.
SHOWER STALL	A prefabricated enclosure for a shower. Costs include the connection to a water supply and drain.
SINK (BUILT-IN)	A built-in bathroom basin. Costs include the connection to a water supply and drain.
TOILET SEAT	The seat portion of a toilet fixture.
TOILET (FLOOR MOUNTED)	A toilet fixture whose base is bolted to the bathroom floor. Costs include the seat (bowl), tank, connection to a water supply, and drain.
TOILET (WALL MOUNTED)	A toilet fixture mounted on a wall. Costs include the seat (bowl), tank, connection to a water supply, and drain.
VANITY (METAL)	A metal case used primarily to house a bathroom sink, usually with drawers. Costs do not include the plumbing fixtures.

Source: Reprinted by permission of the copyright owner, Marshall & Swift
© 2003 by Marshall & Swift, L.P.

The important thing to know about the Marshall & Swift cost data is what is included. All of the values given include:

- The replacement cost of removing the existing component and replacing with new materials, including labor, materials, and all connections
- Contractor's overhead and profit
- Workers' benefit packages and insurance

Can you see that for many items, the prices given are going to be high compared to what you could get by having a handyman do the work? In these instances, I use Marshall & Swift more or less as a worst-case scenario, knowing that I can usually beat the prices using my handyman labor. If you're using a general contractor, these prices should be close to what you can expect on bids.

Get the book and use it. It's an excellent resource. But fine-tune your cost estimating by shopping the local market.

Quality of Materials—You Get What You Pay For

In developing rehab plans and developing cost estimates, one of the first decisions is quality of materials. Do I buy the $8-per-square-yard carpet or the $18-per-square-yard carpet? As mentioned earlier, even when using Marshall & Swift you need to decide on economy, or standard, or custom.

To some extent, this is a personal decision. We all know that you get what you pay for. But let me suggest that there is a big difference between what we buy for our personal homes versus what we buy for our rehab properties. Furthermore, let me share with you my own personal philosophy on the topic: Buy cheap on most items and expensive on a few.

This is consistent with my overall rehab philosophy. Because target properties are usually at the low end of the cost spectrum, it doesn't make sense to install high-quality materials when the market will gladly accept "economy" quality. Putting in $10-per-square-yard FHA-grade carpet is perfectly acceptable for the type of houses we are dealing with. The same is true for cabinets, appliances, windows, toilets, and so forth.

The exception is when we are putting in our sizzle features: ceiling fans, sink faucets, towel racks, lighting fixtures, mailboxes, house numbers, and wallpaper borders. When it comes to these items, always buy the more expensive items. I don't mean standard quality. Buy the custom end of the quality spectrum. Remember, it's the sizzle that sells, and we're trying to create the unexpected with a few carefully selected items. So go ahead and splurge on these and make a statement!

The other exception is paint. Always use good-quality standard-grade paints that are always on sale somewhere in your local stores. Cheap paint makes the house look cheap, which is not what we're trying to accomplish!

Next, let's dig in to those nasty contamination issues and see how to deal with them effectively.

Toxic Real Estate

Dealing with Contamination Issues

A little-known secret about my personal background is that I worked as an environmental manager in the oil and gas industry for more than 15 years. One of the lessons I learned from that experience is this: Don't mess with Uncle Sam. Regardless of what you might think of certain "environmental wacko" groups behind some of the regulations governing contamination issues, or what you might think of the sometimes zealous state and federal employees who are charged with enforcing the rules, my advise is to always follow the letter of the law. If a regulation requires you to disclose, then you had better disclose. If it requires you to dispose at a regulated landfill, that's what you need to do. Life is too short to risk getting tangled up with enforcement actions, lawsuits, and lawyers. Having said that, dealing with contamination issues related to investment properties really boils down to using common sense and judgment.

A property with a contamination problem has the *potential* to be a deal-killer. If the problem is extensive, excessively costly to repair and the seller can't/won't fix it or can't/won't give you a price reduction to compensate, then the answer is simple—you walk! On the other hand, if the problem is relatively easy to fix (and many of these problems are) and the cost is accounted for in your rehab cost calculation, then you may want to proceed. Getting answers to the following basic questions will guide you when faced with a contaminated property:

- What is the extent of the contamination?
- Is the problem fixable?
- What is the cost to fix the problem?
- Who will pay—buyer or seller?

The question of who will pay is, of course, the bottom line. In this business, it always gets down to money, and from whose pocket it comes. More on this at the end of this chapter. First, let's explore the major contamination issues and learn about the options for dealing with them.

Asbestos—The Mother of All Contaminants

There probably isn't an American adult alive today that isn't aware, at least in general terms, of the dangers of asbestos. For more than 20 years, hardly a day goes by without some mention of an asbestos cleanup project or court case in the local paper or on the evening news. Since the early 1980s, public and private building owners have spent about $50 billion on asbestos removal, with another $50 billion to be spent in the coming years. Everybody knows that asbestos exposure can lead to serious respiratory problems and deadly lung cancer.

Outside the medical community, the little-known secret is that a person who spends a lifetime living or working inside a building filled with asbestos materials is more likely to die of a lightning bolt than an asbestos-related cancer! After years of creating public panic and issuing ill-conceived regulations, government experts at the EPA now concede that leaving asbestos in buildings alone is usually the best course of action. What's going on here? Does this mean asbestos in *not* dangerous? Absolutely not.

Asbestos has caused an estimated 172,000 cancer deaths in the United States from 1967 to 1997. An additional 119,000 cancer deaths are expected before the scourge runs its course by about 2025. This by far, is the worst occupational health disaster of the 20th century.

However, the important point to understand is that an overwhelming majority of all asbesto-related disease and death incidents occurs in the sub-population of industrial workers who were previously exposed to airborne asbestos fibers in the course of their daily job duties. This includes workers such as shipyard pipe fitters, building insulation installers, and asbestos mine workers. In other words, it usually takes prolonged exposure over time to high levels of airborne asbestos fibers to become at high risk for asbestos illness. On the other hand, the cancer risk to those of us who live and work in buildings containing asbestos materials is barely measurable. Unless asbestos-containing materials are damaged and are releasing fibers into the atmosphere, they pose an *insignificant risk.*

Today in the United States, the use of asbestos in building materials, brake linings, or other commercial products is essentially banned. The final stage of the phase-out ended in 1997. But the material was widely used in houses and commercial buildings until the late 1970s.

Asbestos is very common in the types of houses we work with in the rehab business, because we tend to invest in older properties that have been neglected and are in need of moderate-to-extensive updating. What this means is that we need to know where it is typically found and how to deal with it.

Asbestos can be found in a variety of building materials used in the construction of older (pre-1980) houses. Here are the most common areas in which to find asbestos containing materials.

- Roofing and siding shingles made of asbestos cement
- Insulation (ceiling and walls) in houses built between 1930 and 1950.
- Patching and joint compounds for walls and ceilings and textured paint (their use in these products was banned in 1977)
- Soundproofing or decorative materials sprayed on walls and ceilings
- Vinyl floor tiles and the backing on vinyl sheet flooring and adhesives
- Asbestos paper, millboard, or cement sheets on walls and floors around wood burning stoves
- Asbestos blankets or tape around hot water and steam pipes
- Oil and coal furnace and door gasket insulation

How do you know if a particular construction material contains asbestos? Unless you are an expert, you can't tell by just looking at the material. The only way to know for sure is to have it tested at a laboratory. Before we get into that, let's talk about basic asbestos management.

The Golden Rule is this: *Don't Remove It Unless You Absolutely Have To!*

The removal is what causes the danger when dealing with asbestos materials, particularly when working with old, brittle products. Ripping, tearing, or cutting the material out can release the dangerous fibers into the air. You want to avoid removal, if possible.

Because we are in the business of remodeling our houses, we have to do something, right? If feasible, the best course of action is to either encapsulate the material with a commercial asbestos sealant like AsbestoSafe® <www.encasement.com> or cover-up the asbestos material with a protective wrap or jacket. Exposed pipe, furnace and boiler insulation and minor roof or siding shingle repairs (the most common asbestos problems encountered) can be easily addressed with a sealant. If you are installing a new roof or siding, you can oftentimes have the new material placed right over the old (check with your contractor). The asbestos material remains safely in place and costly removal and disposal costs are avoided. This is the obvious choice if you can complete your rehab without removing the old stuff.

What if leaving the insulation or shingles in place is not going to work? If the old roof or siding shingles just have to go? If the old boiler and piping has to be ripped out and replaced? What to do?

The first thing is to have the material sampled and analyzed at the laboratory to confirm you are dealing with asbestos. Many professional home inspectors will handle this for you. Check with the lab to see if they have EPA accreditation for asbestos sampling or you can check online at the National Institute of Standards and Technology Web site <www.nist.gov>. A sample or two is not going to be that expensive, and it could very well result in avoiding the extra cost of asbestos removal if the results turn out negative.

Let's assume the worst case scenario—you have confirmed asbestos containing material and it has to be removed. Now what? Do you have to bring in a small army of guys in moon-suits and put a plastic tent over the entire house? This will cost a fortune!

Relax. This is where some calm thinking and common sense will *save* you a fortune. One thing is for sure, the removal and disposal must be done in a way that insures the safety of the workers involved in the process and is in compliance with regulatory requirements. That said, the rest is negotiable with the contractors you choose. By that I mean you can hire a professional asbestos removal company, which *will* cost you a fortune, or you can work with responsible contractors who know how to get the job done safely and economically.

The good news is that private homes are not covered by the asbestos regulations that apply to schools and public buildings. And roofing and flooring contractors are exempt from state and local asbestos licensing requirements that apply to asbestos removal contractors. However, you should use contractors who have had training in asbestos handling procedures. The main issue is to make sure workers are using approved respiratory protection, gloves, and other protective clothing. You want to make sure that they apply a wetting agent (usually water) to the asbestos material with a hand sprayer that creates a fine mist before removal. This will keep the fibers out of the air and out of the worker's lungs. It will also minimize the creation and accumulation of dust that can cause post-removal cleanup problems.

Oftentimes, you or your contractor can make arrangements with the local asbestos disposal company to provide a special rubber-lined dumpster on the jobsite. Once the removal job is done, they pick up the dumpster and bury the material in their government approved landfill.

On one of my early projects, I thought I'd do the responsible thing and bring in a professional asbestos removal company to handle the removal and disposal of an asbestos-cement-based shingle roof. I about fell over when I received a bid for a mere $6,000! Heck, the new roof was only going to cost $2,500! I did some checking around and found a disposal company who provided the dumpster for $575 and my roofing contractor did the rest. The work was done safely and in full compliance with regulatory requirements—and at a reasonable cost.

Lead-Based Paint—Not the Problem It Once Was

Lead-based paint is another environmental issue that came to the forefront during the 1970s. It was discovered that ingestion or inhaling dust particles of lead-based paint can lead to very serious health problems, such as learning disabilities and kidney and nervous system damage, and that children six years old or younger were particularly vulnerable. Although this type of paint was widely used in residential buildings throughout the country, its use on interior surfaces had declined significantly since the introduction of latex paint in the 1950s. Nevertheless, something had to be done, and by 1978 the use of lead-based paint in houses or other types of residential units was banned.

Although the banning of lead-based paint has taken care of the problem for new housing units built since 1978, the problem remains for the homes and apartment buildings built prior to that time. In fact, HUD has estimated that 83 percent of private housing built prior to 1980 contains lead-based paint. Even with the introduction of latex in the 1950s, lead-based paint was still used extensively on exterior surfaces through the mid-1970s, which has resulted in soil contamination. The bottom line is this—the older the home, the more likely it is to contain lead-based paint.

The most common potential problem areas around a house are:

- Windows and window sills
- Door and door frames
- Stairs, railings, and banisters
- Exterior siding, porches, and fences

How do you know if the house you are dealing with has lead-based paint? Since 1996, the owner/seller of any real estate built prior to 1978 is required by EPA/HUD rules to disclose if any *known* lead-based paint is present in the house. Because testing is *not* required, very few sellers actually *know.* As a result, you will typically get little to no information from a seller. Your best bet is to bring in a professional home inspector. Your home inspector will have a handy-dandy portable x-ray fluorescence machine that will tell you. This device detects not just the presence or absence of lead, but measures the amount of lead present. The inspector can then advise you as to the degree of potential problems associated with planned renovations.

As a real estate entrepreneur, you will need to deal with the lead-based paint issue on two levels. First, in getting the rehab work done in a manner that is safe and economical, and second in dealing with the regulatory disclosure requirements.

Just about any rehab project will involve one or more of the following: removing paint; tearing down walls; replacing windows, baseboards, doors, or plumbing fixtures; heating and ventilation duct work; and electrical systems. All of these jobs likely will require breaking through painted surfaces and thus create a concern about contamination from lead-based paint.

When doing renovations that disturb the old paint and release chips onto the ground/floor or dust particles into the atmosphere, you have to be concerned about two things in particular: protecting the health of those doing the work and making sure that the contaminated particles are not allowed to spread throughout the entire house. Taking a few common sense precautions is all that is required. But it is your responsibility to inform your contractors about the presence of lead-based paint so that they can take the necessary steps.

An excellent EPA publication, *Reducing Lead Hazards When Remodeling Your Home,* is available online at <www.epa.gov/lead/rrpam ph.pdf> (you will need the free Adobe Acrobat Reader software available at <www.adobe.com> to read this file). This provides guidance on how to get the job done safely and how to prevent the spread of lead contamination throughout the house. In a nutshell, the EPA recommendations include:

Before the work begins
- Have your paint tested for lead by a qualified professional.
- Cover interior and exterior exposed areas with plastic sheeting.
- Turn off forced-air heating and air conditioning systems.

During work
- Keep all nonworkers outside of the work area.
- Wear protective clothing and shoes while doing the work.
- Use a properly fitted respirator equipped with HEPA filters.
- Exercise caution when using paint strippers since they contain toxic chemicals.
- Do not eat, drink, or smoke in the work area.
- Do not dry-sand, blast, or power-wash to remove lead-based paint.
- Do not use high-temperature heat guns or open flames on lead-based paint.

After work is completed
- Remove plastic sheeting by rolling or folding inward.
- Wrap construction debris with plastic.

- Vacuum exposed areas with a HEPA filter-equipped vacuum cleaner.
- Wash exposed areas with a general all-purpose cleaner or lead-specific cleaning product.
- Change clothes and shoes before leaving the work area. Machine wash separately.
- Shower and wash your hair right after finishing work.
- Test areas for lead dust contamination after final cleanup.

The creation of dust is the major pathway for lead contamination. It follows then, that the primary consideration when doing rehabs on older homes is to minimize activities and techniques that create dust. This means you and your contractors must avoid *dry* scraping, sanding, brushing, or blasting and instead use *wet* techniques. Burning lead-based paint with open flame torches to make it easier to strip is particularly dangerous because the fumes will contain lead and volatile chemicals that are poisonous when inhaled.

As a practical matter, when doing rehabs on houses containing lead-based paint, you want to minimize actual removal of the paint. Old lead-based paint that is well maintained does not present a hazard and is best left undisturbed. An excellent alternative to removal is encapsulation wherein the old paint is covered with a sealant. A commercial sealant product similar to that used for asbestos is called LeadLock™ <www.en casement.com>. After the sealant dries, you just paint over it with a paint of your choice, and you're done. When compared with the cost and hassle of paint removal, this type of product is the obvious choice.

The second level we must deal with as real estate entrepreneurs is the regulatory arena, specifically the EPA/HUD Lead-Based Paint Real Estate Disclosure Rule. This rule became effective in 1996 and has several provisions that real estate investors need to understand. First and foremost, remember that these requirements *only apply to houses built prior to 1978.* Here are the key provisions that apply to the seller/owner.

- Must disclose any *known* lead-based paint or lead-based paint hazards in the house (obviously, if you don't know about it, no testing or disclosure is required).
- Must provide any records or reports about lead-based paint in the house.

- Must provide your *buyer* with a copy of the EPA pamphlet "*Protect Your Family from Lead in Your Home*" (available online from the EPA <www.epa.gov/opptintr/lead/leadpbed.htm>).
- Must provide your buyer a ten-day period to test for lead, if they choose.
- Your sales contract must include warning language (that lead-based paint may be present) and a signed statement in the contract verifying that the above requirements have been met.

EPA and HUD's strategy is basically one of disclosure. They want to make sure that all homebuyers purchasing homes built prior to 1978 are aware of the possibility that lead-based paint is present, so homeowners can protect themselves and their children. Note that testing is not required and if you or your buyer discovers lead through testing, removal of the lead-based paint is not required.

All indications are that the government's disclosure strategy has been very effective in reducing the exposure of people (especially children) to lead poisoning. In 1998, HUD published a report compiled from 18 federal agencies, *America's Children: Key National Indicators of Well-Being,* which reported that the percentage of children ages 1 through 5 with elevated blood lead levels has fallen from 88 percent in the late 1970s to *just 6 percent.* This phenomenal success indicates that the lead-based paint issue, while still relevant and important, is not the problem it once was. Good news for all of us in the real estate industry!

Radon—Ho Hum . . . Yawn

As a real estate entrepreneur, particularly one who specializes in quick-turnaround projects, I just can't seem to get too excited about radon. Although the issue caught the imagination of the EPA in the early 1980s, it has died a slow death (no pun intended) in more recent years. Just like the hype that accompanied the asbestos issue in its heyday, a nationwide radon scare captured the residential real estate market for a while. As more scientific studies were completed, people have become more realistic about the dangers of radon in their homes.

Certainly, high levels of radon in a home can be a very legitimate health concern. Persistent exposure to this radioactive gas has definitively been linked to lung cancer in some individuals—smokers and uranium miners are particularly vulnerable. EPA's recommended criteria for when a homeowner should consider taking some form of mitigation is 4 picocuries per liter (4 pCi/l) of air. To put that in perspective, the EPA estimates that 93 percent of all homes are below this level. In fact, they estimate that the average home has a radon level of only 1 pCi/l.

With this perspective in mind, it is easy to see that radon very rarely becomes an issue in a real estate transaction. Although incidents of elevated radon in homes have been reported in all 50 states, the "problem" is widely variable and scattered. Keep in mind, adjacent homes can have entirely different radon measurement readings, meaning that a high reading in one house is not an indicator of problems in the entire neighborhood.

If you think radon is a potential problem, there is only one way to find out–test. You can buy a test kit at your local home improvement or hardware store for as little as $10 or, you can have your home inspector include the test as part of the inspection routine. The minimum testing period is 48 hours. If you do it yourself with a kit, you have to mail the test strips to the lab for analysis. There are some specific testing conditions that must be met (like closing all windows) and these are described in the kit instructions or will be provided by your inspector. If you would like advice on test kits or approved radon inspectors in your area, contact your state radon office. A listing of state radon offices can be found online: <www.epa.gov/iaq/contacts.html>.

Radon enters the house either through cracks or holes in the foundation, penetrations into a crawl space, or through well water. To fix a radon problem, you generally have to vent the subsurface soil or crawl-space, seal cracks and penetrations, or, in the case of well water, you are looking at either an aeration or an activated carbon filter system.

EPA has put together a publication outlining various alternatives for radon mitigation: *Consumer's Guide to Radon Reduction,* available online <www.epa.gov/iaq/radon/pubs/consguid.html>. This guide also contains some cost information for the various remediation techniques. The cost information in the guide is based on 1991 data, which in Figure 13.1 I have adjusted to 2003, using CPI factors.

Figure 13.1 Installation and Operating Cost Table

Technique	Typical Radon Reduction (%)	Typical Range of Installation Costs (Contractor)	Typical Operating Cost Range for Fan Electricity & Heated/ Cooled Air Loss (Annual)	Comments
Sub-slab Suction (Sub-slab Depressurization)	80–99	$1,000–3,000	$100–225	Works best if air can move easily in material under slab.
Passive Sub-slab Suction	30–70	$725–3,000	There may be some energy penalties.	May be more effective in cold climates; not as effective as active sub-slab suction.
Drain Tile Suction	90–99	$1,000–2,000	$100–225	Works best if drain-tiles form complete loop around house.
Block-Wall Suction	50–99	$2,000–4,000	$200–400	Only in houses with hollow block walls; requires sealing of major openings.
Sump Hole Suction	90–99	$1,000–3,000	$125–300	Works best if air moves easily to sump under slab; or if drain tiles form complete loop.
Submembrane Depressurization in a Crawl Space	80–99	$1,300–3,000	$100–225	Less heat loss than natural ventilation in cold winter climates.
Natural Ventilation in a Crawl Space	0–50	None ($265–650 if additional vents installed)	There may be some energy penalties.	Costs variable.
Sealing of Radon Entry Routes	0–50	$125–2,500	None	Normally used with other techniques; proper materials & installation required.

Figure 13.1 Installation and Operating Cost Table

Technique	Typical Radon Reduction (%)	Typical Range of Installation Costs (Contractor)	Typical Operating Cost Range for Fan Electricity & Heated/ Cooled Air Loss (Annual)	Comments
House (Basement) Pressurization	50–99	$650–2,000	$200–650	Works best with tight basement isolated from outdoors and upper floors.
Natural Ventilation	Variable	None ($265–650 if additional vents installed)	$125–900	Significant heated/cooled air loss; operating costs depend on utility rates and amount of ventilation.
Heat Recovery Ventilation	25–50 if used for full house; 25–75 if used for basement	$1,600–3,000	$100–650 for continuous operation	Limited use; best in tight house; for full house, use with levels no higher than 8 pCi/L; no higher than 16 pCi/L for use in basement; less conditioned air loss than natural ventilation.
Water Systems: Aeration	95–99	$4,000–6,000	$50–120	More efficient than GAC; requires annual cleaning to maintain effectiveness and to prevent contamination; carefully vent system.
Water Systems: Activated Carbon (GAC)	85–99	$1,250–2,500	None	Less efficient for higher levels than aeration; use for moderate levels (around 5,000 pCi/L or less); radon by-products can build on carbon may need radiation shield around tank & care in disposal.

NOTE: The fan electricity and house heating/cooling loss cost range is based on certain assumptions regarding climate, your house size, and the cost of electricity and fuel. Your costs may vary. Numbers based upon 1991 data, adjusted to 2003.

Unless you are just sealing cracks or adding crawl space ventilation, radon mitigation techniques are not cheap. If you go this route, you should hire a contractor who has documented experience in this specialized area.

Now we get to the difficult part. What should you, as a real estate entrepreneur, do to address this issue? On the one hand, if I advise you to ignore radon, get the rehab done and the property sold–I run the risk of being labeled insensitive (or worse!). If I advise you to always test a property for radon, I run the risk of being called overreactive (or worse!). I think the best course of action is to let you decide, based on your knowledge of the presence of radon in your area and your own personal thoughts. Personally, if I know radon has been an issue in a neighborhood I will test–otherwise, I don't bother. I just get the deal done and move on.

Toxic Mold—A "Growing" Problem

The *toxic mold* or *black mold* problem has come out of nowhere in the last three years to become the hottest issue affecting the real estate industry today. Several high profile Hollywood-types have made the headlines–entertainer Ed McMahon sued his insurance company for $20 million in April, 2002. He claims toxic mold at his Los Angeles home killed his dog. Another LA resident, consumer advocate Erin Brockovich, has spent $500,000 remodeling her 6,000 square foot home, claiming it is teeming with toxic mold. She is suing the builder as well as the seller of the home, Robert Selleck, brother of actor Tom Selleck. A segment about her claims appeared recently on the TV show *60-Minutes.*

This is only the tip of the iceberg. Ground zero for the mold issue is the state of Texas. Insurance companies in Texas really began to worry about mold in 2001, when a homeowner won $32 million in a lawsuit against Farmers Insurance. A jury decided that Farmers had acted fraudulently and in bad faith when fixing water damage in Melinda Ballard's 22-room mansion in Dripping Springs, Texas. Ballard claims the company delayed fixing a relatively small water leak, which turned into an extensive mold problem. The case, under appeal, has resulted in an insurance crisis in Texas as mold-related water claims have begun to proliferate. The state's top five insurance carriers saw their mold claims skyrocket to more than 37,000 in 2001 from 7,000 in 2000 (a five-fold increase). These insurance companies paid more than $1 billion on mold settlements in 2000 and 2001, according to the Texas Department of Insurance. As a result, Farmers Insurance has pulled out of Texas altogether and State Farm Insurance stopped writing new homeowner policies in Texas, California, and Louisiana in 2001.

Texas has accounted for about 70 percent of all mold claims nationwide. California comes in second, but many other states are now reporting a dramatic increase in mold claims. What in the world has caused this sudden, out-of-nowhere crisis? Is it a real public health crisis or just media hype?

I have read every newspaper article and medical and government report I can get my hands on and have come to the following conclusion: *The toxic mold issue is extremely overblown and vastly exaggerated, driven by the sensationalist media, unscrupulous home inspectors and tort lawyers, looking to replace the asbestos goldmine which has dwindled.*

Without question, there is a nationwide crisis regarding mold, but it is an insurance-driven crisis, not a public health crisis. People are letting banks foreclose on their homes because they can't get insurance on them. Or they are taking huge losses just to sell their homes. One Austin, Texas, real estate agent called almost 150 insurance agents trying to get coverage for one of her pending sales. She had eight different offers on the house fall through because of insurance problems. There had been a water leak in the house that was fixed, but no toxic mold. Eventually, the homeowner replaced the air conditioner and roof, and then upgraded the wiring in order to get insurance. The house finally sold for $75,000 less than the $275,000 original asking price.

From what I can glean from the medical literature, there is very little evidence that exposure or inhalation of black mold (*Stachybotrys*) spores results in any adverse effect, *in most people.* On the other hand, there is a small percentage of our population (about 8 to 10 percent) that have adverse allergic reactions to things like pollen, dust, animal dander, some foods—and mold spores. These reactions are typically asthmalike symptoms and are not life threatening. On the extreme end of the spectrum, some people who are hypersensitive to these types of airborne particles and their reactions can be more severe. However, these reactions are rare and are usually associated with people who have a compromised immune system. With respect to the mold toxins that can be produced by some molds, most of the scientific community feels that these never get into the body in high enough levels to cause harm.

From a public health standpoint, mold or black mold is not a serious threat. However, for a real estate entrepreneur it is a very serious threat that must be dealt with head on. This is because you and your buyers must obtain insurance as part of your real estate transactions, and because you must be prepared to correct any mold problems in houses you are renovating.

The insurance issue will vary from state to state. If you currently live in Texas or California in particular, you will have a much more difficult time dealing with the issue. The cost of insurance, if you can get it, has doubled in many areas. In other parts of the country, insurance problems are nowhere near as severe. Eventually, the problem will be addressed through legislation at both the state and federal levels. Consumer advocate groups are very active in trying to get legislation enacted that would require insurance companies to provide coverage at a reasonable cost. Likewise, insurance companies are very active in pushing for legislation that caps or limits the dollar amount of claims. How it all turns out is anyone's guess. Talk to real estate and insurance agents in your area to see what the current status is at any time. You will have to factor in the availability and cost of insurance when considering a rehab project.

What causes mold to grow in a home? It's very simple—water. Mold spores are everywhere and you can't realistically keep them out of your home. Unless there is a suitable substrate to provide food (carpet, wallboard, wallpaper, ceiling tile, insulation) and more importantly, water, the spores cannot grow into mold. The source of water can come from a variety of areas in a typical home: small leaks in water supply or drain pipes, air conditioners or evaporative coolers, roof leaks, cracks in the foundation or basement walls, and condensation of water vapor in the air. In dealing with mold, the overriding principle is this: Prevent, fix, or stop the source of water and you've eliminated the mold problem. Of course, this is easier said than done in many cases.

When you or your home inspector are going through a home, you obviously want to pay special attention to signs of water leaks, water damage, and, of course, the presence of mold. This means looking under bathroom vanities and cabinets under sinks in kitchens, behind refrigerators, in laundry rooms and attics, around window sills and coolers, behind furniture, at ceilings, and a close inspection of basements.

Many times, the source of the water leak is hidden behind a wall or ceiling and goes undetected for a long time. In the case of a bathroom, condensation can get behind loose wall or floor tiles and supply moisture every time someone bathes. Another common situation, particularly in humid climates, is furniture in a corner or against a wall that traps condensation because there is little circulation of air.

What if you find mold? It's not the end of the world! It simply tells you there is a leak or a condensation problem that must be corrected. The most common sources of water leaks and condensation problems can usually be readily corrected once they are discovered. Roofs can be repaired or replaced, piping leaks can be fixed, dehumidifiers can remove water from the air, double pane windows can be installed, and so on. You and your inspector must assess the damage, the cost to eliminate the water source, and the cost to repair the damage. This cost information is then included in the overall rehab cost budget in figuring the maximum purchase price.

On occasion, you will find a house where the mold situation is basically out of control. For example, a sudden water leak occurred that was not corrected immediately. Or the insurance company dragged their feet for months, trying to minimize their financial responsibility (a common occurrence in some areas). Mold begins to grow and grow and grow. I have seen pictures of entire rooms that are engulfed in mold, from floor to walls to ceilings—a total mold disaster. All because leaks were not stopped or the wet areas were not immediately dried out. The cost to repair the damage can become astronomical, particularly if an entire kitchen or bathroom has to be gutted, plus roof, walls and flooring replacements. If you run across this situation, you are better off walking away. There are plenty of other deals out there.

One word of caution regarding home inspectors. In all likelihood they will recommend you buy a test kit (which they sell) or suggest you have them collect air samples (very expensive) to "test for toxic mold," if any evidence of mold is observed. My advice is to forget about it. There is absolutely no benefit to testing. What difference does it make to find out what *kind* of mold is present? If you find mold, you have a water problem that must be corrected, period. Don't get talked into testing, because that is not the issue. The issue is the source of the water and how much it will cost to fix the problem. End of story.

What about wet basements? This can be a huge problem with respect to mold, and otherwise. I saved this one because wet basements can be a one of the most problematic areas to evaluate and fix.

What to Do about a Wet, Moldy Basement

These subterranean caverns can be a value-added feature to any home or be a bottomless money pit if they leak like a sieve. As an investor, you need to carefully investigate any evidence of leakage. Be forewarned—wet basements can be costly to fix and some are not fixable at all.

Your first chore is to check and see if there is any evidence of leakage. This is particularly important in your prepurchase inspection. In many cases, you don't have to be Sherlock Holmes—the basement will be damp, musty, with water stains or visible mold on the walls or floor, and a wet mop in the corner. There may even be a sump pump already installed.

Be on guard when you see fresh paint and particularly wood paneling in the basement. These are frequently used to cover leak problems. If you see wood paneling, look closely in the corners and all around the baseboards for evidence of soggy wood, stains, or cracked/splintered wood. Also look for wet or mildewed carpet around the perimeter of the basement. This could indicate a problem at the wall-floor cold joint.

Of course, if you see visible cracks in unfinished basement walls, your antenna should go up. Be especially vigilant to observe horizontal cracks on interior walls which are an indication of potentially serious problems, such as high moisture soil or hydrostatic pressure on the outside. Basement floors should also be inspected for indications of water intrusion or slab damage, and basement windows should be carefully inspected to see if they open and close and are sealed properly.

Once you have confirmed that the basement leaks or otherwise collects water, your next task is to determine the source of the water and thereby identify potential corrective actions. It's usually a process of elimination, unless the source is obvious. In most cases, the source of the water is either from groundwater coming in from below the house structure or from rainwater and surface runoff. You also need to eliminate other possible sources.

One such alternate source is condensation caused by inadequate ventilation. You can check this by taping a piece of aluminum foil to a wall and wait a few hours to see which side is fogged up. If the side exposed to the air is fogged, you know you have a condensation problem, which can usually be fixed by adding a portable refrigerated dehumidifier. Other potential sources include sewer and water line leaks, a leaky roof, and missing or deteriorated caulking around windows or exterior doors.

About 80 percent of all wet basement problems are caused by poor drainage around the house, either poor surface drainage or a poor groundwater handling system, or both.

Surface drainage problems are usually the easiest and least expensive to fix (but not always). You need to do a careful exterior inspection around the house and observe the slope of the lot, presence of low spots, built-up flower beds next to the house, and roof drainage systems (or lack thereof). As you walk around, ask yourself, "Where does the water go during a heavy rainfall?"

Roof gutters and downspouts are a frequent culprit in wet basements. The trick is to make sure that this water is directed away from house and not allowed to drain or pool next to the foundation. Gutters and downspouts are needed to collect the water—splash-blocks and sometimes subsurface drain lines are needed to carry the water down slope. This will depend on the slope of the lot, soil type, and adjacent topography.

Most lots are sloped to some extent and many have dramatic slopes. You want to make sure water drains away from the house perimeter. This is accomplished by a variety of methods, depending on the site conditions. Sometimes it is as simple as sloping the ground around the foundation so that water drains out and away. Construction plastic can be added to give ever better protection. Subsurface drains or French drains can be used successfully in many instances if they are installed and maintained properly. On larger lots, a swale (artificial depression) can be built to direct surface water off-site.

If all of the surface runoff issues have been addressed and the basement still leaks, then you've either got a problem with the exterior foundation wall coating (if present) or a groundwater problem.

Basements built within the past 25 to 30 years or so probably had some sort of exterior coating applied to the exterior of the foundation wall. The problem is, most of these compounds are not waterproof—rather they are merely asphaltic materials that damp proof the wall. Over time, the asphalt becomes brittle and will crack, just like the concrete or block wall foundation—and bingo, water migrates through the wall.

If the problem appears to be localized to a small area, you might be able to get away with using one of several products on the interior wall (this is the cheap fix that sometimes works). You want a product that will seal the crack and have some flexibility to withstand expansion/ contraction. A good choice would be a liquid waterproof epoxy that is injected into the crack and sets into a flexible seal.

If you're dealing with an older house (or even a newer one with a brittle asphalt coating), the foundation wall probably never was coated and you may have to consider the unthinkable—digging out around foundation and applying a modern waterproofing compound. A variety of synthetic rubber or urethane based compounds are specifically designed to handle this problem. You can even consider cardboard panels filled with bentonite clay for waterproofing, which have been used for years in commercial applications. The problem of course, is the cost and mess associated with all this digging. You're looking on the order of $4,000 to $7,000—ouch!

Speaking of drain tiles, these are clever little 4″ diameter pipes that are perforated with holes to allow water to enter. If installed correctly, these are located at or below the basement floor level, adjacent to the footing on the exterior. They circle around the perimeter of the basement foundation, and drain (hopefully) to daylight down slope or sometimes to a sump pump. These are typically covered with gravel, which keeps silt and mud from clogging the holes. The primary purpose of drain tiles is to handle water from below (rising groundwater).

If you are going to waterproof the basement wall, properly installed and operating drain tiles are an absolute requirement. If fact, most waterproofing manufacturers will not warrant their product unless drain tiles are installed and working. An added benefit of drain tiles is that you can use them (if a riser to the surface is installed) in dry weather to wet the soil around the house to regulate the moisture content. This is real important if the house is built on expansive clay soils that expand and contract with moisture variations.

An alternative to excavating externally, is to excavate internally. This means installing an interior de-watering system, complete with sump and pump. This can be either a baseboard-style drainage channel on top of the basement floor, or a sub-floor drain tile. The sub-floor drain tile system requires the contractor to break out the basement floor around the perimeter and is the preferred method when dealing with groundwater seepage. These internal systems are usually cheaper than the external dig out fix, typically in the ballpark of $2,500 to $4,000— not an inexpensive fix.

The worst situation is the case where you have very shallow ground-water under pressure and your basement just happens to cross that seam. You could be sitting on a gusher! The truth is, the house never should have been built there in the first place and the basement may not be salvageable. This is the type of situation where you might consider drilling water wells to pump the water off-site, but you're probably better off filling in the basement with dirt and calling it a crawl space.

I think you see the potential nightmares that basements can become. In any real estate purchase transaction involving a basement, perform your due diligence with caution and care. Again, as an investor you might be better off just walking away and finding another deal.

Water Wells and Septic Systems—Look Out!

For all you city slickers, talking about water wells and septic systems is like talking in a foreign language. But in cities and rural areas all across the country these are very common. In fact, about 25 million homes are equipped with septic systems and about 15 million homes receive their water from private wells. The reason for a brief discussion here is that both of these systems can be a major source of contamination and therefore should be checked out carefully if they are present in any proposed real estate transaction.

There is no EPA or other federal oversight regarding the operation of private water wells. However, most states and cities do regulate the installation of new wells and oftentimes regulate the repair of existing wells. This leaves the issue of whether an existing well is operating properly and is free of contamination to the owner—or to you as a potential buyer. This means that you *always* have the water tested as part of a purchase transaction. At a minimum, the test should include coliform bacteria, nitrates, total dissolved solids (salts), and Ph. This level of testing only costs about $25. If you suspect the possibility of other types of contamination, add more test parameters. Of course, you will want your home inspector to check out the basic functionality of the system—is there adequate water pressure, for example. Is the water discolored or have an odor?

If water quality testing indicates contamination outside of acceptable levels, it's all over—you don't under any circumstances want to buy the property. If there are mechanical problems with the well, it's just like any other repair item. Factor in the repair or replacement cost with all others in your rehab cost estimate and go from there. Keep in mind, however, that the cost may be a deal killer. It's essential to find out up front and not get caught holding the bag.

Septic systems should likewise be tested as part of the upfront due diligence inspection. The septic tank and the associated leach field are the main components of the system, and are the components susceptible to failure. Symptoms of failure could include:

- Gurgling sounds in pipes or drains
- Sewage backup in drains or toilets
- Pooled or seeping liquid in the backyard or presence of mushy spots
- Lush green grass in portions of the back yard (above the leach field)
- Unpleasant odors indoors or outdoors

The biggest problem with septic systems is the lack of proper maintenance—the tank is not pumped on a regular basis (every two years, depending on size of tank and size of family) and the maintenance chemicals are not added on a regular basis. Fixing septic system problems is doable, but not cheap. A tank replacement will run about $1,500 to $2,000, but the biggie is leach field replacement—$6,000 to $20,000, depending on size and design. Again, problems need to be discovered up front by using a good home inspector.

You've Found a Problem—Now the Question Is, Who Pays?

Here's the situation—you're evaluating a great fixer-upper property and in the course of doing the inspection, you or your home inspector discover an environmental problem. It could be drainage related (wet basement, mold), asbestos roofing, radon, lead-based paint, water well or septic system. It doesn't matter. What does matter as an investor is the cost to correct the problem, your risk as to whether it can be fixed, and who pays.

We've seen in this chapter that many of these environmental-related problems can be corrected for a relatively minor cost. A little sealant here, a little ventilation there, a portable dehumidifier—minor costs that can simply be added to your rehab budget without major impact. However, we've also seen that fixing some of these problems can be very expensive.

How you address this usually boils down to the seller you are dealing with. If the seller is the homeowner, you always have the option of making an offer subject to the seller fixing the problem prior to closing. This will work if the problem is relatively minor and relatively inexpensive to fix. If the seller doesn't have the money up front, you can ask that sufficient funds be escrowed at closing from the seller's proceeds to cover the cost. If the seller refuses to cooperate, your only choice is to reduce your offer price. In other words, you add the cost to your rehab estimate, thus reducing your maximum purchase price. Obviously, you will encounter situations that are so costly that it just won't pencil out for either party. It's walkaway time. Just be glad you were smart enough to find the problem and *not* buy the property.

The seller may also be either a bank or a government agency like HUD, that now owns the property through foreclosure. In most instances, these sellers market the property "as is" and will not consider spending any money to fix problems. That only leaves you with the option of reducing your purchase offer price—or just walking away.

In summary, the main idea when dealing with environmental-related issues is to approach them with a level head. Many of these problems can be dealt with in a very cost-effective manner. You don't want to miss out on a great deal, just because of a little black mold under the bathroom sink caused by an ill-fitting water supply line connection. Big deal—you can fix that yourself in less than two minutes!

But, if the cost to fix the problem is so overwhelming, or there is any uncertainty as to whether the problem can be fixed, start looking at other properties. These are deal killers that are just too risky–even if the seller wants to *give* you the house!

Now that we've learned how to deal with these nasty environmental problems, we're ready to focus on exactly what type of renovations we need to make on the typical rehab project. I like to call this whole process "kissing frogs!"

Kissing Frogs

Renovations That Make You Money

*Y*ou all remember the story of the frog prince, the ugly, wretched little frog who was transformed into a handsome prince when kissed by a princess. That's what you're going to learn how to do in this chapter— you're going to learn how to kiss frogs and turn them into handsome princes!

Underimprovement and Overimprovement

In the rehab business, the basic challenge in making renovations is to decide what improvements to make and therefore, how much money to spend. If you underimprove the property by being a cheapskate and doing the bare-bones minimum, you are only hurting yourself in the pocketbook. Underimprovement simply transforms the house from a junker into an average, plain-Jane, run-of-the-mill house. Although you wouldn't spend a lot of money fixing it up, you could never expect to maximize your profit on resale. In fact, with an underimproved property, you run the real risk of not being able to sell the property at all—at least not within any reasonable time frame. Because a plain-Jane house has no distinguishing features, it becomes lost in the sea of mediocrity, along with all the other listings on the market. Such a house creates no excitement or desire in the buying public—it just sits there, languishing in obscurity.

Your goal in renovating a house is to create just the opposite effect. You want your house to stand out from the crowd, to create excitement and desire in the marketplace. When people see your finished product, you want them to say, "This is the one. I want it, and I want it now!" To accomplish this goal, you must plan on spending money and sometimes, spending a lot of money.

Do you run the risk of overimprovement? You may be surprised at the answer: No! I know what you're thinking: "If I spend too much money and make the house fancier than the neighborhood, I'll never get my money back!" Did this thought come to mind? If it did, it's because you are used to thinking in retail terms. You buy the house retail, or maybe a little below, you spend a lot of money fixing it up, and then sell it. You may or may not make any profit and you could even lose money with this approach.

However, your system is fail-safe! This is because no matter how much you decide to spend on improvements, that amount is subtracted from your maximum retail value (MRV) to arrive at your maximum purchase price (MPP). In other words, any extravagance is already factored into your buying price (along with your profit and expenses) so that if you buy at your calculated price, it's impossible to overimprove a property.

The problem is that, while you don't run the risk of overimproving per se, you do run the risk of not getting to purchase the property to begin with. This is because your calculated price is so low that the owner can't afford to sell it at that price. Overimprovement is a problem only to the extent that it creates an unrealistic and otherwise unacceptable low-ball offer price. Obviously, this is an undesirable effect that you want to avoid.

The Basic Renovation Strategy

You need to get good at selecting the right mix of improvements that will produce the maximum retail value for the neighborhood and incorporate features that create excitement and demand in the marketplace. Thus, your two complementary goals with your selected improvements are to create value and create marketability. One without the other is not acceptable within the context of your overall business strategy.

For example, if you renovate the house just enough to sell at maximum retail value for the neighborhood, you could easily find yourself sitting on a house that doesn't sell for six months or more. It's a nice house, but because it has only mediocre market appeal, it may not sell for quite some time. This does not fit in well with the strategy of getting in and getting out with your profits quickly. You cannot overlook the marketability or sizzle factor that must be incorporated into each and every rehab project. Only through creating both value and marketability can you consistently meet your investment objectives.

Know Who Your Buyer Is

Before you pound the first nail or put on the first coat of paint, you need to stop and think about what you are doing. You are about to create a product that you hope to sell quickly and at a profit. Do you know anything about your prospective buyers? In any business pursuit, success comes only to those who have a clear understanding of *who* their target market is and what product they want to buy. Violate this principle and you are asking for trouble.

First of all, you need to know in general who your target market will consist of. Considering the fact that most of your activity will be in the lower price range of houses, it is logical to conclude that your prospective buyers will most likely be in the low-to-moderate income bracket. Furthermore, it tells you that they will more than likely be first-time homebuyers. In fact, recent statistics from HUD indicate that first-time homebuyers are almost 50 percent of today's market.

If your primary market is first-time buyers, that must mean that they are currently renting, right? Who are renters? According to a recent Fannie Mae National Housing Survey, renters tend to be young (50 percent between the ages of 18 to 34), and mobile (more than 50 percent have lived in their current residence less than three years). Almost half of all renters place buying a home near the top of their priorities—talk about a pool of motivated buyers! As a rehab business person, it will be your job to help show them how to buy a home (for more on this, see Chapter 16).

But the most important statistic from Fannie Mae's study is this: The majority of all renters (and thus the majority of your future buyers) are women. In fact, more than 60 percent of the renters in the low-to-moderate income group, your primary target, are women.

In a recent study published by the Real Estate Center at Texas A&M University, a most remarkable and profoundly important statistic was revealed: A woman makes the house-buying decision 85 percent of the time. Those of us in the business for some time knew this, at least qualitatively, but it is something that you must never forget. If you can sell her, you can sell the house! First and foremost, your renovated creation must appeal to the woman—the ultimate consumer of your product. Understand this, and you know who your target customer is. Now let's find out what it is she wants.

Two Rooms That Really Count—Kitchen and Bath

The question is, what exactly is the woman interested in when she is looking at houses? Market research from a variety of sources has conclusively shown that she is interested primarily in two rooms in the house: first, the kitchen and second, the bathrooms. This is not to say that she will ignore the other features, or lack thereof, of the house. It simply means that these two rooms in particular are a priority and that you'd better do an outstanding job making these two rooms very attractive.

In developing the rehab plan on any house, you need to always emphasize the kitchen and bathrooms as your first priority. Dollars spent on these two rooms will always meet the two basic investment criteria: increase in value and increase in marketability. I discuss what renovations to make in each of these rooms in a later section of this chapter. First, let's get a glimpse of the big picture.

The Basic Renovation Philosophy

Earlier, you learned that your basic renovation strategy is to make improvements that increase value and increase marketability. In the next section, I discuss a formula that identifies specifically what renovations will meet that criteria. First, you need to develop an overall philosophy or starting point for your renovation projects. From this, you can create and implement a more detailed game plan for any given house.

If you are to achieve the objective of selling your house for maximum retail value, you need to think about how a potential buyer is going to finance the purchase. If I haven't made this clear before, let me state it emphatically now: This is a cash business—all cash going in and all cash going out. In other words, you want to pay all cash when you buy and you want to receive all cash when you sell, if possible.

For you to receive all of your earned equity and pay off your short-term lender, you need the buyer to obtain new financing for the property. Because your target market is primarily first-time homebuyers of low-to-moderate income, there is a good chance that they likely will come into the market through some government-backed program such as VA, HUD, FHA. The point is, you do not want to exclude this important potential buyer by ignoring minimum standards of acceptability for funding. The property and its components must be in reasonably good working condition in order to be fundable through these programs. If you assume the property will need to meet the minimum standards for FHA insurance, following are some of the minimum standards you must be aware of.

Must-Have Items

- Smoke detectors
- Safe installation of water heater
- Attic insulation
- Doors and windows sealed and in working condition
- Minimum two-year remaining life for the roof
- No chipped or defective paint surfaces in houses built prior to 1978 (lead issue)
- Plumbing, electrical, and heating systems in good working order

Cannot-Have Items

- Rotten or worn-out countertops
- Termite damage
- Leaking roofs
- Masonry or foundation damage
- Drainage problems
- Broken plaster or drywall

In looking at this list, it is very evident that you cannot expect to "poor-boy" the job with just cosmetic renovations and get by with it. This then forms the starting point for all of your rehab projects. The basic philosophy is as follows: Repair all structural and mechanical defects and cosmetically rehab all visible features.

This makes sense doesn't it? If you expect to get top dollar for your house, everything needs to be in good operating condition and all of the visible features of the house need to sparkle.

What do I mean by the phrase "cosmetically rehab all visible features"? I'm talking about all of the house features other than such components as the roof, electrical, plumbing, and heating systems (which are covered in the structural and mechanical defects portion of the philosophy). For example, carpeting, interior and exterior paint, cabinets, kitchen and bath fixtures, lighting, tub enclosures, countertops, and landscaping—all of these features of the house need to either be new or look new. If any feature does not meet this standard, you need to cosmetically upgrade it by either replacing it or improving it (e.g., by applying fresh paint on wood cabinets).

To get top dollar, the house must sparkle! This is a hard lesson for some people to learn. In fact, it took me quite a while to learn it, too. The natural tendency is to conserve your cash and only rehab those items that are absolutely necessary. Again, this prudent, conservative approach is appropriate only when you buy retail and then sell retail. In this case, your profit opportunity is so thin that you certainly will lose money unless you become a landlord and let inflation bail you out over time. This is no way to run a business! By including all of the necessary and desirable rehab expenses in the purchase price calculation, you forever eliminate the issue of overimprovement!

The Myth of Return on Rehab Expenditures

Some real estate authors have perpetuated the myth that the desirable return on rehab dollars is anywhere from two-to-one up to four-to-one. In other words, for every rehab dollar spent, you should receive an increase in value of between $2 and $4. Under this theory, a $1,000 investment in rehab would increase the value of the house by $2,000 to $4,000. This is both preposterous and irrelevant to the rehab investor!

In the chapter on appraisals, I discussed the fact that the cost of a feature in a house has little direct relationship to its value in the marketplace, as reflected in the appraisal of the property. Figure 14.1 provides you with some sobering statistics to reinforce this concept. This information comes from data in the *2002 Cost vs. Value Annual Report* published by *Remodeling Magazine* (used with permission from Hanley-Wood, LLC). It reflects generalized national average costs and percent recouped, from across the country (regional differences exist and vary by category). A more recent example (2003) of this type of information can be found at <www.remodelingmagazine.com>. On an annual basis, usually around December, they publish their annual "Cost versus Value Annual Report."

Just glancing at this table, you can come to only one conclusion: Remodeling a house is a losing proposition! This conclusion is absolutely true—unless the costs of the remodeling projects were factored into the initial purchase price. Using the formula, every rehab penny is returned and a profit that you determine in advance is accounted for and built into your buying decision.

Your basic rehab philosophy tells you that you will fix any structural or mechanical defects in the house. This may include putting on a new roof, a new heating system, repairing termite damage, or installing new carpeting. These are the basics that you will incorporate, as needed, into every project. Now that you know you are going to get your money back plus make a nice profit, you need to focus your attention on the specific cosmetic rehab projects that will make you money. These are the things that make the house sparkle, create demand in the marketplace, and allow you to sell quickly for top dollar. This is what kissing frogs is all about!

Figure 14.1 Return on Invested Remodeling Dollars

Remodel Project	National Average Cost	National Average Recouped
Bathroom Remodel	$ 9,720	88%
Bathroom Addition	15,058	94
Two Story Addition	69,857	94
Basement Remodel	43,112	79
Family Room Addition	52,251	79
Siding Replacement	7,146	79
Master Suite Addition	69,173	75
Window Replacement	9,424	74
Major Kitchen Remodel	43,213	67
Roof Replacement	11,399	67

The C-K-B-Sizzle Approach to Rehab

I call this the C-K-B-sizzle approach to rehab because it focuses your attention on the four most important features of the house. If your rehab efforts are creatively applied in these areas, you will be handsomely rewarded:

1. Curb appeal
2. Kitchen
3. Bathrooms
4. Sizzle features

Curb appeal is the first priority because unless the house looks attractive when a prospective buyer drives up with their real estate agent (or by themselves), they will never get out of the car to look inside. Remember the old saying, you never get a second chance to make a good first impression. Your goal is to make the house so appealing from the curb that the buyer instantly falls in love with the house and wants to buy it! To achieve this goal, use the checklist in Figure 14.2.

Figure 14.2 Curb Appeal Checklist

❑ *General cleanup.* Remove all garbage, debris, trash, junk cars, and broken glass found on the property. Your city government may be of assistance with the removal of junk cars. While you're at it, you might consider offering "free hauling" to any of your neighbors who have junk lying around that detracts from the character of the neighborhood.

❑ *Roof.* One of the first things people notice about a house when they drive up is the general condition and appearance of the roof. This is a major fear factor for many homebuyers because of the expense and potential damage that a leaky roof can cause. Unless the roof looks new or is new, plan on replacing it. This is a controversial area for rehabbers, but I can tell you from experience that you need to aggressively tackle this issue at the outset. Even if the roof "passes inspection" by a roof inspector, if it looks aged, buyers will be concerned. If they are concerned, they will not be willing to pay top dollar. Just bite the bullet and budget for it.

A visible roof (in contrast to a flat or Pueblo style that can't be seen) that looks good from the curb is an important selling feature. If you have to install a new asphalt shingle or metal roof, select a color that will blend nicely with the paint and trim on the house and that will complement the neighborhood. Gray, beige, or slate blue are often good choices.

❑ *Exterior paint and trim.* This feature of the house needs to be flawless. Cracked or chipped paint is immediately observable and detracts greatly from the appearance and value of the house. If fresh paint is needed, make sure your contractor cleans all surfaces and have any holes or cracks in stucco repaired prior to painting. Any wooden trim that is warped or rotten needs to be replaced. As for colors, I like to drive neighborhoods and take pictures of attractive color combinations. When I get ready to paint a house, I just pull out my file and choose something that matches the style and design of the house I'm working with. Just make sure your choice blends well with the neighborhood.

❑ *Front windows.* These often-neglected items can dramatically improve the appearance of a house. Seriously consider installing bay windows, garden windows, or picture windows in the front of the house. Certainly, these are more expensive than the traditional aluminum frame or wood casement windows. But these decorator windows can create an emotional attractiveness that is simply awesome. I have had people buy a house just because they fell in love with the front bay windows! If the house design is compatible, try to fit them into the rehab plan—they are well worth the extra expense.

Figure 14.2 Curb Appeal Checklist

❏ *Sidewalks and driveway.* These are exceedingly mundane features of a house, but it is these little things that can affect initial impressions. Concrete sidewalks that are cracked or buckled are not only unattractive but also can create a tripping hazard. Concrete is relatively cheap. Often your local city is responsible for maintenance and can be coerced into fixing the problem for free.

   Driveways are equally noticeable and may need attention. If the house doesn't have one, consider putting one in. With an existing asphalt drive, I always put on a new sealer coat. For about $30, it removes any unevenness in color and gives it an attractive appearance. Concrete driveways should be cleaned to remove any significant oil stains. Cleaning agents can be purchased at any auto parts or hardware store.

❏ *Landscaping.* The importance of attractive front landscaping cannot be emphasized enough. This feature is often ignored by rehabbers, but it is absolutely critical to creating superior curb appeal. While rear landscaping may be important in some neighborhoods or parts of the country, it is the front that makes or breaks the whole concept of curb appeal.

   The best specific advice I can give you is to hire a landscaping contractor to design and do the work. This is a very competitive business in most areas and many of the contractors will throw in the design aspect for free. These are the people that are in the business day in and day out—they know what looks good and they know how to keep costs down (if you press them!). Try to keep it fairly simple and low-maintenance. Don't forget that any grass or flower plants will need to be cared for during your holding period. In my area (Albuquerque) I usually go with "Southwest landscaping," which means lots of rock and desert plants and shrubs that require little maintenance.

❏ *Fences and walkways.* An attractive walkway, separate from the driveway, leading to the front entrance is a plus feature for most houses. Creative, yet inexpensive designs can add warmth and flair to the overall front appeal of the house. Bricks in a herringbone or basket weave pattern are especially attractive and can be bordered with railroad ties or flowers to create an exciting appearance. Low-intensity lighting is also very attractive.

   Low-elevation wooden or stone fences in the front of a house can often provide a sense of separation from the hustle and bustle of the neighborhood. Additionally, these barrier features will often create a higher sense of value from buyers, even though their cost is minimal.

Figure 14.2 Curb Appeal Checklist

❏ *House numbers and mailbox.* Although these are very inexpensive items in the overall scheme of things, they are very important to the creation of positive initial impressions. Don't skimp on the cost of these two features. Gold-plated, tile, or wooden house numbers are all very attractive. Mailbox holders come in a large variety of designs—pick out one that's compatible with the neighborhood but one that will add a little flair to the house.

❏ *Porch and front door.* This area of the house creates the important final transition from the outside to the inside. In many of the tract homes built during the booming 1950s, the porch was a feature that was simply omitted. Even with some new construction today, the porch is deleted or given little attention. This is a mistake, because people want and need a front porch to provide a little protection from the weather as they enter or leave a house. The porch also is an area that people can decorate with flowers, lighting, and a welcome mat to greatly enhance the appeal to visitors (and buyers!). Look for inexpensive ways to spiff up your front porch. If your house doesn't have one, consider putting one in. You can typically get one installed for less than $1,000 depending on design.

The front door is your final chance to make an initial statement about the quality of your house. In the older houses that you work with, the front door almost always needs to be replaced. I'm partial to a solid-wood or raised-panel front door with glass inserts. Some people prefer a metal door. What's important is that it be of good quality and finish. The addition of a shiny brass or gold-plated door handle and knocker adds the finishing touch of class. This is important, even in the lower-priced homes and neighborhoods.

One final thought before you go inside—make sure the doorbell works!

The Killer Kitchen for $2,000 or Less

Without a doubt, the kitchen is the most important room in the house, from the perspective of the buyer (i.e., the woman). The kitchen tends to be a focal point for most families, with meal preparation being only part of the equation. Family meetings, gatherings, and discussions are often held in this area of the house. So naturally, the kitchen needs to be a primary target of emphasis in any rehab project.

But let's face it: Rehabbing the kitchen can become a bottomless pit, gobbling up huge amounts of cash. I know people who have spent as much as $40,000 remodeling their kitchen! How could you possibly do an adequate job for less than $2,000? It's really quite simple: Select inexpensive materials and have them installed by a skilled handyman, not by a kitchen remodeling contractor. I'll say more on this later.

First, you need to have a general concept of what your rehab goals are for the kitchen. In descriptive terms, your final product needs to be bright (with plenty of natural lighting, if possible), clean (spotless in fact), fresh, and functional. Using the standard criteria, everything needs to look new or be new. In the older, modest houses that you will normally deal with, you are not trying to create a gourmet kitchen with all the latest gadgets—just a good-looking, functional workstation and gathering place.

Now that you know in general what the kitchen needs to look like, let's take a look at what you find in a typical junker house. This will vary greatly, but here are some normal defects that must be corrected:

- Dark, dreary lighting
- Cracked, ripped, faded vinyl flooring
- Chipped, stained, or outdated countertops
- Outdated or broken cabinets
- Scratched, chipped, or stained sink
- Ugly, outdated, or inoperable appliances
- Grease-splattered walls

The presence of any of these items is unacceptable and must be corrected. Sometimes, all of them are present and you will need to rip out everything and start from scratch. That's OK, because you can still get it done cheaply if you shop carefully and control your material and labor costs.

Still don't believe you can do it for less than $2,000? Here's one I did recently (see Figure 14.3). It was a small 10′ × 10′ L-shaped standard kitchen. It was a simple remove-and-replace job, requiring no additional electrical or plumbing modifications. All materials were purchased at Home Depot and installed by an experienced handyman.

Now granted, this was a low-budget rehab, using materials at the low end of price ranges (except the fancy sink faucet). But it was perfect for the house, which was in a lower-priced neighborhood. The important thing is that a brand new, light and bright kitchen was produced at a very reasonable cost. Indeed, a killer kitchen for less than $2,000!

Figure 14.3 Kitchen Rehab Costs

Item	Materials Cost	Labor Cost	Total
New Cabinets—Base and Overhead	$750	$400	$1,150
New Countertops—Formica	275	75	350
New Vinyl Floor	80	65	145
New Sink and Faucet (fancy)	200	50	250
Total			$1,895

In many cases, a total remove-and-replace is not necessary. For example, several alternatives are available for the big-ticket item—cabinets. If you've got older, solid wood cabinets that are basically in good shape but a little worn out—just have them sprayed with a fresh coat of paint (usually white) and install new, good-quality handles. This simple treatment can result in an outstanding transformation that looks great. I've done this many times with excellent results.

Another trick is to just replace the cabinet doors and drawer fronts. If they match well, you're done. If not, you can either paint the old cabinets or cover them with a matching peel-and-stick hardwood veneer or vinyl laminate. A company called Quality Doors in Cedar Hill, Texas, 800-950-3667, has an excellent selection of doors, drawers, and veneer if you want to pursue this option. This will work fine for homes in the lower price ranges, but I would caution you not to try it on midpriced or expensive homes—the marketplace just won't accept it.

Unless you are very talented and experienced, stay away from the unfinished cabinets. It's very difficult for the amateur to get these to turn out looking good.

Here's my advice on appliances: If the existing ones are old and worn out or they are olive green, harvest gold, copper, or red, get rid of them pronto! White or almond are the only acceptable colors at the present time. I generally replace the stove if necessary, usually with a good-quality used one (check your Yellow Pages for a supplier). If a dishwasher is already installed but needs to go, I'll replace it. If not, I usually do not go to the expense of putting one in from scratch because of the plumbing and electrical hassles. I do not install a replacement refrigerator, unless it's negotiated when I sell the property. In that case, I'll usually throw one in just to make a deal.

Microwaves are a different story. I almost always buy a little microwave that mounts under an overhead wall cabinet. It's a relatively inexpensive item that is unexpected in most of the lower-priced homes you will work with. Its purpose is to generate "oohs" and "aahs" from the buyer and is part of the sizzle package that I discuss later in this chapter.

The more you know about kitchen renovation techniques, the better. Make it a life-long learning project because it, in many respects, is the centerpiece of your real estate rehab business. Figure 14.4 offers a checklist of a few tips that I've collected along the way.

Bathrooms to Die For

Following the kitchen, the bathroom is the next important room in the house. It's high traffic, high use, and usually high maintenance. One reason that this room needs to be perfect is that people just don't want the hassles of having to renovate this area. Instead, they are willing to pay top dollar if everything is neat, clean, tidy, and pretty.

Make no mistake—this room is important to both genders, but for different reasons. Women tend to view the bathroom from an aesthetic standpoint. Is it clean, is it colorful, is it pleasing to the eye? Men, on the other hand, tend to look at it from the "hassle factor" point of view: How much of my time and money am I going to have to spend on this room? As a rehabber, your goal is to produce a room that meets the needs of both genders. The final product must be very pleasing to the eye and it must be completely finished—nothing left to be done. If you accomplish these two goals, you have significantly added value to the house and its marketability. You've done your job!

Bathrooms can be an absolute nightmare because of one thing— moisture. Here you have a room, typically quite small, that is basically a steam room. Water or water vapor is everywhere. This, of course, can cause a lot of wear and tear on wall surfaces and on the flooring. More important, water can cause severe damage when it is allowed to seep behind or underneath wall coverings and flooring. The first priority in

Figure 14.4 Kitchen Renovation Tips

- ❏ Use the free computer-aided design services at the larger home improvement centers such as Home Depot and Lowe's to lay out your kitchen.
- ❏ Measure the distance between walls and measure the height of walls, from floor to ceiling.
- ❏ Measure distances between all doors and windows in both vertical and horizontal dimensions. Trim is part of the door or window. Pinpoint all electrical outlets, water lines, plumbing, and gas lines on the drawing, measuring to the centerpoint of each.
- ❏ Check and double-check all measurements to within one-eighth of an inch.
- ❏ Buy your appliances before you buy your cabinets—you need to know their exact measurements to lay out the cabinets.
- ❏ Provide a minimum 15" clearance between the countertop and the bottom of the overhead wall cabinets.
- ❏ Never use valuable counter space for a microwave—install a built-in or mount under a wall cabinet.
- ❏ Consider a garden window above the sink or a skylight, or both, to promote natural lighting.
- ❏ Correct any unevenness in subflooring before installing vinyl or cabinets.
- ❏ Hire a skilled, experienced handyman for cabinet and countertop installation.

bathroom rehab is to seek and eliminate any internal leaks in the plumbing and to replace any damaged wood or drywall. This is a must. Soft spots or mold in the flooring or behind the shower tile are unacceptable—their presence will immediately raise a red flag to any prospective buyer. Tear it out and fix the problem. If you don't do right, it will cost you money on resale.

I hate bathtubs. Now, don't get me wrong—I like to soak after a long hard day, just like everybody else. But when it comes to a rehab project, they can be a real pain in the neck. My first rule of thumb is, never replace or remove a tub unless there is no other alternative. You're talking a major expense because you typically have to cut out walls or doors, not to mention the subflooring. Fortunately, it is rare that a tub needs to be replaced. Support and subfloor problems usually can be fixed from the inside. The tub itself, unless it's a total wreck, can be inexpensively refinished (for $125 to $250) in place to look like new. Unless the tub can be cleaned to really look good, have it refinished. It's well worth the minimal expense.

The shower tile also can be a source of great aggravation. In a routine rehab job, it's chipped, cracked, discolored, moldy, missing, or just plain ugly. Many times, you can get away with having the tile regrouted and refinished to look like new. Another good alternative these days is to paint the tile with a good epoxy paint. It's a bit on the pricey side (about $35 a quart) but it sure beats doing a total remove-and-replace. Epoxy paint is also a good solution if you have to replace just one or two tiles and can't find a match.

Tub enclosures, if present, are often in junky condition and need to be replaced. I like to put in a clear glass enclosure with a nice gold-finish frame. It adds a touch of class, particularly in the lower-priced homes. Shower curtains are fine if you don't want to spend the money or go to the trouble of putting in an enclosure. The reality is, they're not very expensive and they're real easy to install. I consider an enclosure to be part of the sizzle package.

For most of the houses you work on, in the lower price ranges, vinyl or linoleum flooring in the bathroom is just fine. It looks good and wears well and, best of all, it's cheap to install. In a midpriced house, I usually go ahead and install a tile floor. You can get a decent one put in for about $10 a square foot installed. They look great and again, add to the sizzle.

Toilets. For the life of me, I can't figure out why rehab people always ignore the toilet. When people buy houses, they always notice the condition of the toilets. Do yourself a big favor—if there is anything wrong with the toilet, put in a new one! If it's chipped, cracked, faded, stained, discolored, whatever, replace it. A new one, with the wax seal, will cost all of $125 installed.

If the bathroom has a window, make sure it's in good shape and looks good. Otherwise, replace it. If it needs replacing, consider adding a little garden window or other unusual design. Think sizzle!

The bathroom vanity, medicine cabinet, sink, towel racks, faucets, paper holder, and lighting are another chance for you to use your creativity and make a statement. Good-quality, attractive fixtures are available in a wide variety of choices, and they can be purchased very inexpensively. This is another opportunity to add a little sizzle for just a little extra money. Do it right and spend the extra money by upgrading these items. Make the finishing touches to the bathroom look fancy and unexpected.

Of course, the very final touches will be the paint and wallpaper or ceiling border. Some people say, let the new owners pick their own wallpaper or border. I say baloney! Put it in yourself because it adds so much to the visual impact of the room when it's time to show and sell the house. It doesn't matter if your choice is not exactly what your buyers would have chosen. You want to produce a finished product in move-in condition. Wallpaper is cheap and the buyers can change it if they like. But most people don't want to bother with it. If it looks good, they will appreciate the fact that they don't have to do anything!

One last bathroom note: Make sure the exhaust fan is working. And if it sounds like a meat grinder, fix it or change it!

It's the Sizzle That Sells

As the old saying goes, "The steak is fine but it's the sizzle that sells!" This is normally associated with selling cars, but it is a powerful tool to use in your rehab "bag of tricks." The philosophy is basically this: Each and every house that you rehab must have several unexpected sizzle features that make the house stand out from the crowd. This is an absolute must if you expect the house to sell quickly and for top dollar. Unless the house is distinguished from all the competition on the market, it will languish and cost you money.

The possibilities are of course, endless. The idea is to choose one or two features that are a little expensive and a bunch of smaller things that, added together send the message of uniqueness and charm. Maximize value and create extraordinary market demand. That's what you're trying to achieve.

I've referred to it as the sizzle package and that's what it is—a package. Each house is different and you need to noodle out a unique package for each one. This is where a little creativity and flair really come into play. Whatever you do, don't leave this step out—you won't maximize the potential success of the project without it!

Fish ponds, laundry chutes, workshops, security systems, tree houses, bay windows, garden windows, decks, and covered patios are some of the things that I have added to create uniqueness. One of my fa-

'orite big-ticket items, especially for the lower-priced homes, is to add a hot tub. For about $1,000 or less, you can get a really nice used hot tub—just look in any weekly or Sunday newspaper. Here's the psychology of it: How many people shopping for the lower-priced homes expect to find a hot tub? None! How many people, even if they had the money, would spend it on a hot tub? Very few. How many people would like to have one, if it was already included in the price of the house? Most people would love to have it! How do I know this? The house I bought a few years ago and the one I'm currently living in came with a hot tub on the deck off the upstairs master bedroom. I never would have bought one on my own—I'm too cheap! But because it came with the house (along with a pool) it's great! If you can find a spot for it, a patio or a deck, include it in your rehab budget and put one in. Trust me—it will sell the house.

The smaller items to add sizzle are also numerous. Pick and choose from among the following and then come up with some of your own ideas: tiled entry, built-in bookcase, microwave, trash compactor, mirrored closet doors, fancy light fixtures, fancy sink and water fixtures, skylights, garage door opener, butcher block insert in countertop, wood stove, ceiling fans, miniblinds, drop stair scuttle into attic, wallpaper, borders, chair rail in dining room, and built-in ironing board. Some of the items are more expensive than others, but I think you get the idea—use your imagination and make the house something special!

Let's move on and find out how you're going to get all of this work done.

OK, I Bought the House—Now What?

Getting the Work Done

*N*ow the fun begins! You've found the house, developed a list of renovations, prepared an offer and got it accepted, arranged your financing, and closed the deal—now, you're ready to start on getting the rehab work done. To get you in the right frame of mind, let me remind you about what business you are in: You're in business to buy and sell properties at a profit—you're not in the construction business!

Why You Should Never Do the Work Yourself

I know as sure as I'm sitting here at my computer, that some of you are saying to yourself, "If I do the work myself, I'll save a bundle." Am I right? I know you're thinking that because I used to think it myself. After several years of doing all or most of the work myself, I became pretty competent at many of the repair jobs. I put in hundreds and hundreds of hours of time. But the truth is, the quality of my workmanship was mediocre at best and, in some cases, even less than mediocre. Frankly, some of the work looked like a do-it-yourself project and probably cost me money in marketing time and resale value.

Finally, I came to realize that I was not particularly talented in all of the areas I needed to be and began wondering if there was a better way. Wouldn't the final product look a lot better if I hired talented people to do the work? Could I get the job finished a lot faster and get the house sold a lot faster if I hired the work done? Wouldn't my time be better spent out looking for deals rather than installing cabinets?

The turning point for me was when I realized that I could hire someone else to do all of the work and still make the same—or more—profit. How is this possible? You already know the answer: by simply including the cost in the buying formula. When the cost of repairs, including the cost of contractors, is included in the maximum purchase price formula, it doesn't cost you a dime in profits to hire the work out to professionals. Once you fully appreciate this concept, you'll never again pick up another paintbrush! Regardless of your handyman talents, it just doesn't make economic sense for you to spend your valuable time doing repairs.

Handyman or General Contractor?

One of the first decisions you'll need to make is whether to look for a general contractor or a handyman to do the work. Actually, this is a decision you should make before you buy the property, because it can have significant cost ramifications. What is the difference between the two?

General contractors are typically licensed, bonded, insured, and normally will provide full-service rehab management for your project (note that not all states require general contractors to be licensed). They will coordinate the hiring of all necessary subcontractors, schedule the work, supervise the crews, handle any permits and inspections with local officials, purchase materials, and pay the subcontractors as work is completed. They may or may not have their own crews, but in any event, will bring in the needed labor to complete the rehab. Basically, general contractors provide a turnkey service, start to finish. All you do is write the checks.

In contrast, handymen almost never have licenses, insurance, or bonding. Although they may agree to "supervise" subcontractors when they are on-site, it will usually be your responsibility to hire them and pay their bills. Handymen are talented in many of the routine construction and repair tasks but may have little or no skill in some of the more complex jobs like electrical, plumbing, carpeting, roofing, and heating and air-conditioning. It just depends on the individual—some have more skills and experience than others. In using this alternative, you will be the general contractor.

With this brief contrast, I think you can start to sense the advantages and disadvantages of each. General contractors are professional renovators and project managers. This is their full-time occupation and they probably belong to one or more trade organizations. If you hire the right person, your rehab will be a hassle-free experience and the final result will be excellent. The disadvantage is, of course, cost. Because of their overhead structure and project management responsibilities for the subcontractors, you will be paying anywhere from 20 percent to 50 percent more for contractors' services.

Going the handyman route, you will save much of that 20 percent to 50 percent incremental cost. But you will pay a price for that savings, in terms of your time and effort. In essence, you become the general contractor with many of the associated duties. You must do the hiring and firing of all the subcontractors, schedule the work, supervise and inspect, coordinate permits, and handle all the payments to the subcontractors. Handymen can do many of the tasks at a much lower cost but you will need to bring in the crews for the more specialized jobs. The bottom line on this option is that you will save money but it will require a lot more of your time.

Which option should you choose? There really is no right or wrong answer here. It depends on your needs, the scope and complexity of the rehab work, and the availability of your time and money. Here again, you might want to do a little self-assessment. Do you really have the time and skills needed to tackle the job of being your own general contractor?

I have used both options very successfully at different times. I prefer the handyman option because of the cost savings. Once you find and develop your handyman and the various subcontractors for the specialized jobs, it's not that much additional work. But this route is not for everyone. You may be in a situation where your spare time is very limited. In this case, you just won't have the ability to do all the legwork associated with being your own general contractor.

Even if you have the time, if you have little or no rehab experience, let me suggest you start out using a general contractor. Think of it as a great learning opportunity, because that's exactly what it is. Watch and observe as the contractor hires and directs the crews, enforces quality standards, and manages the process. This is an excellent way to learn the technical aspects of rehab and the management skills needed for a successful rehab project. The incremental cost you will pay is simply an investment in your training and education as a rehab specialist.

Let's assume you will be using a general contractor. The next step is to get bids and negotiate a contract. Before you do that, you need to develop a scope of work. This tells the contractor exactly what work you want accomplished.

Developing a Rehab Plan Scope of Work

The rehab plan that you developed in connection with your purchase decision now becomes the centerpiece of your activity. You need to review it, fine-tune it, and add in the necessary detail in order to get bids on the work. You will need to do this whether you choose to be your own general contractor or you decide to hire one.

The quality of the bids you receive and your ability to control costs will depend largely on the level of detail in your rehab plan. The idea is to identify as specifically as possible all of the work that you want performed and the type and quality of materials you want used. You are transforming the generalized rehab plan into a checklist of tasks and specifications, which, in total, make up the rehab plan scope of work. Figure 15.1 is a sample form that includes details of a rehab job. In describing the work you want performed, you must be as detailed, comprehensive, and specific as possible. No detail is too small. If you have already selected certain brands, models, or colors for any items, put it in your scope of work. To give your contractors a little leeway and perhaps allow them to use some creativity, insert the words, "or approved equivalent." This means that they can approach you with an alternative brand, model, or whatever, but that you must approve any such substitution.

Get the idea? You want to put in as much detail as possible in order to eliminate discretion or uncertainty on the part of contractors bidding on the work. The more detail provided, the better, because it captures all of the tasks in the rehab project and will allow you to evaluate bids on an equal footing.

Figure 15.1 Sample Rehab Plan Scope of Work

Task	Specifications
Remove and replace roof.	Standard asphalt shingles, blue-grey in color
Remove and install new kitchen cabinets—base and overhead.	Inexpensive fiberboard with upgrade hardware handles; obtain dimensions during site inspection
Paint exterior stucco.	Patch cracks and use good quality exterior paint; two coats required
Landscape front yard.	Southwestern style; contractor to submit conceptual design with bid
Install tile entry. Area approximately 3' × 4'.	American Olean, 4" × 4" glacier white with marble finish, or approved equivalent
Remove and install new toilet in master bathroom.	Kilgore low-flow or approved equivalent
Remove and install new carpet.	Approx. 130 square yards of FHA-grade with ½" pad

Once you have developed your scope of work, you will need to prepare a brief set of bidding instructions. This simply gives your contractors specific directions on how you want their bid proposals formatted, along with some of your requirements. Figure 15.2 is a sample set of bid instructions that can be used for this purpose. Several of the important contracting concepts that are included in this instruction sheet are discussed in the contracts section of this chapter. For now, let's figure out how to find good general contractors to get bids from.

Figure 15.2 Bid Instruction Sheet

Project Location: _____

Property Owner/Client: _____

General Description: This project involves the renovation of the single-family house at the above-indicated location. This house is intended to be resold immediately upon completion of all work; therefore, time is of the essence. At completion of work, all systems and subsystems of the house are required to meet appropriate local building codes and minimum FHA construction standards.

Scope of Work: Bid proposals are to be based on the scope of work attached hereto. This will be considered the base proposal. Contractors may submit additional work items or alternatives specifications. However, these are to be identified as such and costs provided separately.

Proposal Format: For each identified task, contractor shall specify units/quantity, price and total cost to complete the task. Overhead and profit may be identified as a separate line item. Contractor shall identify material cost mark-up percentage. Costs indicated in this proposal will be considered not to exceed values for subsequent contracting purposes.

Lump-sum bids (for the entire project) or time and materials bids will not be accepted.

Proposals shall identify any subcontractors and include copies of their proposals.

Start and Completion Dates: Bid proposals should identify the earliest approximate start date and earliest approximate completion date for this project. Firm dates will be negotiated and included in final contracts.

Project Site Inspection: Contractor will meet with Owner at the project site at a mutually agreed date and time. Clarification of tasks and specifications will be made at that time.

Proposal Due Date: All proposals are to be submitted to Owner no later than _____
_____ .

How to Find Your General Contractor

If you're starting this process from scratch, you need to know that a successful search is going to take you considerable time and effort. Unless you already know of one or more good candidates, you're in for a very challenging experience. Your job is to locate at least three competent, honest, experienced, reliable, and reasonable people who are interested and willing to bid on your project—not an easy task. Be prepared for at least a little (and sometime a lot) of frustration as you go through this process. It's normal and unavoidable.

First, let's set out some basic criteria that you should use to evaluate potential candidates. Here are three general characteristics that I would recommend:

1. The contractor should have experience managing rehab projects similar in scope to your project.
2. The contractor/company should have been in business for at least five years.
3. The contractor should be licensed (if required), bonded, and insured.

The five years in business criterion stems from recent research that indicates approximately 96 percent of all contractors go out of business within the first five years (similar to many other types of start-up businesses). This is an important issue to consider, particularly when warranties are part of the equation. You want contractors who have passed the five-year mark, indicating that they have successfully built their businesses and will likely be around for the long haul.

Where do you find these people? Anywhere you can! The absolute best source is a referral from friends, neighbors, or acquaintances who have had major remodeling work done by a general contractor and are satisfied with the outcome. Ask, ask, ask anyone and everyone you know. Talk with real estate agents, electricians, plumbers, building supply stores, or anyone else in the industry. Check out the small classified ads in your local papers. The smaller, low-overhead contractors will often advertise here. Stay away from the ones with big display ads in the Yellow Pages. These are the big outfits with big overheads and high prices. And never, ever consider anyone doing door-to-door solicitations—most of these are high-pressure scam artists that prey on the naïve and unsuspecting. In some of the larger cities, you may find contractor referral agencies, associations, or councils listed in the phone book—if all else fails, give them a try.

With names in hand, you are ready to start calling your candidates. This initial contact is very important. Your goal is to determine their availability, interest level in your project, and the extent to which they meet the general criteria discussed previously. How easy were they to reach? Did they promptly return phone calls? How responsive were they to your questions? These intangibles are important because they help define the type of service you might expect in the future.

For those who pass your initial screening, the next step is to arrange for them to meet you at the house for an on-site tour. As mentioned previously, you want at least three contractors to prepare bids. I would suggest you meet with them individually, with appointments spaced out over a couple of days. The advantage of this approach is that if some good ideas are developed in your initial interviews, you may want to change the scope of work and ask the subsequent contractors to also bid on the revised information. Otherwise, just have them include any proposed changes to the scope in their proposals, as indicated on the bid instruction sheet.

Review the rehab plan scope of work and listen to their responses carefully. Also review the bid instructions you have prepared. Ask about how they price their services, and how they handle change orders and mechanics' liens. If everything seems to check out, give them the scope of work and ask them to prepare a bid. Make sure they know when you expect to receive their proposals.

Selecting Your Contractor and Signing the Contract

You know your budget and now you have the cost proposals in front of you. What's your initial impression? Who has done the best overall job in terms of options, cost-saving ideas, presentation, schedule, and, of course, price? Price alone should not be the determining factor. You have personally met with each of them at least once. Which one do you like, on a gut-level basis, the best? Make your choice and call to set up an appointment to finalize your agreement in the form of a contract. This will be the last opportunity before work begins to negotiate the scope of work, cost, and key contract provisions.

Before you actually enter serious contract discussions with your chosen contractor, you need to do your due diligence on the person or company. Ask your contractor for several recent work references and give them a call. Most contractors will show you photographs of their projects, which is fine, but it only tells half of the story. You really need to get feedback directly from their customers. This is also the time to call the state licensing board to verify compliance with any licensing or registration requirements. And don't forget to call your local better business bureau to check out any consumer complaints.

If you have followed the advice to deal only with reputable and licensed individuals who have been in business at least five years, they will undoubtedly have their own standard contract. If they do not have a contract to work with, you have probably picked the wrong person.

Do not be intimidated by any of this. It's just paper with words on it that you can cross out and initial if you don't like any of them. Read the contract very carefully and ask questions about anything you do not understand. Always seek competent legal advice if you have any concerns or unanswered questions.

Now, let's review some contract provisions that you want to make sure are included. If they're not, you (or your attorney) or your contractor will need to prepare an addendum to include them. Several of these items are further discussed following this listing:

- The scope of work and any agreed-upon changes thereto
- The cost proposal and any agreed-upon changes thereto
- A provision stating that the costs for the job components are not to exceed values. Any cost overruns are the responsibility of the contractor, unless a written agreement provides otherwise.
- A change-order provision that requires any addition or deletion from the scope of work to be approved by both parties, in writing
- A minimum warranty of one year (from date of completion) on all materials and labor. Appliances and similar equipment may have "limited" warranties.
- Schedule of payments
- Start date and substantial completion date
- Cleanup procedures, both daily and at job completion

- Contractor's responsibility for obtaining building permits, compliance with zoning and building regulations and government inspections
- Mechanics' liens and how they are to be handled by the contractor
- Breach of contract and dispute resolution provisions
- Notice of right to cancel contract
- Requirement for contractor to maintain insurance for personal injury, property damage, and workers' compensation

Change Orders

If you don't want to get taken to the cleaners, make sure there is change-order language in your contracts. Change orders refer to changes made by the contractor (or you) during the course of the job that are different from the original scope of work—for example, using a more expensive flooring material or more expensive cabinets, or adding a new fence when a fence was never discussed previously. The way to avoid problems in this situation is to include change-order language in the contract that specifically states that any change requires the signature of both parties. Make sure the contract includes this clause, discuss it with your contractor, and enforce it religiously during the project. Most contractors will have preprepared change-order forms that are used for this purpose. Figure 15.3 is an example of a change-order form.

Schedule of Payments

The contract should clearly state the total amount due and when it is due. A reasonable payment schedule would be as follows: a 5 percent down payment when the contract is signed; another 15 percent upon commencement of work; 30 percent at the halfway point (should be defined by completion of specific tasks; e.g., all kitchen tasks); 30 percent at "substantial completion" (discussed later); and the final payment of 20 percent to be paid within 30 days following final completion. Remember, contractors are paid in full, they have no real incentive to fix any problems that you discover after they walk out the door. It is customary and an accepted practice to withhold payment of 10 percent to 25 percent of the total job cost for a period of up to 30 days after completion. This gives you the upper hand in getting any deficiencies promptly

Figure 15.3 Scope of Work Change Order

Change Order # _____   Date: _____

The following is a clarification or change to the original contract dated _____
between:
Owner: _____

Contractor: _____

Property Address: _____

This change order is made in order to modify, change, or clarify the scope of work under the above-referenced contract. This change order is made a part of the contract and supersedes any previous specifications and agreements. The changes or clarifications are as follows:

Total Additional Charge (+) for This Change: $_____

Total Credit or Reduction (–) for This Change: _____

Amount of Original Contract: _____

Additional Charge from This Change Order (+)   _____

Credit/Reduction from This Change Order (–)   _____

Adjusted Contract Amount: _____

Contractor is authorized to proceed with the change in work specified in the change order.

Approved by Owner: _____ Date: _____

Approved by Contractor: _____ Date: _____

corrected. It also coincides with the 30-day limitation in many states for subcontractors to file mechanics' liens (check the limitations in your state).

Substantial Completion

You and the contractor must agree on a date that the work will be substantially complete. This means all of the work is basically completed, except for some of the final finishing touches. Examples of finishing touches would be things like missing cabinet doors, molding, a light fixture, touch-up painting, and other similar items. At this point, the house is completed and functional, with a few odds and ends of a minor nature that are missing or yet to be completed. It is very important that you and the contractor take this date seriously, particularly when considering that you are on a fast track to get the house finished and sold. In view of this, I would suggest that you include a substantial completion clause that incorporates a penalty provision for missing this date. The amount of penalty is negotiable but it should be of sufficient magnitude ($50 to $100 per day) to induce compliance with the completion date. The language should read something similar to this:

All work done under this contract shall be substantially completed by _____ . Failure to complete by such date will entitle owner to deduct $ (____) per day for each day beyond such date. The date of substantial completion may be changed as a result of change orders or other factors. However, any change in this date must be agreed upon in writing by both parties.

Mechanics' Liens

Most states have laws that allow anyone who supplies labor or materials on a job site to record a mechanic's lien if he or she is not paid. Mechanics' liens are not to be treated lightly—if one is recorded on your house, it is a cloud on the title that must be cleared prior to selling the house. Theoretically, a contractor can foreclose on the lien and take the house. However, this rarely happens because any mortgage loans are senior to the mechanic's lien and the contractor would therefore be responsible for maintaining payments on these mortgages.

Problems can occur when an unscrupulous contractor receives payments from you but fails to pay subcontractors. The subs will then place mechanics' liens on your house, even though you paid the bill—not exactly a fair situation, because you could end up paying the bill twice.

The solution to these problems is to have your general contractor obtain a signed waiver of lien each and every time a subcontractor is paid (see Figure 15.4). You need to make sure it is in the contract that the contractor is responsible for this and will sign an "unconditional" lien release for all work under his or her supervision. Language similar to the following should be included in the contract:

> At each payment made by Owner to Contractor, the Contractor will provide to Owner acknowledgment of payment from each supplier and subcontractor as well as from the Contractor for all materials, equipment, and labor provided by the date of the previous payment. Upon final payment, the Contractor will provide Owner a written unconditional waiver or release of payment from all suppliers, subcontractors, and from the Contractor.

Dispute Resolution

Disputes or disagreements with your contractor are not uncommon and should probably be expected. Most of the time, they are just little issues that are easily worked out and solved. The key to resolving these inevitable problems is prompt and courteous communication. Always treat your contractor with the utmost respect. This above all else will keep things under control and moving forward. However, situations can develop where things unravel, tempers flare, and you hit a brick wall. You just can't get the problem resolved to your mutual satisfaction. This could occur either during the work phase or after the job has been completed. In anticipation of this potential situation, your contract should have a dispute resolution or arbitration clause specifying that such disputes will be settled by arbitration. The concept is great because it avoids the costly and time-consuming option of litigation. But be cautious about who will administer the arbitration. Contractors will want their trade association named as the arbitrator. Don't fall for this one, for obvious reasons (do you think a trade association would actually decide in your favor?).

Figure 15.4 Waiver of Lien

State of _____   Date: _____

County of _____

TO ALL WHOM IT MAY CONCERN:

Whereas _____ the undersigned _____
has been employed by _____
to furnish _____

_____
for the building located at _____
Lot No. _____ Block No. _____ Addition _____
City of _____
County of _____
the undersigned for and in consideration of the sum of $ _____ dollars
and other good and valuable considerations, the receipt whereof is hereby acknowl-
edged, do hereby waive and release any and all lien, or claim or right to lien, on said
above described building and premises under the Statutes of the State of _____
_____ relating the Mechanic's Lien, on account of labor or materials or both,
furnished or which may be furnished, by the undersigned to or on account of the said

_____
_____ for said building or premises.
Given under hand this _____ Day of _____ 20 _____

_____
          Signature

A good choice is The American Arbitration Association (800-778-7879; <www.adr.org>) or the National Academy of Conciliators (214-638-5633). You could also check with your county bar association, state attorney general's office, or local better business bureau for suggestions on mediation or arbitration services. Whomever you and your contractor mutually decide on needs to be named in the contract. Suggested language would be as follows:

All claims and disputes between the parties that relate to this contract shall be resolved by arbitration that shall be provided by _____, unless the Owner and Contractor mutually agree to resolve them by other means.

Breach of Contract

Sometimes, in spite of all the precautions you have taken, you end up hiring someone who becomes a nightmare. This is the situation that goes well beyond relatively minor disputes that occur while the work is in progress. Examples are endless, but typically relate to shoddy work and/or schedule problems that the contractor has been unwilling or unable to correct. The chances of this are very slim, if you've really checked the person out as discussed previously. In the event it does happen and you feel the contractor has violated the agreement, you want a provision in your contract that allows you to promptly cancel it and bring someone else in to finish the job. Suggested contract language would be similar to this:

Should Owner become dissatisfied with Contractor's work, a written notice shall be made. If the problems are not corrected to the Owner's satisfaction within five days, Owner has the option to terminate this contract and make arrangements to finish the job by whatever means are reasonable. Owner will deduct these costs from the amount due the Contractor. All disagreements over payments due and owing will be resolved in arbitration as provided.

In the event you end up needing to invoke this termination clause, always do so in writing. This can be done with either a telegram or a certified letter with return receipt requested. This will ensure that you have proof the contractor was notified of your action.

Right to Cancel

Federal law, as administered by the Federal Trade Commission, requires that when a contract is entered into at your home, the contractor must provide you with a cancellation form and information about your cancellation rights at the time you sign the contract. This requirement gives you the right to cancel the contract within three days of your signing it.

This is an excellent law because it protects homeowners from the high-pressure sales tactics of some of the unscrupulous operators. However, it is unclear as to whether it applies to a situation involving an investment property that you do not occupy. But to make it applicable to you, add the following to your contract:

> Owner reserves the right to cancel this contract within three days of signing.

Again, if you decide to exercise this option for some reason, do so in writing.

Now that we've covered the main provisions you want in the contract, it's time for you to sit down with your contractor and negotiate the final agreement. I would suggest you do this at your residence or place of business—in other words, on your turf. Go over all the details and contract provisions one by one until all the issues are settled. Talk it all out and make sure you both have a clear understanding of each other's expectations. So many potential problems can be put to rest at this stage, if only the parties take the time to discuss them. It's much better to do it now, in a relaxed atmosphere rather than during the heat of the battle when the work is in progress. Again, if you are uncomfortable with this process of contract negotiation or if you have any unresolved questions, get your attorney involved.

Funding Control—Handling the Money

Payments to your contractor should always be made with a check, not cash. A check gives you additional hard evidence that a bill was paid in the event of a future dispute. If for some reason you pay cash for some work, be sure to get a receipt that fully describes the work performed and get the signed lien release.

An alternative to you writing checks, getting receipts, and worrying about lien releases is to use the services of a funding control company or escrow company to disburse funds. For a small fee (typically 2 percent to 3 percent), this third party will handle all of these details for you. One of the safeguards in using this system is that funds will not be released unless and until you have approved the work in writing. This gives you considerable leverage in dealing with sloppy or unacceptable performance by the general contractor or subcontractors. In some instances, you will not have a choice in using this type of service because a portion of your renovation funds will have been held in escrow anyway. Whether you're getting the money through a private lender or some federal program such as 203(k), a certain portion of the total loan amount will usually be placed in escrow and released in stages as work is completed.

Here's how it works: The money for the rehab work is put into an account at the funding control company (or escrow company). As each part of the project is completed, the general contractor issues vouchers to the suppliers and subcontractors for their work, as of a specific date. The suppliers and subs send (or deliver) the vouchers, along with invoices and receipts, to the funding control company for payment. Prior to issuing the checks, the company usually inspects the job site to ensure completion or check with you for your approval.

Companies that provide this service can be located in several ways. First, your contractor may know of such a company through previous experience. Your lenders (private or bank) likely will be able to suggest a company that they have used in the past. And finally, you can call around to the escrow or title companies in your area and ask if they can provide this service.

Some contractors do not like this arrangement because of the added hassle factor. If you decide to go this route (highly recommended on bigger projects), just let your contractor know that it is a nonnegotiable issue. If the contractor refuses, call up the next person or company on your bid list.

How to Find Your Handyman

If you've decided to tackle the job of being your own general contractor, the first person you will want to look for is the handyman. To me, the excellent handyman is the most unappreciated person in America! Handymen are worth their weight in gold, although you can hire them rather cheaply. They are multitalented, clever, and can save you big bucks in the execution of your rehab plan.

The problem is finding the excellent handyman. In any community, there are dozens of handymen, but only a few would fit into the excellent category. It will be your job to seek these individuals out and get them involved with your projects. How do you go about doing this? You follow the same procedure discussed previously for locating the good general contractor. Ask, ask, ask everyone you know and look for ads in the classified section of the newspaper.

Sooner or later you will find one or two people who might fit the bill. Tell them about your project and let them tell you about their capabilities. Ask them about their recent projects and see if they are willing to give you any references. Do they have any insurance or a license (it's at least worth asking)? If this discussion sounds promising, set an appointment to meet at the project site. Once there, review the rehab plan scope of work as you walk through the house. If the chemistry is good, continue on with the discussions. If not, you'd better just move on.

As you review the checklist of tasks, listen for any ideas they may have on cost-saving or alternative approaches. This will give you an idea of their creativity and skill levels. This would also be the time to begin discussions of costs. You'll want to get an idea of what their hourly rates are, but whatever you do, do not agree to being charged on an hourly basis. If you decide to have them bid on a portion of the work, let them know that you want them to bid each component separately, as a line item. As discussed previously, never accept a lump-sum bid for the work they are proposing to do. Again, let them know that their costs are to be firm, not to exceed values, and any change will require your written approval.

The subject of contracts gets a little sticky when dealing with handymen because they typically work without them. Remember, handymen usually have no license, no insurance, and no bond. Nevertheless, I would strongly suggest you have a written contract with your handymen, even if it's just a simple agreement you prepare. Many office supply and stationary stores carry blank contracts that you could use. If you can't find anything locally, try calling Wolcotts (800-421-2222; <www.wolcottsforms .com>). They are a Los Angeles–based legal form company. With any of these fill-in-the-blank forms, remember that you can cross out or add language to meet your needs.

How to Find Your Specialized Subcontractors

These people are not really subcontractors because you will be contracting with them directly. But I call them subcontractors to distinguish them from the general contractors. The people I'm talking about here are the flooring contractors (carpet, vinyl, or tile), roofing contractors, electricians, and other specialists that you may need to bring in to supplement the work done by your handyman. If you're working with a general contractor, he or she will handle this task, but probably not as well as you could on your own, because the financial incentive is just not there.

I have found one of the best ways to find good-quality specialists that offer the best prices is to go out to new subdivisions under construction and talk to the workers. Many times I have found carpet layers, heating and air-conditioning installers, and landscaping workers that work for a big contractor but moonlight on the side (evenings and weekends). These people are highly skilled in their craft and are willing to work on the side for considerably less than what the boss (big contractor) would charge you. The bonus is that they will often get you the materials at cost so you just pay for their labor. What a deal!

Another good place to look is the small classified ads in the local paper. This is where the moonlighters and the small guys (with low overhead) advertise. Forget looking in the Yellow Pages. This is where the big contractors with the big overhead and the big prices advertise. You'll never get a good deal shopping in the Yellow Pages for contractors.

The exception to this approach is when you need very expensive work done and want a warranty or guarantee. This would include such jobs as roofing, major electrical, and foundation repairs. For these jobs, you want to hire a company, not an individual. And the company needs to have the financial wherewithal to provide and back up a guaranteed product. The only way to get the best price on these jobs is to bid them out, using the procedure discussed earlier.

Six More Tips for Working with Contractors

Working with contractors on a rehab project has the potential to be an absolute nightmare. Over the years, I have had to deal with everything from shoddy work to outright fraud along with a variety of behavioral problems. Things can get ugly from time to time and you need to expect this and prepare for it. It is almost unavoidable, particularly in cases when you are forced to fire someone because of nonperformance or lousy work.

But many problems can be avoided simply by communicating extensively before and after the work starts. You need to take the lead in this area, initiating full discussions of your desires and expectations. Get everything you can think of out on the table and in writing before work begins; don't be afraid to express any appropriate criticisms as work progresses. Open and frequent communication is the key.

That said, there are a number of other tips that you should be aware of that can help you in the various aspects of dealing with rehab contractors. Here are six that may be of benefit to you:

1. Once you have received bids on a job, always look for opportunities to further negotiate a better price. Let the contractors know that you have received competing bids and begin asking questions that require them to justify their figures. At the end of this discussion, always ask, "Is this the absolute best price you can give me?"

2. In interviewing prospective handymen or general contractors, be alert if they ask for a large up-front payment. This indicates that they have financial problems and will likely be trouble throughout the job.

3. Work out the payment schedule in advance and put it in the contract. At the start of the job, never give a contractor more than 20 percent (including the down payment). This is money at risk because no work has been completed. After that payment, don't pay additional money until a good portion of the work has been finished to your satisfaction. And of course, hold back 10 percent to 25 percent at the end to deal with any work defects you may discover after final completion and to allow for the mechanics' lien filing period to end.

4. Plan on being on-site as much as you can, particularly early in the project. This will allow you to reiterate your expectations and correct any unacceptable behavior. Make your presence felt early and set the tone for your work standards. You're paying the bill and if you are not getting what you bargained for, you need to take corrective action immediately.

5. Do not hesitate to fire anyone associated with the project who is not performing, displays behavioral problems, or in any other way jeopardizes the success of the project. This would include your handyman, general contractor, or any of the subcontractors. Take action early and swiftly. You've got a lot of money at stake and cannot afford to risk it on someone who doesn't cut it.

6. Protect yourself by diligently checking to make sure that your general contractor has an active workers' compensation insurance policy. Don't just take his or her word for it; make the contractor produce documents and call the insurance company if you have any uncertainty. If you're using a handyman, contact your insurance agent and add a workers' compensation rider. It doesn't cost much and you'll be able to sleep a lot better at night.

Managing Your Rehab Project

A comprehensive rehab project is a complex set of activities that can easily get out of control if not managed properly. The two biggest problems are cost control and schedule control. A big part of your job is to keep the project on time and within budget. You can only do this if you set up a process to capture and monitor progress over time. Of course, you will need to take corrective action when the inevitable problems crop up.

The important thing is to have a plan and monitor progress. You don't want to make this too complicated with computer databases and daily reports. After all, you're rehabbing a house, not building a skyscraper.

You've already developed a comprehensive rehab plan with all of the planned tasks and activities. You also have developed a detailed budget. With respect to the rehab plan, all that remains for you to do is to develop a time line for all of the components and the overall project. Obviously, some tasks need to be completed before others can begin, while other tasks can be worked on simultaneously. Your handyman or general contractor will likely have firm ideas on the sequence of how they want to accomplish the work. Weather conditions may be a factor in scheduling the outside tasks; however, I would suggest making the external painting and front landscaping a high priority. This will allow you or your real estate agent to begin marketing the property almost immediately (without scaring people off with horrible curb appeal). Sit down with your handyman or general contractor and work out a schedule that is acceptable to both parties.

To keep on top the of the budget, you will need to closely monitor expenditures as they occur. Regardless of whether you use a handyman or a general contractor, you must keep in daily contact with them to track the spending patterns. Remember, you've set the contracts up on a firm bid price, with a not-to-exceed provision for each job component. This is where your contractors may try to push the envelope and claim certain items were not included in the initial scope of work. Be fair when something unusual comes up or you've added tasks, but don't be duped by illegitimate claims. And don't forget, your written approval is required to change the scope of work and any incremental costs.

Managing the rehab process is not rocket science, but it does require you to pay close attention to the details. Set up a master project file and keep good records. If you follow the procedures I've outlined, you will achieve an acceptable outcome. Certainly, you will become more proficient at this with each rehab you complete. Frequently ask yourself, how can I do this better? There always is a better way, and it's up to you to find it.

Well, you're almost done. Now, let's find out how to get your masterpiece on the market and sold quickly so you can collect your hard-earned profits!

Getting Paid

Quickly Selling Your House for Top Dollar

*Y*ou're on the final leg of your journey. You've bought your raw material, transformed it through a value-added process into a desirable finished product, and now you're ready to sell it at full retail value and convert your paper profits to cash. This is what the rehab business is all about. But let me tell you in advance that this last leg of the process can be the most difficult. It is in a sense the weakest link in the chain of events that comprise the rehab business. Why? Because it is the part of the business where you have the least amount of control over the outcome.

On the surface, the selling process appears straightforward. Find a buyer, sign the contract, close the deal, and collect your check. That is the process, but it is so full of uncertainty because so many things can go wrong, even under the best of circumstances. We are now dealing with the human element, where emotions and feelings play a big part in the equation. In addition, we are dealing with the inherent conflict of people's wants and desires, coupled with their financial strength. Combine all of this with the inconsistent lending policies of financial institutions and you have a situation that can be very volatile and uncertain.

Given these caveats, your mission is clear. To sell your house quickly and at top dollar, you must be proactive and assume as much control over the process as you can. This is no time to become passive and leave things to chance. Many new players will be interjected into your life—buyers, lenders, real estate agents, escrow companies—and you must learn to interact with them effectively and ensure that they perform their tasks well. This will require persistence, follow-up, and constant attention to the details.

The Six Key Elements of Your Marketing Strategy

You need to begin planning your marketing strategy or exit plan before you actually buy a property. It's not good enough if you wait until the rehab is complete because your buying strategy should be intertwined with your selling strategy. For example, did you assume a loan that can be passed on to your buyer or can you create an assumable loan when you buy? If a new loan will be required, what will conventional or FHA lenders require in terms of physical condition of the house? Start planning your strategies on the front end so that you can begin implementing them on the day you close your purchase.

There are six key elements of any marketing strategy, regardless of the product you are selling. Here's a summary of them, put in the context of selling your rehab property:

1. *Sell a product people want to buy.* If you have not created a house that people want to buy, you will not get it sold for top dollar. This speaks to your rehab plan and the sizzle features that you should have included. Certainly, people want to buy houses to live in, but what distinguishes your house from all the others on the market? Your product must have something about it that is unique or unusual, compared to competing products. If not, your house is mediocre and likely will languish on the market and cost you money in holding costs. Create demand by including features people really want and can't find at a comparable price. This is a key element to your marketing strategy.

2. *Know your customer.* In devising your marketing plan, it is imperative that you have a good knowledge of your buyer's profile. Assuming you're working at the lower end of the price

range with your rehab investment, your primary target customer is the first-time homebuyer. We've previously discussed some of the characteristics of this buyer. In terms of selling the house to this buyer, you will need to be prepared to help in overcoming several potential problems—fear, down payment, and loan qualification being the most common.

3. *Make it easy to buy.* With many products, sales will increase dramatically if you make it easy for a customer to buy your product; for example, by providing a postage-paid order form or a toll-free number. When selling a house, it's a little more difficult to "make it easy," but there are some things you can do. For instance, you could create and offer assumable financing or sell on a wraparound mortgage. You could work with a nonconforming lender in advance and put together a financing package that might include you carrying back a second mortgage coupled with a low down payment requirement. Work up a summary of the requirements for the first-time homebuyer financing programs being offered by lenders in your area. What else could you do to make it easy for your buyers? Think!

4. *Offer incentives.* Your house will sell much faster if you are offering some additional incentives. This would include incentives to your buyer and incentives to your real estate agent, if you are using one. A common incentive for the buyer is to offer a home warranty program that you and/or your agent would purchase. How about a health club membership? What incentive would motivate a real estate agent? There's only one (money), and I'll discuss that further in a later section.

5. *Fair price.* People will not buy a product if they think they're getting ripped off. In terms of selling a house, this means that you never price it very far above current market value. You want to receive top dollar for your creation, but if you overprice it, you will see a lot of resistance in the marketplace. Your price should be fair and based on recent sales in the neighborhood. If it's listed at a higher price than recent sales, you better have good justification for the price; for example, it's in much better condition or it has a much larger lot compared with the recent sales.

6. *Advertise your product constantly.* To sell your product quickly, you must get the word out to people who may be interested in buying. You must devise as many avenues as possible to put your product in front of as many people as possible. Just putting an ad in the Sunday newspaper isn't going to cut it. You must plan on a multimedia approach, which is sustained constantly and continuously until the house is sold. Anything short of an all-out, sustained advertising effort will only cost you more in the long run with holding costs.

These are the basic elements of a well-coordinated marketing strategy that you need to think through, devise, and implement. I'll be discussing several of these in more detail in the sections that follow.

Should I Use a Real Estate Agent or Sell the House Myself?

Be honest with yourself. This is a very important question. I know you want to save and pocket the 6 percent commission, but are you really the best person for the job of marketing your property? It's not just a question of knowledge. It also involves such issues as ability to maximize market exposure, availability of time, ability to prequalify buyers, personality, and selling skills. If you don't score high in all of these areas, plan on getting professional help in the form of a competent real estate agent. Otherwise, you're just kidding yourself and could end up wasting large amounts of money, large amounts of time, and potentially killing otherwise viable deals. Some of us are just not meant to be involved in sales. Don't make it an ego thing—make it a business decision.

I have a strong bias toward using a real estate agent to market properties. Why? Because I know the value that their service can bring to the table. Even if you're good in all of the areas necessary to complete a sale, you cannot even come close to the market exposure capability of getting your property listed on the MLS system. If you really mess up and choose the goofiest agent out there, you still have a better-than-average chance of selling the property because every other agent in town will know your house is available. The laws of probability are in your favor when more people who are working with buyers have access to your property.

Still want to do it yourself? Go for it, but just remember that time is of the essence and the longer your property sits on the market, the less profit you will make. The successful rehab investment depends on speed–buying quickly, getting the rehab done quickly, and getting the property sold quickly. Stumbling along in any of these areas is going to cost you money.

For those of you who just can't shake the idea of selling the home yourself, I can recommend a resource for you to consider. It's a book written by an associate of mine and can be found at my Web site <www .rehabwiz.com>.

How to Select Your Real Estate Agent

The number-one criterion for selecting a real estate agent to handle the sale of your property is that the agent be a selling agent, not a listing agent. Remember, many agents specialize in one or the other, although most agents do both. How can you tell? You have to ask. Over the past six months, how many listings has the agent received and how many sales has he or she made? You want an agent who is a "top gun" selling machine, someone who lives and breathes the selling side of the business.

There are many horror stories out there about agents, like the one about the hapless couple who walked into a real estate office one Saturday morning and listed their house with the "nice young lady" agent who had floor duty that day. They signed a six-month listing. Unfortunately, they didn't know that she really was a full-time legal secretary moonlighting as a real estate agent on the weekends. As you might expect, the house sat for six months without a single offer.

The agent you want is one who is active in the neighborhood your house is in or at least active in that price range. Remember, some agents specialize in first-time homebuyers at the lower price range, while others specialize in the upper-end "executive" homes. Look at realty signs in your general area and look at the Sunday newspaper. The agent you want has his or her mug shot in the paper and maybe even on a billboard along the highway. This agent is in the business full-time and is very successful.

The next step is the face-to-face interview. The best advice I can give you on this is to talk little and listen a lot, at least at the beginning of your meeting. Let the agent lead the conversation and you just sit back and listen. Make the agents work for the listing and demonstrate their skills. Are they shooting from the hip or do they really know their stuff?

What price are they suggesting you list the house? Are they persuasive and passionate or boring in their presentation? Observe them from the eyes of prospective buyers.

After this initial assessment, it's time for you take control of the meeting and get down to business. Ask them to specifically describe their marketing plans for the house. Nail them down on such issues as frequency of newspaper advertising, distribution of flyers, and holding open houses. You want to clearly communicate your expectations of performance and get commitments from the agents. Ask them specific questions about how they intend to attract buyers and how they prequalify buyers. If your house is targeted at first-time homebuyers, is the agent experienced in working with loan programs designed for these clients?

I would suggest you go through this process with at least two agents. This will give you a basis of comparison and allow you to make a choice. Which agent seems to have the best overall "package" and which has the best chemistry with you? Make your decision and call for the next meeting.

The second meeting is intended to finalize the listing agreement and to further clarify your expectations of performance. It is also the time for you to exert control, to the extent you can, over the selling process. Let the agent know that you intend to be an active seller, and are not just passively handing the job off to the agent.

The Three Key Provisions of the Listing Agreement

When your agent arrives to take your listing, he or she will most likely have a listing agreement already filled out (these are standardized forms). However, your challenge is to get three provisions added or modified. You are going to have to do some negotiating to get these provisions inserted in the listing agreement. Not all agents will agree with all of them but most will. If you run across an agent who will not cooperate, move on to the next agent on your list.

1. Limit the listing agreement to a period of 90 days. The agent likely will ask for a six-month (180-day) listing but this is entirely one-sided and unnecessarily puts your profits at risk. The agent needs to know that you *pay for performance* and that if the house is not sold within 90 days, you intend to list with someone else. Say it and mean it.

2. Insert a buyout provision that allows you to buy out the listing agreement in the event you produce a buyer of the house on your own. This is critical, as it places your agent on notice that you are not going to sit around and do nothing. You want fast action and if you happen to find a buyer on your own, so be it. You will agree not to go out and advertise for buyers, but if you happen to find one through your contacts in the community, you want the ability to consummate a deal without having to pay a full commission. It also tells the agent that you only pay for successful performance.

Offer $500 to buy out the contract if you produce a buyer during the first 45 days and $750 if during the last 45 days. This is a fair compensation for the expenditures the agent will make for advertising and other marketing expenses. You may get some grief over this provision, but I can assure you it is achievable and has been used by investors all around the country. This approach is much better than trying to get a nonexclusive agency agreement whereby only the person who obtains a buyer gets paid. Most agents won't work under this type of agreement. By maintaining the normal exclusive right-to-sell arrangement combined with the buyout agreement, agents feel much more secure. They will get paid for their expenses at a minimum and they will receive the full commission if they (or any other agent) produces a buyer. Suggested listing agreement language would be something similar to the following:

> This listing agreement is modified to reflect agreement between the parties of a buyout provision, as follows:

> In the event that the seller, through his own independent contacts, produces a buyer for the listed property, this listing agreement can be canceled by the seller by payments to the listing agent in accordance with the following schedule. Seller will pay listing agent a sum of $500 to buy out this agreement during the first 45 days and a sum of $750 during the final 45 days of the 90-day listing period. This compensation is in consideration of listing agent's efforts and expenses in marketing the property and fully discharges all obligations under this agreement. No additional compensation or fees will be due to the listing agent or listing agent's broker.

> Seller agrees that during the term of this agreement, he will not actively advertise the property in an effort to secure a buyer and will cooperatively work with the listing agent in all marketing

efforts. However, the seller may secure a buyer through his own independent contacts, if such buyer has not been previously shown the property by the listing agent or by any other real estate agent.

3. Offer an attractive selling bonus for quick results. Nothing provides a more powerful incentive to a real estate agent than money, so make it the centerpiece of your listing agreement! Here's what I suggest. I call it the 8-7-6 commission package. Instead of the normal 6 percent commission, offer 8 percent if the sale occurs within the first 30 days and 7 percent if a sale occurs within the second 30 days. The commission would revert to the standard 6 percent during the final 30 days of the listing. Pay for performance, that's the philosophy. Essentially, what you're saying to your agent is this, "Get out there and quickly produce a buyer who ends up at the closing table and you get a nice bonus. Wait until the last 30 days, and you get the normal 6 percent commission. Don't produce one within 90 days and you get nothing—not even a second chance." Although you will want to say this in a more diplomatic manner, that's the message you want your real estate agent to get. Pay for performance. The following is suggested language to modify the listing agreement:

This listing agreement is modified to reflect agreement between the parties of a revised compensation provision, as follows:

Seller agrees to pay broker a commission of 8 percent if the property is sold to a qualified buyer within 30 days from the effective date of this listing agreement. Seller will pay broker a commission of 7 percent if sold between the period of day 31 and day 60, following the effective date. Seller will pay a commission of 6 percent if a sale occurs after day 60 and no later than day 90 from the effective date.

Commissions are not due and payable unless said sale results in a closed transaction.

Apartment-Dwellers—Your Prime Marketing Target

Based on the profile of your *most likely buyers,* they have never owned a home before and are currently living in an apartment. That being the case, why not work with your agent to develop and implement an apartment-dwellers marketing program as part of the overall marketing strategy. This program would consist of flyers that would be distributed to apartment buildings in the general area of your house. The flyers would be designed to overcome the most common concerns of these buyers, such as affordability, down payment, and credit history issues, and would include a picture of your house and financing available for first-time homebuyers. You might even persuade your agent to hold weekly seminars for prospective buyers from this group.

It's important that you offer to help with the distribution of the flyers to the apartment buildings. This is part of your commitment to be proactive in the selling process and it shows your agent that you are willing to help him or her earn their commission. Spend a couple of hours each week out hitting the bricks with your agent. This is a powerful marketing tool, because it targets a large pool of potential buyers who are highly motivated to buy, if they can be shown that their dream is achievable.

Will You Help with Financing?

This is a key question that you need to answer before the house goes on the market. In fact, it's one you really should make at the time you buy. Are you going to offer seller carry-back financing?

In an ideal market, we all like to cash out, get all of our profits, and move on to the next deal. And, in many instances that is exactly what you will do. Remember, even under less-than-ideal market conditions, there is always a demand for good-quality housing at the lower end of the price range. This is precisely where your rehab investments are focused.

But there are times when local market conditions may be such that additional incentives need to be offered in order to get a quick sale. Lower demand due to excess inventory on the market or general economic recession are two common instances where you might want to consider this option.

Let me be clear about what I mean here. I'm not talking about creating a nonqualifying, assumable loan or selling on a wrap. Those are different options I'll discuss in later sections. What I mean is a situation where the buyer cannot qualify for a 95 percent or 97 percent LTV loan through Fannie Mae or FHA due to some problem with credit history or whatever. But the buyer can qualify for a 75 percent or 80 percent LTV loan from a nonconforming lender or finance company. This type of loan, coupled with a down payment and a seller carry-back second mortgage, will allow the deal to happen.

Let's say you have a house you're selling retail for $70,000 and you have a buyer who can qualify for a 75 percent LTV loan at a local finance company. This would amount to $52,500. The buyer can come up with $4,000 for a down payment. You would then carry back a second mortgage in the amount of $13,500. Done deal.

How much cash would you walk away with at closing? That depends on your acquisition cost and your share of closing costs, including any real estate commissions. You'll have $52,500 plus $4,000 to pay off any loans and closing costs. Anything left you can put in your pocket. Plus you have a $13,500 mortgage paying you a nice monthly income. Or you could sell your note at a discount for cash (to an investor or note broker) and be done with the deal.

Your willingness and ability to structure such a deal can have outstanding benefits to your bottom line. Why? Primarily because offering this kind of deal means you can sell quickly (more potential buyers can qualify for the financing), thereby reducing your holding costs and you can sell for top dollar. Whenever you offer good terms, you can always name your price, within reason.

This can be an excellent strategy, particularly if you plan for it in advance. If you can buy and rehab the property cheaply enough, you will be able to get your costs and some of your profit out at closing. Plus you'll be earning a good interest rate on your remaining profit if you choose to keep the second mortgage. The key to making this strategy work is knowing a lender who offers loans to people with less-than-stellar credit or with higher debt ratios (or both). These loans are offered by what are known as nonconforming lenders or by finance companies.

Nonconforming Lenders and Finance Companies

A nonconforming loan means a loan made to a borrower who does not meet the requirements of Fannie Mae, FHA, or other conventional lending programs. It could be for any number of reasons, such as a prior bankruptcy, slow payment history, debt ratio too high, self-employment, or a new job. If they do have a recent history of stable income and a debt ratio of up to 50 percent, however, borrowers may qualify for a 75 percent to 80 percent LTV loan in the secondary mortgage market or through a finance company. A nonconforming lender could be any mortgage company offering B, C, or D loans (mediocre, poor, or bad credit rating) or a finance company offering similar loans. Nationally known finance companies that may offer this type of financing include Commercial Credit, The Associates, American General, Ford Motor Credit, AVCO, and Beneficial Finance, to name a few.

If you intend to offer seller carry-back financing under the scenario just discussed, it is very important that you or your real estate agent make contact with several of these sources of funding. The idea is to make contact well in advance of your marketing program and learn their loan requirements. Your agent will then be well versed in prequalifying potential buyers, and some of this information should be included in marketing materials. The importance of showing people who otherwise think they can't qualify for a home loan how they can achieve their dream of home ownership cannot be emphasized enough. Flyers should dramatize this point and all newspaper advertising placed by your agent should include the words, *owner will help with financing.* These words are extremely powerful and will make the phone ring off the hook!

Creating an Assumable Loan with a Private Mortgage

Want to sell your house tomorrow without the need to hire a real estate agent? Offer your house for sale with an assumable loan! This is another option in a slow market when you need to induce buyers and you're willing to carry some of your profit in a second mortgage. It requires you to negotiate an assumption provision with your private mortgage lender.

Normally, a rehab loan from a private lender will be for a short term, usually two years or less, and will be nonassumable. However, some private lenders are willing to allow an assumption for an additional fee and to extend the loan to a balloon in five to seven years. This is particularly true after the rehab has been completed and the house is in tip-top shape.

Under this scenario, you would attempt to negotiate a higher LTV loan with a 15- or 20-year amortization schedule and a balloon in five to seven years. For example, you might be able to get a loan of up to 70 percent of the full retail value. You would then need to carry the balance, less the down payment, as a second mortgage. In this situation, the private lender will normally want to qualify the new borrower in order to feel comfortable that the payments will be made. But be assured, the lender's qualification standards will be nowhere near the stringency of a bank, because his or her mortgage is secured in first position with at least 30 percent underlying equity.

Anytime you can sell with assumable financing, you can sell tomorrow and sell at top dollar. If you structure the deal correctly at the outset, by buying well below market value, and then sell with assumable financing, you can usually cover all of your costs and receive some of your profit at closing. The remaining profit will earn a good interest rate until it is paid off with the balloon in five to seven years.

As you begin working with private mortgage brokers and lenders, this option of creating assumable financing will become quite easy. Your lenders will get to know your capabilities in producing a good quality product and will gain considerable confidence in your abilities. If you don't need all of your profits right now, this is an excellent alternative that allows you to quickly move your properties. And as we know, speed is very important in the rehab business.

Getting the Buyer to the Closing Table

This is your number-one mission in life—getting the buyer to the closing table. All of the blood, sweat, and tears that you have given up to this point have created only paper profits. Getting a buyer to the closing table is your chance to turn those paper profits into cash.

If you are using a real estate agent, all of the steps involved in this process are generally his or her responsibility to coordinate. Let me urge you to never, never, never just turn it over to the agent and forget about it. You must follow the progress of every detail and double-check to make sure everything is completed in a timely fashion. Here again, you need to exert your brand of control, to the extent you can. After all, no one involved in the process has as much at stake as you do. Now is not the time to let your guard down and relax. Keep pushing—you're almost there!

Your first step, once you have received an acceptable written offer and before you sign the contract, is to check out the buyer. Don't ever agree to take your property off the market until you or your agent has confirmed the buyer's qualifications. If the buyer will be getting new financing, has he or she been prequalified by a lender or at least by the agent? You need to feel comfortable that the buyer will be likely to get the needed financing. Has anyone pulled a preliminary credit report? You or your agent can get this done quickly by any of your respective lender contacts. This is especially important when dealing with first-time buyers who may have marginal financial qualifications.

Again before you sign, find out exactly how the buyer intends to finance the purchase. Which lender, if any, has the buyer chosen? Does the buyer have the necessary down payment in the bank? When working this end of the market, I have learned to be a little skeptical. You can't entirely prevent people from making misleading statements, but at least exert some level of due diligence before you take the property off the market. Is the buyer's loan application going to be dead on arrival or does it appear that they have a good shot at it? Talk it over with your real estate agent and one of your lender contacts. If everything seems to check out, sign the sales agreement, drink a toast, and prepare for the next phase of continuous and persistent follow-up.

Most sales agreements require the buyer to make a loan application within a specified period. Follow up with your agent to make sure that this was accomplished. If not, you'd better get your agent fired up to find out why not. There is no excuse for missing this deadline, particularly if your agent produced the buyer.

Once the buyer has made his or her loan application, it's pretty much a waiting game. The paperwork is enormous and seems like it takes forever to finish, but this doesn't mean you or your agent should just sit back and do nothing. Your agent should be in contact with the lender's loan processor on a weekly basis. Your job is to make sure that this contact has been made. Keep pressing.

Your agent should be checking on the status of various loan documents, including the buyer's credit report and the appraisal on the house. Many lenders wait to order the appraisal until the loan is approved, wanting to save the applicant the appraisal fee in the event the loan is denied. To heck with that! Try to get the lender to order the appraisal immediately—and collect the money from the borrower. You might even consider including this in your contract: Buyer agrees to pay lender for appraisal at time of loan application. This will eliminate this phony issue and will eliminate any potential delays in getting the appraisal completed in a timely manner. As an appraiser, I don't know how many loan closings I have seen unnecessarily delayed because the loan processor forgot to order the appraisal! Ridiculous! Don't let this happen to you.

The next milestone occurs when the lender finally announces that the loan has been approved. It's high-five time, but not time to celebrate—yet. There's still plenty of paperwork to get done and potential obstacles to overcome. This is no time to let up! Get your real estate agent to check with the lender on the status of the title policy, termite inspection report, survey, loan payoff letters, and the buyer's hazard insurance policy. Follow up and keep the pressure on, because the closing date will not be set until all of these documents are in hand.

Finally, the glorious day arrives—the buyer goes to closing and the deal is done. Payday has finally arrived! Pick up your check and take your family out to celebrate! It's been a long and tortuous journey, but today is the day that makes it all worthwhile.

Now that your juices are flowing, it's time to start thinking about doing it again and again and again. It's time to start thinking about ditching your day job and making a secure future for yourself. Let's find out how to operate this as a real business.

Graduate School

Advanced Strategies for Operating a Rehab Business for Maximum Profit

We've covered the basics of a rehab investment from beginning to end. You've gotten a taste of what it's all about and a glimpse of the profit potential that the investment has to offer. Once you get out there and do a few deals, things will start falling into place for you. Your own personalized system will begin to take shape. Sooner or later, you will ask yourself, should I be doing this full-time? Of course, each of us must decide what is best for our particular situation. But many dream of someday being on their own, released from the drudgery of working for someone else. You are looking for an opportunity to pursue long-term financial security without the constraints of a nine-to-five job. The real estate rehab business offers you that opportunity, on a silver platter.

Most people, myself included, start out in this business on a part-time basis. That's just common sense. Get your feet wet, learn the ropes, and then decide whether to pursue it full time. Some of you have already decided that this is what you want to do. Others just want to test the waters and see how things develop. This chapter is intended for either camp. I want to show you the potential this business has to offer, to discuss some of the more advanced techniques, and to give you some ideas on operating as a full-time business. The choice is yours.

Profit Potential of the Rehab Business

The real estate rehab business is essentially a manufacturing operation. A raw product is purchased wholesale and is transformed into a final retail product. Like all manufacturing businesses, profits are based on margin, or the difference between cost and sales price.

In earlier chapters, I've suggested to you that your *minimum* net profit or margin should be no less than $10,000 on any rehab project. I want to emphasize that this is the minimum profit that you should accept. In evaluating a potential deal, if you can't see at least $10,000 net profit, move on to another deal. It's just not worth your time and effort to get involved for anything less.

As you become more adept at finding bargain properties and negotiating better deals, your profit margins will increase. At some time, you will expand your operations into more expensive properties. Higher-priced properties carry more risk because of supply-and-demand factors, but the profit margins increase dramatically. A $50,000 profit on a $250,000 house is not at all unusual and the amount of time and effort is basically the same.

The other factor is how many projects you complete. On a part-time basis, you could comfortably do two to three houses in a year, with little impact on your current lifestyle. Anything above about six houses a year and you're getting into a full-time operation; however, I know of some people who are doing as many as 50 to 60 houses a year. Obviously, this level of activity requires several people to manage the operation.

For a better idea of the profit potential, take a look at different profit margins and frequencies in Figure 17.1. How much money do you want to make next year?

Advanced Techniques for Finding Bargains

Without a doubt, finding and acquiring bargain properties is the most important aspect of a real estate rehab business. You're not in business unless you can develop a continuous stream of houses on which you can make offers. And you're not managing your business properly if you're not spending about 80 percent of your time on the acquisition process.

Figure 17.1 Profit Potential of the Rehab Business

How Much Do You Want to Make Next Year?

Profit Margin	Number of Houses per Year			
	3	6	12	24
$10,000	$30,000	$ 60,000	$120,000	$240,000
15,000	45,000	90,000	180,000	360,000
25,000	75,000	150,000	300,000	600,000

Why such a heavy time commitment on the acquisition process? Because it takes that much time to find and buy properties at wholesale prices.

It would be nice if you could just call up your real estate agent and say, *George, I'd like to buy a house today at wholesale—what do you have?* Unfortunately, it just doesn't work that way. It takes a lot of time and hard work to consistently purchase properties that meet our major investment criterion—that will make you money.

In the sections that follow, I discuss a variety of techniques that are proven strategies for finding candidate properties. Some of these techniques may not fit in with your particular situation or market conditions. You will need to pick and choose those you think will work best for you. Sooner or later, you will hit on a combination of techniques that match your style and market conditions.

In earlier chapters, we worked on techniques wherein the seller has already identified himself to the world, either through a real estate agent or by placing a FSBO ad somewhere. Now we're going to get into the more creative stuff. The focus of our attention turns to potential sellers whose houses are not even on the market. If everybody else is chasing after the same deals, why don't we do something different? Why not pursue properties where there is virtually no competition? Let's do it.

In the techniques that follow, the initial goal is to identify handyman properties and the names and addresses of their owners. Once this is accomplished, we will then initiate a long-term, periodic direct-mail campaign specifically focused on our target audience. During this phase, the objective is to elicit a "selling response" from these owners, and get them to call you when they decide to sell, much like a real estate agent who "farms" a particular neighborhood for listings. In this way, you get first crack at the property before anyone else in the world.

Getting Rich by Driving Around

One of the most important and valuable activities you can undertake as a real estate entrepreneur is to get out and drive around the neighborhoods in your community. It is the only way to observe characteristics and determine trends. How else are you going to find out where the marginal areas are, which neighborhoods are improving, and which ones are going downhill? Beyond these important tasks, getting out and about affords you the opportunity to spot fixer-upper properties.

Your job at this point is to jot down the street address of every candidate. You might even want to take photographs (I use a digital camera—there is no film or processing cost and I just download the pictures to my computer). It doesn't matter if the house is vacant, boarded up, or full of life—you're trying to build a database of potential candidates that might meet your investment criteria. You know the clues you're looking for—curled up roof shingles, chipped and faded paint, cracked stucco, broken windows, cowboy landscaping (weeds and dirt), abandoned cars, cars on blocks in front yard, and so forth. Obviously, you can't see the inside of the house, but these external clues at least indicate poor maintenance. If I'm in a new area, I like to park the car and walk around the streets. Not only can you see the houses better, it gives you a chance to talk to any of the neighbors who might be outside. I just tell them I'm looking for a house in the area, maybe one that needs a little work, and ask them if they know of any houses like that. Be simple, straightforward, and honest. Because you are a stranger, you usually don't get a lot of information, but sometimes you do. It's worth the effort.

By the way, while you're out driving, don't hesitate to stop in on any FSBOs that look interesting and be sure to make a note of any listed property that looks like it might have potential. Not all handyman specials are identified as such in the MLS.

Keep driving (and walking) and jotting down addresses. Go to as many different neighborhoods as you can. Over a few weeks or months, you want to build up to at least 100 and preferably 500 target properties. Remember, this is a numbers game and the more you have, your successes will be more frequent.

Once you have your list of target properties, the next step is to find out the property owner's name and address. You have several choices—look them up through the MLS system (see your real estate agent) or go down to the county courthouse (clerk, recorder, or tax assessor's office) and manually look them up. Another choice would be to contact someone you're acquainted with at a title company or real estate appraisal office—they also have instant access to this information. If you have to go to the courthouse, don't be intimidated. Most counties will have one or two employees whose only job is to assist the public in obtaining information. Keep in mind, this is public information.

Without question, this is a lot of work. Well, who said it was going to be easy? But let me ask you this—do you think any of your competition is going to bother to do this work? No way. What you have created for yourself is virtually *priceless*. Whether you have 20 names and addresses or 2,000, you have gold in your hands. Let's think about what you have. Here's a list of fixer-upper property owners. The houses are falling apart and they look terrible, at least from the street. Something has probably gone wrong in the owner's lives, and it is highly likely that they will either want or need to sell in the near future. How much would you pay for such a list? You couldn't afford it, because as I said, it is priceless! You have information that nobody in your town has. And you are going to use this information in a way that will allow you to buy property before anyone knows the property is available. This is your competitive advantage. Let's look at some more techniques to find candidate properties.

College Students as Bumblebees

I call this the *bumblebee* technique because it reminds me of how beehives operate! Here's how it works: Hire a couple of college students (I'll show you how to find them in a minute) to go out into the neighborhoods and look for fixer-upper properties, as we described above. They buzz around, gather up the goodies, and bring them back to you! It's that simple. You're hiring them to go out and do what I described earlier in driving around. After you start getting really busy, it's important for you to find ways to delegate work to others.

I use college kids for this work, but you can use anyone who has a car and a camera. The important thing is to get them trained so they bring back the exact information you need. You don't want to be paying for useless information. Here are the five steps to follow:

1. Give them a map showing three or four neighborhoods you want them to research.
2. Give them a written description of the type of houses you're looking for; use the list of clues discussed earlier.
3. Tell them you want a photograph of each house—I give them a photograph log sheet (see Figure 17.2 for an example) so they can keep track of which photo goes with which house address.
4. Give them a written priority list: boarded-up, vacant, FSBO, and occupied, in that order. I tell them to ignore all REALTOR®-listed properties (no sense in paying for information your real estate agent should provide for free).
5. For each property, you want them to record the street address. If it is vacant or boarded up, ask them to talk with a neighbor to see if they can get the owner's name and whereabouts (sometimes the county records are inaccurate or not up to date and a neighbor can often provide good information). If it is a FSBO, ask them to record the phone number also.

I provide the film and developing because I usually can get it cheaper than they can. You can also set it up on a straight reimbursable basis, whatever works for you. The next issue is compensation. How do you pay for the work? You need to think this through for yourself, based on your local circumstances, but here's what I do:

- $10 for each vacant or boarded-up house with owner's name
- $7 for each vacant or boarded-up house without owner's name
- $5 for each FSBO with phone number
- $2.50 for each junker, address only

You'll notice that I pay a premium for vacant or boarded-up houses. Why? Because in my community, they're relatively rare and hard to find.

Figure 17.2 Photo Log

Date _____

Roll # _____

Frame #	Address	Status Vacant, FSBO, Occupied	Comments Owner's Name, FSBO Phone #

In your area, they might be common, so you would adjust your pay scale accordingly.

How do you find your bumblebees? I go over to a local community college, get permission from the front office, and place a few flyers on bulletin boards. You'll get plenty of calls with this ad:

> Help Wanted—Do You Have a Camera and a Car? Take Outdoor Pictures of Houses in Your Neighborhood. Will Pay $2.50 to $10.00 per Picture. Call Kevin at 222-1122 for Details.

You'll need to work out a budget for this work and maybe space it out over a couple of months, depending on your cash-flow situation. How many leads do you want? Only you can answer that question. If you're using this technique, I would suggest you target at least one new neighborhood a month and more if you can afford it. You want to build up your pool of owners' names as fast as you can.

If one of your "student bees" works out good for you, you might also want to consider training him or her to do your county records research. As you will find out, this work can get tedious—for me, it's well worth it to pay someone $5 per hour to do this kind of work.

Referral Network

I have not had much luck with this idea but others have, so I'll briefly mention it. The idea here is to get other people you know (or make contact with) to refer names of people to you. If you end up buying the house they refer, you pay them a referral fee, typically $200 to $250.

In the rehab business, you're looking for a very special type of homeowner, not just anybody who is interested in selling their house. As a result, it's hard to get people interested enough, because there is not a very frequent payday.

Do you like a challenge? Okay, here's the challenge. Can you think of a type of person (or occupation) who would come in frequent contact with owners of handyman special properties? If you can solve this puzzle, you would have an excellent referral source that could make you a lot of money.

Here's one I heard about the other day from a mortgage investor here in Albuquerque that might work out for you in the rehab business—disability insurance agents. Apparently, approximately 40 percent of the people who end up on disability also end up in foreclosure. Because many properties in foreclosure are poorly maintained, these would be good candidates. The angle here would be to work with disability agents whose clients are in financial trouble, with the idea of purchasing properties before any foreclosure proceedings begin, if possible. This just might be a win-win opportunity for both parties. If you could develop such a relationship, you would obviously be in a position to act well in advance of any competitors.

Direct Mail—Your Secret Weapon for Success

Without a doubt, a well-designed, targeted direct-mail program has the potential to dramatically increase your success in finding bargain properties. The advantages of direct mail versus telephone contact or door-knocking are, in my opinion, substantial. You control all aspects of the interaction, including timing, content of the "conversation," and frequency. You don't have to worry about rejection or the inefficiency of playing telephone tag. It's a private, powerful method of establishing a rapport with your seller, prior to actually meeting. Perhaps best of all, when the homeowners decide to sell, they call or write you (instead of you calling them), giving you a psychological edge in the initial phase of the interaction.

With your list of names and addresses of property owners, you're ready to kick off your direct-mail campaign. There are many, many options at this point for you to consider. For example, format could be a letter, postcard, brochure, or flyer; postage could be first-class or some form of bulk rate; envelopes could be plain or have your business return address on them; you could use printed address labels or hand-write them on each envelope; you could photocopy a form letter addressed to "Dear Friend" or individualize each letter. The nuances and combinations are almost endless, but let's not get bogged down in too many details! You need to select a method that is workable for you, given any limitations on budget resources or equipment availability.

I have a good computer system, so I compose a form letter, create a name-and-address database, merge the files and produce individually addressed letters and labels for the envelopes. With a computer, I can also design layouts for postcards and have them reproduced at any print shop. I do the same with flyers and brochures. It is absolutely amazing how easy and fast it is to produce high-quality direct-mail pieces right at your home or office computer terminal.

If you don't have access to a good computer system, then you will just have to pay others to help you with this program. Here is what I would suggest: Develop a standard message that will go on all letters, postcards, or brochures. Go to Kinko's or some other copy center and have it reproduced on your letterhead or brochure paper. Many of these copy centers have computers that you can "rent" and do your own design and layout. If you want, they can do it for you, usually at a reasonable cost. Many direct-mail gurus suggest using plain envelopes (no return address on them) and hand-written addresses. This looks like a personal letter from a friend and therefore it will always be opened!

Figure 17.3 is an example letter you could mail to your list. It's designed to attract attention (headline) and a selling response. You can use this example as is or change it to suit your style and needs.

The principle of persistence in direct marketing tells us that we will need to send out several mailings to each homeowner over time in order to get a response. You could send the same letter or create something a little different each time. For example, you could send a letter, then a postcard, then a flyer, then another letter, and so on. The point is, you want to get your name and message in front of each homeowner on a frequent schedule (e.g, quarterly, semiquarterly) so that when they are ready to consider selling, you are who they think of first.

The principle of benefits in direct marketing states that we must emphasize the benefits to the customer (homeowner) in doing business with you. Notice that in the sample letter, the key benefits (hot buttons) are clearly identified and highlighted. Whether it's a letter, postcard, flyer, or whatever, emphasize the benefits to the customer of doing business with you. If you fail in this regard, you will be like the Maytag repairman—the phone will never ring!

Realize that your direct-mail program is a long-term effort that will only begin to pay off with sustained effort. But when it starts to generate business, you will be in an enviable position—getting the chance to buy

Figure 17.3 Sample Direct-Mail Letter

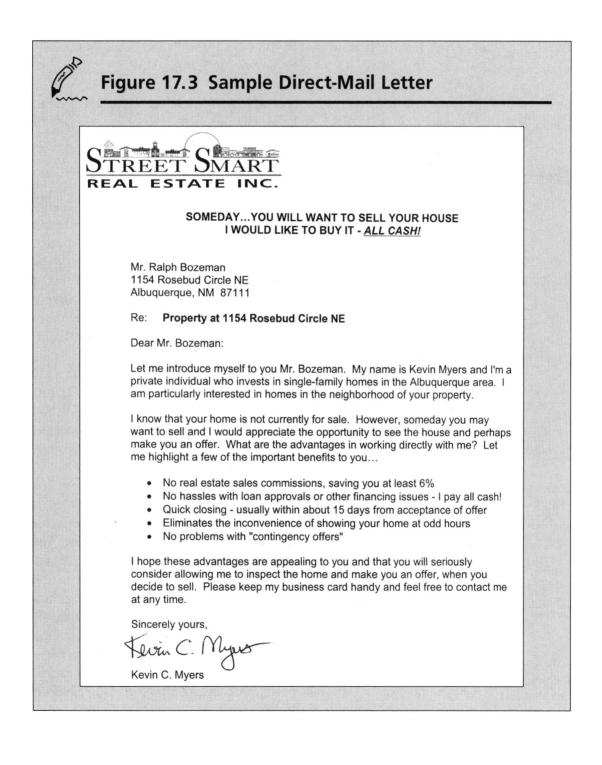

STREET SMART
REAL ESTATE INC.

**SOMEDAY...YOU WILL WANT TO SELL YOUR HOUSE
I WOULD LIKE TO BUY IT - *ALL CASH!***

Mr. Ralph Bozeman
1154 Rosebud Circle NE
Albuquerque, NM 87111

Re: **Property at 1154 Rosebud Circle NE**

Dear Mr. Bozeman:

Let me introduce myself to you Mr. Bozeman. My name is Kevin Myers and I'm a private individual who invests in single-family homes in the Albuquerque area. I am particularly interested in homes in the neighborhood of your property.

I know that your home is not currently for sale. However, someday you may want to sell and I would appreciate the opportunity to see the house and perhaps make you an offer. What are the advantages in working directly with me? Let me highlight a few of the important benefits to you...

- No real estate sales commissions, saving you at least 6%
- No hassles with loan approvals or other financing issues - I pay all cash!
- Quick closing - usually within about 15 days from acceptance of offer
- Eliminates the inconvenience of showing your home at odd hours
- No problems with "contingency offers"

I hope these advantages are appealing to you and that you will seriously consider allowing me to inspect the home and make you an offer, when you decide to sell. Please keep my business card handy and feel free to contact me at any time.

Sincerely yours,

Kevin C. Myers

Kevin C. Myers

properties before anyone else in the world knows the house is for sale. That's a competitive advantage that you definitely want in your bag of tricks.

Now, let's return to the foreclosure market, where bargains abound for the more skilled and knowledgeable investor.

Preforeclosure Market

Buying a house from sellers in default on their loans can be a very lucrative transaction. The sellers don't have the money to make house payments and are usually three or four months behind in payments. They know they are about to lose their house and totally destroy their credit for many years to come. Sellers in this situation are typically very motivated. If you can solve their problem by bringing the loan current and out of default, and give them some additional money to move out and get relocated, you can often buy a house at a substantial discount. For an example of this, see Figure 17.4.

In this case, you negotiate an agreement with the seller to bring the loan current ($4,000), pay the foreclosure fees to the bank ($1,000), pay the seller $5,000 in cash, and assume the existing $68,000 loan. You have a total cash outlay of $10,000 and own a house that you bought for 65 percent of its market value. Your 45 percent equity is worth $54,000. You'll make even more when you fix it up and sell it for $145,000!

Is this a pie-in-the-sky example? Not at all—this kind of deal happens every day in the foreclosure market. I'm sure your next question is, "How hard are these deals to find?" The answer is, if it were that easy, everyone would be doing it and everyone would be making a ton of money. The reality is that in any given community, there are a few highly skilled, experienced, knowledgeable investors who find this kind of deal day in and day out. The rest of the participants (competitors) may be getting their share of deals, but the "pros" excel at this game because they probably do it full-time and have developed a system (some use sophisticated direct-mail techniques) that allows them to dominate the local market.

The preforeclosure market, although highly competitive, can be exceedingly profitable. You can participate in this market with relatively small amounts of cash and can quickly reap huge rewards. Some people who specialize in this area do so without any cash—they find the deals

Figure 17.4 Preforeclosure Deal

House Market Value	$120,000
Mortgage Balance	68,000
Past Payments Due	4,000
Foreclosure Fees	1,000
Payment to Seller	5,000
Acquisition Price	$ 78,000 = 65% of Value

and quickly pass them on to another investor for a nice finder's fee of $3,000 to $10,000. Success requires a tremendous amount of time and energy, intimate knowledge of market values, a clear understanding of the local foreclosure procedures, and the ability to act very quickly. Most of all, you have to be knowledgeable and skilled in solving a number of potentially sticky problems:

- Meet face to face with a distressed seller and negotiate a sales price.
- Get the seller to sign a sales contract.
- Get loan balances from the lenders.
- Research other encumbrances or liens to get clear title.
- Overcome the ever-present due-on-sale clause.
- Get the seller to move out of the house.

These are the typical problems that must be solved in almost every preforeclosure deal. To be sure, there are solutions to all of these issues, but I'm not going to discuss them here, because they really are outside the scope of our subject matter. If you're in the rehab business, this market is probably not where you want to focus your efforts, at least initially. As you become more experienced and knowledgeable, this is a great place to find exceptional deals, but you have to be able to devote the time and effort to learn how to operate in this unique arena.

At this time (2003), the economy is in the dumps and has been for a couple of years. Foreclosures are at a high rate in many areas of the country, in spite of the low interest rate environment. This has resulted in a great opportunity for investors who know how to work the foreclosure market. And this point in the real estate cycle has once again opened up the possibility of using the *short sale* technique for acquiring properties in foreclosure directly from the banks, prior to the actual foreclosure sale (auction) on the courthouse steps.

The short sale technique works like this: You find a property in foreclosure (or even one that will soon be in foreclosure), contact the lender(s) holding the mortgage or deed of trust, and make an offer to purchase the property if the lender will discount the amount due on the loan in default. For example, let's say the loan in default has a balance of $110,000. You offer to buy the property if the lender will discount the balance due on the note to $85,000. If they agree, you've just created an additional $25,000 in equity/profit on the deal! If the property has no equity to begin with, this is a great way to create some!

Right now, many lenders are receptive to this type of transaction because they are willing to take their losses, get the nonperforming asset off their books—without having to go through the expense of foreclosure and subsequent property management and selling costs. This is the perfect time to get in on the short sale opportunity. However, as the economy improves with time and foreclosures decrease in volume, the bankers/lenders will revert back to their normal foreclosure process and will not be receptive to short sale offers. Strike while the iron is hot!

Public Auction Market (Trustee's/Sheriff's Sale)

The second phase of the foreclosure process is the trustee's or sheriff's sale. At this point, the homeowner has not cured the delinquent loan (and an angelic preforeclosure investor has not saved the day), so the property is scheduled to be sold at auction to the highest bidder. If no one bids at the auction, ownership reverts to the lender. If someone other than the lender is the high bidder, the proceeds from such a sale go first to the foreclosing lender, and if there are sums above the loan, these go the homeowner in most jurisdictions. Any junior mortgage liens, established after the time of the mortgage being foreclosed, are extinguished at the conclusion of the sale. Thus, the buyer receives the property free and clear of the subject mortgage, as well as any mortgages that were added later. However, any senior mortgages and certain tax liens (such as an IRS tax lien) remain attached to the property and become the responsibility of the new owner. This is why it is absolutely mandatory that you always research the title before going to an auction.

This market provides some excellent opportunities for anyone in the rehab business, because you often can buy houses at a discount of 25 percent or more below market value. Many of the properties that end up at auction have been trashed by their soon-to-be former owner (or renters). The process is quick and efficient. No pesky real estate agents are involved, eliminating the entire concept of commissions and other potential go-between problems. Competition? Depending on where you live, the condition of the property, the loan amount versus value, and local market conditions, it could be just you and the lender (who will bid at or sometimes below the loan amount). There may be other bidders who are interested in the same property and will be in competition with you (all trying to buy the property for as little as possible). That's okay, because you will have done your homework and set a not-to-exceed price before you show up at the auction. If you get the winning bid, great. If not, no big deal—there are plenty more opportunities in the pipeline.

Are there any disadvantages to this market? Indeed, there are two big ones. First, in most cases, you cannot inspect the home other than by viewing it from the outside. If it is vacant, you could walk around and peek in windows, but that is about it—no roof inspection, no termite inspection, or any other interior inspection. Obviously, this limitation creates a great element of risk that you need to carefully factor in to any bid. You will just have to make some assumptions, based on what you can see in the neighborhood, from the exterior condition of the house, and through the windows (if the house is vacant), and what information you might be able to get from adjacent neighbors. If the house is poorly maintained on the outside, assume the worst for the inside and calculate your bid accordingly.

The second big disadvantage, and perhaps the biggest obstacle for most investors, is the requirement in most jurisdictions to immediately (or shortly thereafter) pay all cash for the property. This means you must show up at the auction with a cashier's check in the amount of your planned bid. If you don't have the cash or can't come up with it (from friends, family, partners, joint-venture investors, or private lenders), you just can't be a player in this market, period.

Another potentially big issue is the right of redemption period following the sale. As discussed earlier, this can range from zero (no redemption after the sale) as in many deed-of-trust states (and some mortgage states) up to six months or even a year. You'd better not roll the dice on this one. If you go in and renovate after a sale that involves a redemption period, you could theoretically lose all the money you put into those repairs. The original borrower could conceivably come up with the money equal to what you paid at auction (plus some specified amount of interest) and "steal" the house back, all fixed up, at no additional cost to him or her. Do you know of any attorneys or other similar citizens of outstanding character who might want to "help" a client or friend in such a deal? You'd better believe that they're out there. Play it safe and wait to make the big repairs until after your redemption period is over.

Is this a good market for the rehab business person? This is one of the best, if you have (or can get) the money to play. The profit potential is excellent, particularly with a house that needs repairs. The amount of time and effort needed to succeed in this market is minimal in comparison to the preforeclosure investor.

Five Success Steps for the Public Auction

Here are the five major steps that will ensure a profitable acquisition in the trustee's or sheriff's sale marketplace:

1. Develop an intimate knowledge of local market values so that you can accurately estimate the "as-is" and "after-repaired" value of any property under consideration.
2. Thoroughly research the title of each property under serious consideration in order to understand the full extent of all liens and encumbrances.
3. Develop a written estimate of projected repairs and include a healthy contingency factor because you have not inspected the inside of the house.
4. In developing your bid, use the maximum purchase price formula, with the contingency factor adjusted for increased risk.
5. Set for yourself a not-to-exceed bid amount and write it in blood that you will not bid over this amount!

These are the most important factors to ensure your success. If you're serious about possibly participating in this exciting and rewarding marketplace, I would suggest that you play the game "on paper" several times before you do it for real. Follow the notices of default and notices of sale in your local newspapers. Do the research on several good prospects, including development of market values, repair costs, and a proposed bid amount. Attend the actual auction to observe the participants, the atmosphere, and, of course, the outcome. Only by going through several dry runs will you gain the experience and confidence you need to become a serious and successful player.

Putting Together Your Own Dream Team

You cannot operate your rehab business in a vacuum. Your success, to some extent, will depend on your ability to assemble a good-quality team of advisers. These people could include all of the following: real estate agent, attorney, accountant, appraiser, mortgage broker, home inspector, handyman, and general contractor. Each of these people has specialized knowledge that you need to effectively operate your business. Select your advisers carefully, because bad advice from any one of them could significantly affect the profitability of your venture.

Wouldn't it be nice to have an adviser who knows the rehab business inside and out and is available to share that knowledge with you? Someone you could bounce ideas off and brainstorm with to come up with options? Someone to help you get focused on a strategy and moving forward? This type of person would be a huge asset to your personal dream team.

Believe it or not, this person might be available right under your nose. A real-live mentor or coach who is more than willing to help you out. The best place to find such a person is at your local real estate investment club. Most communities of any size will have an active club. If not, look for one in your closest larger city or consider starting one yourself. Some clubs meet weekly and others meet monthly. They are great places to meet other investors, lenders, agents, and other people interested in investment real estate issues. Many clubs have an active speakers' program where local and outside experts are brought in to give seminars on current topics. These are great places to find a mentor and to network with others willing to help you out.

Should I Incorporate My Business?

This really is a legal and tax issue that you should discuss with your professional advisers. Having said that, let me give you my two cents' worth. If you are employed full-time in another job and doing real estate rehab on a part-time basis (two or three deals a year), I would say that you probably do not need to form a corporation. However, if you are doing this full-time and derive your primary income from buying and selling real estate, then you'd better think seriously about being incorporated. Why? Have you ever heard of dealer status under IRS rules?

Should the IRS ever determine that you are a real estate dealer, your life will change forever, particularly if you have been doing deals for several years and they start digging into prior years' returns. If you make all of your income from buying and selling real estate, then by definition you are a dealer. You buy real estate with the intention of quickly selling it at a profit (in contrast to a long-term investment).

Once you are considered a dealer, all your income is treated as ordinary income and is also subject to self-employment tax. Profits from the sale of your houses and rental income (there is no depreciation offset if you are a dealer) fall into this category. There is no such thing as a long-term capital gain if you are a dealer. And another catastrophe—installment sales are not recognized. By that I mean that if you receive a $15,000 note payable over seven years in connection with the sale of one of your properties, the IRS says that you are subject to tax on the entire $15,000 immediately!

One way to minimize your exposure to this cruel and unusual punishment is to conduct your day-to-day real estate transactions through a corporation. Income you receive from the corporation is considered salary or dividends such that you personally could not be considered a dealer (although your corporation could be). Moreover, you should keep any rental properties you own separate from the corporation. Rentals should remain in your personal account so that you can use the tax deductions against your personal income.

Another big advantage to operating your business as a corporation is limited liability. Owners and stockholders of corporations are personally shielded from creditors and from some types of lawsuits. Because a corporation is a legal entity, it is legally separate from its owners. If your corporation buys properties in its name and does not pay its debts, the creditors usually cannot get their money from your personal assets (assuming you did not personally guarantee any loans such as you would through nonrecourse loans). Sole proprietors and partners, by comparison, are personally liable for all business debts.

One misconception that people have is that a corporation entirely insulates them from lawsuits. It does not work that way. Certainly, you are protected from lawsuits brought against your corporation, but the corporate shield will not protect you from unlawful acts or acts of gross negligence. In any case of personal injury, you likely will be dragged into the lawsuit personally. So in general, you are fully protected against creditors but you have limited liability protection regarding lawsuits. Yet it sure beats no protection at all, as is the case with a sole proprietor or straight partnership.

What type of corporation should you choose: C corporation, S corporation, or limited liability corporation? Again, seek the counsel of your legal and tax advisers. Personally, I favor the S Corporation (I have two of them) because they provide the limited liability protection and pay no federal income tax. Similar to a sole proprietorship or partnership, all the S corporation profits pass through to the owners (stockholders), who are taxed at their regular individual rates. There are other advantages, but let's not get too boring!

Speaking of Income Taxes

I've touched on income taxes in the last section, so I'd better expand on it a little bit here. Be forewarned, I'm not an accountant or tax attorney, so take whatever I say with a grain of salt. Better yet, make an appointment and go talk with an accountant who does this stuff day in and day out. I hate taxes, so it's an issue that I don't like to think about—gives me a migraine!

The first thing you need to know is that what we're talking about here is income taxes relative to the sale of your *investment properties.*

This has nothing to do with the sale of your personal residence, which is an entirely separate matter. Secondly, *depreciation* is applicable *only* to rental properties and is *not* applicable to your personal residence or to properties that you buy and quickly sell.

Let's take the scenario that you will be dealing with on a typical buy, rehab, and sell project—after all, that's what this book is all about! The bad news is that the profit you make on the deal (the difference between what you paid, plus the cost of the rehab and the sales price) is considered *earned income* and is taxed as *ordinary income* at your personal income tax rate. In other words, it's as if you had a second job and the income is added to any other personal income you may have. Yes, in essence you are taxed as if you are a dealer, as discussed in the previous section, because in fact you are a dealer by definition. On this issue, there is no *good* news!

This scenario assumes your intention was to buy and quickly sell, and it assumes you did in fact do that in a period of less than 12 months. On the other hand, if your intention was to acquire the property as a long-term rental and you own the property for more than 12 months prior to selling, you most likely will qualify for capital gains tax treatment (a maximum of 20 percent and as low as 10 percent for individuals in the 15 percent tax bracket). I say *likely will qualify* because if you are buying and selling properties frequently, including properties held greater than 12 months, the IRS could (in its infinite wisdom) consider those to be dealer properties as well. That's why it is so important to run your quick turnaround deals through one entity and hold your long-term rentals either personally or through a separate corporation or partnership.

Okay, that's enough of this tax stuff—I feel a migraine coming on.

Operating to Maximize Profits

Once you're up and running, maximizing your profits is the name of the game. It's an ongoing continuous process of improvement. How can I do this better and more efficiently? What it really boils down to is control. The more control you exert over every aspect of your business, the more profitable it will become. This requires you to pay close attention to all of the details so that nothing slips through the cracks. It also means that you consistently replicate the things that work.

As I've discussed previously, speed is one of the secrets of success in the rehab business. Speed in buying, speed in rehabbing, and speed in selling are all very important. Speed in the buying process is worthy of special mention. When you're out in the marketplace looking for bargains, you must be prepared to act quickly in making your offers. If you dillydally around, someone else is going to scoop it up while you're still daydreaming! Be prepared at all times to make offers if the right opportunity presents itself.

One of the big stumbling blocks for many people is financing. How am I going to pay for all this, particularly if I don't have much money to start with? If you can get good at negotiating wholesale deals, the money will come. The turning point for me was discovering the availability of money through private mortgage lenders. Once you get out there and find these sources of funding and establish a relationship with one or more brokers, your worries are over. They have the capability of providing you with an endless flow of mortgage money, if you can find the good deals.

As you begin developing your own set of skills and expertise, you will soon be ready to tackle multiple projects simultaneously. This is when the big money starts rolling in. To do this successfully, you must make the transition from a worker bee to a project manager. This does not mean that you have to hire employees. It just means closely supervising and coordinating the work of others (independent contractors). This is where you really have to follow the advice of small-business guru Michael Gerber, who suggests that you work on your business, not in your business. Coordinate, control, and duplicate systems that work.

One of the things I emphasized in the last chapter was that you should use a real estate agent to market your properties. I truly believe that this is the best option for most people. But I know human nature—as you become more experienced, you will want to try to go it alone. The best advice I can give you on this topic is to begin developing a buyer's list as soon as possible. This is simply a list of people who have called you in response to ads that you've placed. As often happens, people call and what you currently have to offer doesn't fit their needs. Get their names and phone numbers, because the house you buy next week could very well be a perfect match. Wouldn't it be great to be able to sell your house before you even start renovations? It can happen with a good buyer's list.

Building Your Business and Investing Your Profits

Good businesses, ones that endure, are built on word of mouth, otherwise known as referrals. The best endorsement any product or service you can get is from a satisfied customer or vendor. Treat people fairly and the returns to you will be compounded exponentially.

I have found this to be particularly true with buyers of my properties. Try to include a home warranty package—either a commercial one that you have purchased or guarantee the house yourself for a reasonable time period. If something goes wrong, get it fixed immediately. People will remember you and tell their friends, neighbors, and relatives—all potential future clients. This is how you build a strong future for your business.

As things get rolling along, your profits will start rolling in, more money than you probably thought possible. This isn't a get-rich-quick scheme—you will work your butt off for the money. But it will come and you will deserve it! The question is, what will you do with your new-found wealth?

Far be it from me to tell you how to spend your hard-earned money, but I can't resist giving you a little advice! First things first—splurge a little! Get that new car you and your spouse have been wanting and maybe even take a jaunt down to Mexico. You and your family deserve to feel good about your accomplishments.

As soon as you can, start investing your money so that it will grow. There are many ways to do this. Certainly, you could buy and rehab more houses, but how big do you want your operation to get? I would suggest you consider real estate–related investments that are less hands-on in nature. Specifically, I think investing some of your profits in mortgages or "paper" is one of the best alternatives out there.

You got a glimpse of this in Chapter 10 on the power of compounding available through investments in private mortgages. You become the lender to another rehab operator or a homeowner. You are in on the deal at its inception and through your private mortgage broker, and know all the details about the property and the people involved.

This is a big advantage compared with just buying "discounted paper" through a note broker who did not originate the loan and may know little about the players or the property. My observation of people who routinely invest in discounted paper is that they focus too much on yield with insufficient attention paid to the property or the people involved. This is just my opinion, for what it's worth!

Most private mortgages are funded in the 9 percent to 12 percent range, with additional profit potential if the borrower defaults. You mean a private lender can actually make more money if the borrower defaults and the lender forecloses on the property? On those rare occasions when foreclosure does happen, the private lender has the opportunity to make a bundle. If you're the lender and foreclose on a 50 percent LTV loan, you have the chance to sell the house at full value and make a 100 percent profit! You may have some attorney expenses for the foreclosure, but these are minor amounts compared to the profits.

This is why some investors make private loans, in hopes that a foreclosure situation will occur. Indeed, some private lenders like to specialize in loans on property headed for foreclosure. It's just another opportunity for a huge profit center upon reselling the house.

Another avenue of investing in paper is the one we discussed in the last chapter—seller carry-back financing. I think leaving some of your profits in a second mortgage, earning 9 percent to 12 percent, is an excellent investment opportunity. You know the property top to bottom and you know all about the buyer. You *are* an informed investor. And at 12 percent, your money will almost double in five years!

A wraparound mortgage is another form of seller financing that you might consider offering in certain circumstances. The wraparound is a mortgage or trust deed created by the seller, which secures a debt that includes the balance due on existing mortgages plus the additional amount you as the seller are loaning to the buyer. The mortgage is written as a single loan amount, with a single interest rate, and with one monthly payment amount. Title to the property is transferred to the new buyer (unless the wrap involves an existing land contract or real estate contract). However, the existing loans are not assumed by the buyer and remain the responsibility of the original borrower. An escrow company typically is used as the control point to handle the administration of the loan. Payments received from the new buyer are used to continue payments on the existing loans, and monies in excess of this amount are distributed to the seller as profits. Let's take a look at a sale of a property for $155,000 with a $135,000 wraparound mortgage (see Figure 17.5).

The key element of any wraparound loan is the amount of interest charged relative to the underlying loans. In this case, the seller is receiv-

Figure 17.5 Wraparound Mortgage

Total Sales Price	$155,000
Less Buyer's Down Payment	−20,000
Amount to be Financed	$135,000
Existing Mortgage at 7%	$100,000
Amount Loaned by Seller	35,000
Wraparound Loan at 10%	$135,000

Seller's yield is 3 percent on the $100,000 existing loan balance and 10 percent on the $35,000 remaining equity. Total first year yield is 18.6 percent, or $6,500 interest.

ing 10 percent on the $135,000, which includes the $100,000 existing mortgage. But he or she is only paying 7 percent on the $100,000. The seller's profit is 3 percent on the $100,000 plus 10 percent on the $35,000 remaining equity.

In addition to the substantial profit potential, there are several other key advantages to selling on a wrap:

- It allows you to offer total financing without requiring the buyer to qualify at a bank or other lending institution.
- Because of the financing incentive, you can sell at top dollar.
- It may allow you to overcome any due-on-sale clause contained in underlying mortgages because the loan(s) remains in your name (or the original borrower's name if you did not originate the loan).

The obvious disadvantage to selling with a wrap is that most of your profits remain tied up in the property. If you want or need all of your cash immediately, this is probably not the best option for you. However, you could sell your wraparound mortgage for cash but you would have to take a substantial discount from face value. The discount would not be as much as a standard 30-year note, because the blended interest rate is much higher. If you know up front that you will sell the wrap, it is best to contact a note broker in advance to assist with structuring terms that will net you more money. For example, if you included a balloon in seven years, the cash value today would be much higher.

Is selling on a wrap a good strategy? It is if you're in a tight market and need to offer financing to induce a buyer. It's an outstanding strategy if you can afford to leave your money invested for the long haul. It's an excellent retirement investment that can make you huge profits over time.

How about investing in rental property? Buying property and becoming a landlord—is this a bad investment strategy? Of course not. It is an excellent long-term investment strategy if the timing of your purchase and sale is in harmony with your local real estate cycle. It's much like investing in the stock market. Buy when prices are low and nobody wants the stock, and sell when the market is hot. What is the status of your local real estate market? The answer to this question will guide you in the timing of your rental purchases.

Still Not Sure about Doing Rehabs? The Wholesale Alternative

At this point, you have all the information you need to go out into the world, find the perfect fixer-upper, get your offer accepted, line up your financing, close the deal, complete a fantastic rehab to put the property in doll house condition, sell the property quickly and then laugh all the way to the bank! Whew!

But maybe you just don't have the confidence quite yet that you can pull it off, right?

How about this for an alternative? You go out into the world, find the perfect fixer-upper, get your offer accepted—and then sell (assign) your contract to another rehab investor for a quick $2,000 to $10,000 profit and you move on. Your investor actually buys the property and does the rehab and makes the big bucks. A very simple process.

I call this the *wholesale alternative.* You're actually getting a property at a wholesale price, marking it up slightly to make your profit, selling the contract to another investor who actually does the rehab and sells the property at full retail value. In his famous book *Nothing Down for the '90s,* best-selling author Robert Allen refers to this technique as the "Earnest Money" option or "Offer to Purchase" option.

Please do not confuse this type of transaction with some of the bad press you may have seen on an unscrupulous property flipper. In this scenario, a dealer, lender, and an appraiser all work in cahoots (illegally) to bamboozle an unsuspecting homeowner and the government (usually FHA/HUD). They go out and buy an old house at a cheap price, maybe throw a coat of paint on the inside, and then find a prospective home-owner, dummy up a loan application and sell the house for no money down at an outrageously high price. At some point, the parties involved usually get caught and end up paying the price for their fraud.

In the next chapter you will find several examples of our entrepreneurs using the wholesale alternative, doing it the right way (legally and ethically) and making lots of quick cash! It's a very good alternative for those who are not quite ready to tackle the rehab project themselves. For more information on the wholesale technique, visit my Web site <www .rehabwiz.com>.

Momentum—The Secret of Business Success

One of my favorite movies is the Billy Crystal classic, *City Slickers.* On the trail ride up to Colorado, Mitch (Billy Crystal) keeps trying to get Curly (Jack Palance) to reveal the secret of life—"the one thing." In the business world, "the one thing" is building and maintaining momentum. You have to get energized and create focused activity to keep it alive. As we learned in physics class, the only way to overcome inertia is to apply energy.

We must also remember the advice of Ernest Hemingway who wrote, "Never mistake motion for action." To accomplish our goals, we must engage in activities that are meaningful and that lead us to completing the tasks at hand. Work out your business plan. Line up your partners and private mortgage brokers. Start calling FSBOs and driving the neighborhoods. Begin interviewing handyman prospects and contractors. Take seminars, read books, subscribe to newsletters, and join your local real estate investment club. Make things happen and create your own future!

Success Stories from the Field

*I*n contacts with my students and various real estate investor groups around the country, I am exposed regularly to success stories from the field. Since publication of the first edition of this book, I have been flooded with incredible success stories from around the country and even overseas! I have updated this chapter to include a few of these new stories because I know how much you folks love reading about them!

These stories come from ordinary people like you and me, who not only have taken the time and effort to learn the basic investment techniques taught in this book, but have gone out into the marketplace and put the ideas into practice. A few have gone on to achieve extraordinary financial success in real estate. Many, however, are just quietly plodding along, renovating houses in their spare time, and accumulating a nice nest egg for retirement. Others have tasted success on their first few deals and have decided to pursue the rehab business on a full-time basis.

These stories are an endless source of enjoyment and satisfaction for me as an educator in the real estate investment field. I know that the investment technique is one of the most powerful and rewarding avenues available for the small investor to accumulate wealth and otherwise achieve financial success. The challenge for me is to effectively teach the techniques and then motivate people to go out and put them to good use. These are the two sides of the equation. The second side, motivating people to get out into the marketplace and get started, is always the more difficult. Perhaps by sharing a few of these success stories with you, I can stimulate you to put these ideas into action.

The stories that follow are real. Several of the people involved have asked that their privacy be protected and I have honored that request. What's important is that these people took an idea and made something happen. As you read their stories, put yourself in their shoes and imagine yourself doing what they did. I think you'll find their accomplishments are within your reach.

Small Town Handyman Makes the Leap

Chambersburg, Pennsylvania—Glenn lives in a small town in south central Pennsylvania (near Gettysburg) and for years had taken on small handyman jobs on the side as a way to make a little extra money. It finally occurred to him that he ought to use his handyman talents on his own properties, so he decided to learn everything he could about real estate investing.

"I bought books (including Kevin's excellent book, *Buy It, Fix It, Sell It: Profit!*) and courses and went to local real estate clubs and seminars. Finally, I got the courage to dive in!"

Glenn found a little fixer-upper that was a FSBO being offered for $23,000 (don't you love the prices in small town America!). The owner was desperate to sell and accepted Glenn's offer of $13,000, with no counteroffer. The best part was that the house had a private mortgage on it with a $7,500 balance that the noteholder allowed Glenn to assume—and it only had 48 months of $196 per month payments! He took $5,500 of his own money and closed the deal. Over the next couple of months, Glenn went to work (mostly on weekends) fixing up the place and spent about $7,000 in the process. After the repairs were completed, he had the house appraised and it came in at $37,500. Had he sold the property at that point, he would have pocketed a net profit of about $10,000. Instead, he rented out the property for $480 per month (giving him a $284 per month positive cash flow) and paid the property off over the next two years. Four years later, Glenn will have a free and clear property worth about $40,000, plus he will pocket about $13,500 in positive cash flow–a great deal for a first-time investor!

Soon after closing on his first deal, Glenn found another fixer-upper he could buy at a foreclosure auction for $20,000. The problem was, he had used all of his available cash on his first deal–he didn't have the $20,000 cash that was required to buy the house at auction (remember, you have to pay cash at auctions). So, the enterprising Glenn found two friends who were willing to split the deal three ways with Glenn providing the expertise and his partners providing the money. The three amigos then went to work, spending about $9,800 in repairs over a couple of months. One weekend while they were working on the place, a real estate agent stopped by and said he had a buyer that wanted the house and was willing to pay a full price offer of $67,900. Bingo! They accepted the offer, completed the work and walked away with a net profit of $35,000 ($67,900 – $29,800 invested – commission and closing costs).

According to Glenn, "I am now searching for my third property and I'm very excited, as are my partners. I don't mind splitting the profits as we also split the risk and the work."

Finance Companies as a Source of Bargains

Tampa, Florida–Leandro is a former school teacher who decided to start investing in rehab projects just a few years ago. Full of enthusiasm but little knowledge, he plunged ahead. He had read about finding bargain properties from bank REO departments, so that's where he began his search. Unfortunately, he was given the runaround with each bank he called. Finally, after several weeks of frustration and no progress, he hit upon an idea–how about checking with finance companies? Sure enough, several had REO properties that they were dying to get off the books and they were willing to accept just $100 for a 60-day option to purchase.

At that time, Leandro had not learned how to tap into the world of private mortgage lenders. So, with lots of ambition but no money, he decided to try to "flip" these properties to other investors. On his first deal, he found a three-bedroom, two-bath fixer-upper that he got for $18,000, all cash. Leandro next ran an ad and within three days sold the property (actually he sold his option) at $24,000 for a quick $6,000 profit. Encouraged by his success, he found another property through a finance company. This was a three-bedroom, one-bath brick house that needed a lot of work. He bought the house (on a 45-day option contract) for $10,000 and quickly sold it to another investor for $17,600—a nice $7,600 profit!

Since these early successes, Leandro recently found a couple of private mortgage brokers in his area. He now has four properties under contract that he located through finance companies and plans to devote himself full-time to the rehab business. With the availability of financing in place, he has found his niche and is off and running.

First-Time California Rehabber Strikes Gold

Benicia, California—Bill is a computer systems analyst living in the Bay Area of Northern California and a long-time do-it-yourself remodeler around the house. His interest in real estate investment was recently sparked after taking a weekend seminar at the local community college. He also discovered *Buy It, Fix It, Sell It: Profit!* while browsing at Barnes & Noble and this really got him motivated!

Bill hooked up with a local real estate agent and began scouring the countryside looking for a bargain property. The duo spent numerous hours out looking at properties, but nothing seemed to fit. Then finally, his agent got word of a potential bargain in nearby Pittsburgh, California. It was a 20-year-old, one bedroom, one bath, 1,200-square-foot ranch with a "Florida room." The house was vacant and a total mess—junk piled everywhere, but on closer inspection it needed mostly minor repairs and updates in the kitchen and bath. Best of all, the owner lived in Oregon and was very motivated to sell (gotta love those out-of-state owners!).

Comparable sales in the neighborhood showed the value would be about $118,000 to $125,000 in tip-top condition. Bill submitted an offer of $79,000 and it was accepted. Because he had good credit, he was able to get a 95 percent loan at 9 percent with no points and 30 years fixed. It pays to have good credit and a good banking relationship! Everything was all set—then disaster struck!

A day before closing, a fourth-grade vandal broke into the property and had a little fun—to the tune of $7,000 in damages. Ouch! Bill and his bank decided they weren't going to eat these costs, so they went back to the seller who reluctantly agreed to a $10,000 price reduction. So, he ended up closing the deal for $69,000.

Now the fun started–renovating this little palace! Fortunately, Bill found a great contractor who ended up living at the property until it was ready to put on the market about a month later (why can't I find contractors like this?).

"I put $18,000 of my own money into rehabbing it. Interior and exterior paint, new kitchen cabinet fronts from Quality Doors (as you mention in your book, Kevin), a small microwave, small deck (sizzle items), new carpet, tub enclosure, new vinyl in bath and kitchen. I replaced all the broken windows from the vandalism, and put up a 20-foot-long, 6-foot-high wooden fence to eliminate the path through the property by the school children."

After a couple of false starts with buyers, Bill signed a contract with a young, first-time homeowner family, and got full value at $125,000. The buyers got a conventional FHA loan and cashed Bill out of the deal. After closing costs, his check at escrow was $45,750, giving him a net profit of about $27,000.

"As you suggested in your book Kevin, I took a trip to Mexico and paid off some bills!"

Calling All FSBOs

Phoenix, Arizona–Larry decided he wanted to give fixer-uppers a try. But there was a problem. All of his friends advised him that he needed to do all the work himself in order to make any money at it. Larry had a little experience around construction, but not much free time. Finally, he bought a home-study course that taught him how to incorporate into the purchase price formula the cost of hiring contractors to do the work. With this breakthrough, Larry decided to get active and to start looking for his first property.

Larry had some real estate experience, so he felt comfortable with the idea of calling for sale by owner (FSBO) properties. He figured that with FSBOs he just might stumble on to a real bargain. One weekend, after calling on about 30 ads in the newspaper, he called an owner who seemed very anxious on the telephone. The owner had a fixer-upper and wanted to sell immediately. His price was $40,000. Larry made an appointment and started researching the neighborhood. He started getting really excited when he discovered the after-repaired value for the neighborhood would be about $70,000.

When Larry drove up to the house, he knew he had uncovered a gem in the making. It was a two-story house, not bad-looking from the outside, and in an older but attractive neighborhood. The inside turned out to be a real mess. The kitchen and two bathrooms would have to be redone, all flooring would need to be replaced, several windows had cracked glass, and the house needed a new asphalt shingle roof. With all the upgrades, Larry quickly figured the repairs would cost about $16,000. As Larry was preparing to leave to go home and crunch the numbers, he asked the classic question: How much would you take if I offered you all cash? Larry about fell off the front porch when the owner quickly replied, $28,000. Just as quickly, Larry said, I'll take it!

Larry arranged for a 65 percent LTV private mortgage that covered the purchase cost and the rehab cost—a real-life no-money-down deal. He hired a general contractor to do all of the work and the job was completed in about two and a half months. He found a good real estate agent who was very active in the neighborhood and had the house sold in 40 days for $68,000. When Larry walked out of closing with a check for almost $15,000, all he could think was, I've got to go out and find another deal just like this one!

Appraiser Builds a Rental Empire

Spokane, Washington—Dean, a real estate appraiser, got started investing in real estate after reading all the nothing down, creative financing books that were in vogue a few years ago. He bought a couple of condos with maximum leverage and rented them out. The problem was, he was constantly facing months of negative cash flow due to periodic vacancies and upkeep requirements. He thought about getting out of investment real estate altogether. Dean then discovered this book, decided that buying cheap fixer-upper houses made a lot of sense, and decided to give it a try.

With his first deal, he partnered with an acquaintance who had money and bought a foreclosure on the courthouse steps. Dean and his wife worked on the place themselves, nights and weekends for a three-month period before it was ready to sell. Unfortunately, the Spokane market was very soft at the time and the property was competing with many other houses that were for sale. Eventually, he and his partner decided to rent the house, and he ended up walking away from the deal without realizing any profits. His partner, with whom he is still good friends, continues to keep the house as a rental.

Next, Dean went down to his bank and obtained approval for a $50,000 line of credit on his personal house. He also put his new truck up as collateral and got an additional $25,000 line of credit. It was a risk, but Dean felt that if he found the right deal, it would be worth it. He found a good Fannie Mae REO house through a local agent who specializes in fixer-uppers. This time, after the rehab work was done, he decided to go back to the bank, refinance the property at 80 percent of appraised value, and then rent out the property. The numbers worked great—the refinance allowed him to pay off his line of credit loan and put a few thousand bucks in his pocket. Dean then rented the house and was able to get about $300 per month positive cash flow. Now, he had found his niche! Buy fixer-uppers cheap, get them fixed up, refinance them to pull out equity and rent them out with a positive cash flow.

It has been two years since Dean got started on his new venture. He eventually learned to hire handyman workers to get the rehabs done and his real estate agent brings him deals before they even get into the MLS. He now has 15 properties, with two more to close very soon. His properties provide him about $3,400 per month in positive cash flow. And, he and his wife figure that they have been able to pocket about $100,000 during this period as a result of the refinance activity.

Dean plans to get his portfolio up to 25 properties within the next year or so. Then, the plan is to just sit on them, building equity for retirement and enjoying the positive cash flow. Not a bad plan for a young man who is only 36 years old!

South African Teacher Discovers Rehab Profits

Pietermaritzburg, South Africa—John, his wife Mary, and their three children live in this small city northwest of the coastal town of Durban. John is a teacher working for the KwaZulu-Natal province. He began searching for a way to supplement his salary when he realized that he would not have enough money to send his daughters to the university. John's search ended when he found this book at Amazon.com while surfing the Internet.

"I knew that I had struck gold because the book was written in straightforward English (my second language) and it was presented in such a way that it was clearly understandable."

John's first effort was a bank REO property he found on the Internet in the nearby town of Prestbury. It was a three-bedroom, two-bath house. His initial calculations were that in fixed-up condition (maximum retail value) the house would be worth about $22,900 (these figures are in U.S. dollars converted from ZAR, South African Rand) and would take about $4,600 in rehab costs to get it in tip-top condition.

After five offers, the bank finally accepted John's last offer of $14,300. He immediately started on the rehab. Within three months he had completed the project (rehab costs came in a bit higher at $7,500) and had the house sold for $27,600. A nice, tidy $5,800 net profit on his first deal. He was very happy!

Experimenting with the "driving around the neighborhood" technique discussed in this book, John went driving every Sunday afternoon for three weeks. He finally located what he was looking for—a empty house in a "fairly mid-class neighborhood." The house was locked up but "by peeping from the outside, I could see that it was a fixer-upper." John checked with the neighbors and discovered that the house had been a rental and the owner was African Life Insurance Company.

The next day, he called the insurance company in Johannesburg and found out that yes, indeed, they wanted to sell the property. In chatting with the company secretaries, he further found out the company had paid $9,000 for the house and another $4,500 in fees and taxes. He figured that they had about $13,750 invested. Without even inspecting the interior, he made them an offer of $14,300 because he had become familiar with values in the area and knew the house would sell for at least twice that amount in fixed-up condition. The offer was immediately accepted!

John called his contractor crews and got to work. He spent about $6,500 on rehab costs and sold the property four months later for $32,300—and made a very nice profit of $11,575!

In his first year of part-time effort, John completed two deals and made a total of $17,375 (a huge amount in South Africa). He has just bought his third property and is expecting to make about $12,000 on this deal. John loves his part-time job and is now planning to retire from teaching within five years to devote full time to rehabbing houses. The best part is:

"I now have no more worries about my daughter's education. Inspired by your book, Kevin, I now have the ability to run a steady business in order to pay for their university fees."

A good man, a good father, and maybe a good inspiration for *you* to get busy and follow in John's footsteps!

Focus on the Finished Product

Country Club Hills, Illinois—Sandy and Al are an interesting couple. Sandy got burned out after a 20-year-plus career as a registered nurse. Al worked for ten years as a model in New York and Chicago and later owned a porcelain refinishing business. The couple began their real estate investment activity by buying an old fixer-upper. They turned a nice profit on their first deal and were hooked.

The two of them make a great team. Al is now a full-time rehab investor and acts as his own general contractor. Sandy works a couple of days a week as a computer and music teacher but spends the rest of her time working on the creative aspects of each rehab project. Her specialty is creating exciting and appealing interior features, always with an eye for the contemporary design. They too have found that the sizzle features sell, and they put in the effort to create excitement and demand in the marketplace. This focus on producing a quality finished product that sells quickly is the key to their success and a source of great personal satisfaction.

Al and Sandy have purchased mostly bank REOs through a real estate agent, but the niche they like best is the "get rich by driving around" technique. They love to drive the streets looking for beat-up old houses located in decent neighborhoods. Using their home computer, they can access a local database that gives them the property owners' names and addresses. They then contact the owners to see if they would be interested in selling. If they get a positive response, the home interior is inspected and an offer is made—all this before anyone else in the world knows the house is for sale! That's the power of this remarkably effective bargain-hunting technique.

Al and Sandy have completed four projects during the past year, with an average net profit of $15,000. They typically buy with an all-cash offer, using a private mortgage broker to finance the purchase and rehab costs. On one of their recent projects, they purchased a house for $22,900, spent $9,000 on the rehab, sold the property for $57,900, and in the process pocketed a net profit of $13,000. The entire process took only 108 days, from purchase to sale.

First Rehab Project Nets $18,000 Profit in 30 Days

Camden, New Jersey—Ralph considers himself as a newbie in the real estate rehab arena. He recently made a career change and decided he wanted to explore quick turnaround real estate techniques. He thought the best way to jump-start his education was to attend one of my workshops (check my Web site <www.rehabwiz.com> to see if any workshops are currently being offered).

Following the workshop, with the *How to Get Up and Running in 30 Days* checklist in hand, Ralph went to work looking for bargains. While he was looking at properties and doing research on neighborhoods, he also spent numerous hours getting the business side organized—talking with insurance companies, mortgage brokers, real estate agents, and a couple of lawyers.

A month or so later, Ralph closed on his first deal. It was an uninsured, HUD fixer-upper property—three bedroom, one bath row house with about 1,620 square feet. He bought it through a local agent who specialized in the neighborhood, but, made a deal with the agent on the front end—he would buy the house only if the real estate agent had clients who wanted to buy the house after it was fixed up. No problem—she had two people lined up in a matter of days.

A couple of key ideas Ralph picked up at the workshop were immediately factored into the business plan—use neighborhood-based real estate agents *and* contractors from the local community. Don't try to import your brother-in-law!

As with many uninsured HUD properties, the condition of house was poor. The house had been vacant and suffered from extensive vandalism. All of the internal plumbing and heating pipes were missing but amazingly, the hot water heater and boiler were left and in good condition. Of course, the house needed carpeting, flooring, patching here and there, and paint inside and out, but nothing major.

Ralph's real estate agent came through as promised—the house sold for $45,000 and the sale closed only 30 days after he bought it!

Here are the financials on the project.

Purchase Cost:	$15,500
Rehab Cost:	8,800
Sales Cost:	2,700
Sales Price:	45,000
Net Profit:	18,000

How did Ralph finance this project? After talking with 15 mortgage brokers in the area, he decided to finance this one out of pocket. Although he identified several hard money lenders that he intends to use in the future, he wanted to reduce his holding costs on his first project to maximize his profit.

Once you start doing projects and begin to accumulate profits (after your trip to Mexico!), you can do what Ralph and I do—pay cash for your deals and thus dramatically reduce your transaction costs, thereby increasing your profits.

With the first project under his belt, Ralph is looking to the future. He plans to do three or four projects a year in the Camden area and is looking for projects in other areas as well. He's also considering a multifamily unit and doing some research on commercial properties. Look out—we may have the next Donald Trump!

Retired Truck Driver Pursues His Dream

Chicago, Illinois—James had wanted to get involved in real estate investing for about eight years. He had attended several seminars, but his 30-year-plus truck-driving career kept him too busy to get involved. Finally, he retired and began actively pursuing his dream of full-time real estate investing.

As a newcomer to the real estate field, James decided the quick turn, rehab, and sell technique was the best opportunity for him. Although he had no prior experience, James made a very smart move by developing relationships with several experienced professionals to help him through the process. He works with five different real estate agents, primarily looking for newly listed bank REO properties that are in need of repairs. Additionally, he has been working with Dave and Bobbee, private mortgage brokers (at the same company) who have taken him under their wing. These brokers have not only provided the funds needed to complete his projects, but also have provided technical advice on getting the rehab work done and getting the property sold. James uses general contractors for the rehab work and sells the properties through real estate agents.

Without a doubt, James is making all the right moves as a new investor. He has surrounded himself with experts to advise him and is spending most of his time looking for properties to buy. James has decided to specialize in foreclosure properties as the technique for finding bargains. He has made offers during all three stages of the process (pre-foreclosure, public auction, and bank REO), but has been successful only at the bank REO stage so far.

On his first project, James purchased a single-family house from a bank REO department for $15,500, all cash (obtained from the private mortgage brokers). He hired a general contractor for the rehab work and spent $8,000 on the renovations. The property was then put back on the market and was quickly sold for $55,900. James walked out of closing on this deal with a nice net profit of $23,000—not bad for a novice investor on his first deal! His second project is now in progress and he is targeting a net profit of about $20,000. Go get 'em James!

Car Dealer Goes Full-Time as Investor

Rancho Cucamonga, California—Sam is another rags-to-riches hero who has just recently quit his full-time car dealer management job (making $250,000 per year) and is now pursuing his dream as a real estate entrepreneur. He is accumulating his wealth the old fashioned way—playing by the rules and working hard!

Sam, an immigrant from Lebanon in 1988, got into the car business about 12 years ago and it worked out very well for him. He eventually advanced to a senior management position, was able to start a family (three children), buy a house, and pay it off by the age of 35.

"In spite of my financial success at my job, there was something missing from my life—something that would allow me to enjoy the essence of life and fulfill my long-term goals. What I really wanted was the personal freedom of being my own boss, having my own business and report only to myself."

Sam stumbled on this book at a neighborhood Barnes & Noble bookstore.

"I took the book home and read it cover to cover in one day. This is the only book that I've read in one day in my entire life! Then I gave it to my wife and asked her to read it. After she finished it, we looked at each other and said, 'Let's go for it!' And that's exactly what we did."

Sam and his wife Lamia worked out a very specific plan; they would buy fixer-uppers, get them fixed up, and immediately sell them for a profit. Lamia would get her real estate license so she could search for deals and earn 3 percent on each end of the transactions. They would obtain a line of credit on their paid off house, raise their credit limits on their credit cards and apply for unsecured loans. This was their plan and they went to work putting it into action.

Over the next two years, Sam and Lamia (who did get her real estate license) bought and sold seven houses, and made a little over $100,000 in profits! This was a part-time venture because Sam kept his job at the dealership during this initial period. Here are the averages for their first seven rehab projects.

Average Purchase Price:	$125,000
Average Holding Period:	3 months
Average Profit per House:	$ 15,000

More recently, Sam and Lamia decided to purchase a new home in Rancho Cucamonga. They found a brand new 3,600-square-foot home with a great view that the builder was offering for $525,000. After some tough negotiations, they purchased the house for $457,000 (including Lamia's $8,000 commission). They paid 50 percent down payment from the line of credit on their existing home and then paid off the balance a few months later when their house sold. Now they're cooking! They are sitting on a free and clear home worth $525,000 (per appraisal) and were granted a $500,000 line of credit "to play with."

One day, Sam was sitting in his office and got to thinking about what was going on at his new subdivision. He realized that the builders who had built his new home were just starting on the final phase of development. Within the next three months, they were going to build on the best lots with the best views. He stopped by and had a talk with the builders. They were asking $540,000. Sam offered $470,000 with $8,000 to Lamia for a real estate commission.

"They thought I was crazy!"

I said, "I'll pay cash."

"We settled at $480,000 with $8,000 going to Lamia."

"I then sold my new house that we had just moved in to nine months earlier for $525,000, making a quick $50,000 profit, and we moved into a beautiful new home with a spectacular panoramic view. Again, the house is free and clear and I have another $500,000 line of credit to play with."

Sam just e-mailed me to let me know he had quit his car dealership job and was going to be working on his rehab business full-time. He and Lamia have set a very ambitious goal for this next year—they plan to re-hab and sell 36 homes with a total profit target of $500,000—and I have no doubt that they will achieve it!

Should I Sell the Contract Wholesale or Rehab?

Cincinnati, Ohio—Jill, who lives in a suburb near Cincinnati, has been doing wholesale deals to rehab investors for some time. She has learned how to find the bargains, get them under contract, and then flip the contract to rehab investors for a quick profit. Over time, she began to learn how to actually orchestrate a rehab project herself and finally decided to tackle her first project.

Jill has developed several techniques for finding bargain properties in her market. One of her favorites (because of her success) is using direct mail to contact property owners to inquire about a possible sale. Prospects? Any number of possibilities, including following preforeclo-sure notices, divorce notices, and estate sales, and researching owner-ship of abandoned buildings.

Here are the details on the project she planned to rehab herself.

Purchase Cost:	$40,000
Rehab Cost Estimate:	10,000
Value after Repairs:	80,000
Finance and Selling Costs:	5,000
Potential Net Profit:	25,000

The house was a three-bedroom, one-bath ranch fixer-upper, with about 950 square feet of living area. It had central air-conditioning and gas forced-air heating, all appliances, and is located in a popular suburb with an active market. The mechanical and structural systems are all in good shape, but every square inch of carpet, vinyl, wall, and ceiling needed to be redone; in addition, the kitchen counters needed replacing, an electrical upgrade was required, and some updating work in the bath was needed—about $10,000 in repair cost is what she estimated.

Jill had established a good business relationship and track record with a local hard money lender. He has been a good source for locating rehab investors who purchase her wholesale deals. On this deal, she obtained a $43,000 loan to close the deal and walked away from closing with $1,400 in her pocket! A classic nothing down, cash at closing deal. The terms of the loan were 3 points (very good) at 10.5 percent for one year, interest only.

Within a day of closing on this deal, Jill unexpectedly received a $60,000 all cash offer from one of her wholesale clients (rehab investor). Her investor could close very quickly and was anxious to do so.

Wow! What to do? Jill could go ahead and wholesale it and walk away with a quick $17,000 profit, or she could go forward with the rehab and sell it retail for a net profit of about $25,000.

Jill decided to accept the $60,000 offer, take her profits and move on to the next deal.

Sure, she bypassed the incremental $8,000 in profits but, in her case, it was a question of time commitment. Also, it was a question of opportunity cost. She had the chance to take a large chunk of the profit potential via selling wholesale, and decided she didn't want to devote significant amounts of her time for an incremental $8,000. She had recently been working on a couple of large acquisition projects that have very large profit potential and felt she now had the chance to clear her schedule to finalize these deals. A very reasonable resolution of her dilemma, under the circumstances.

A final note on how this wholesale deal was accomplished. You will notice that Jill borrowed the money and closed the $40,000 purchase in her name. This was done because she had intended to go ahead with the rehab herself.

If you know in advance that you are going to transfer the contract to another investor, there is no need to get a loan and close the transaction yourself. You simply *assign* your contract, or do what's called a *simultaneous* or *double closing*. In this case, a simultaneous closing would have been the choice because Jill would not normally want an investor to know that she was making $17,000 on the transaction!

Jill has developed the skills for finding the good deals and turning a good profit quickly. That's what the quick turnaround investment philosophy is all about!

A Partnership That Works

Milwaukee, Wisconsin—Cheryl, Charles, and Theresa met at a real estate seminar and decided they wanted to work together on rehab projects. Cheryl was previously a branch bank manager, Charles had worked in construction and home remodeling, and Theresa was (and still is) employed as a laboratory technician manager. What is interesting about this partnership (actually they formed a corporation to conduct their real estate business) is the way they utilize each others' strengths to get their projects completed and capitalize on their overall investment strategy. Basically, they have developed a buy, rehab, refinance, and hold strategy, using small apartment buildings (typically a two-flat unit) as the focus of their attention.

Cheryl, with a background in business and marketing, coordinates the purchase of properties, the short-term financing through private mortgage brokers, and the property management duties for the completed rentals. Charles handles all the rehab work, acting as the general contractor for each project and hiring all of the necessary subcontractors. Theresa, while maintaining her full-time job, takes care of bookkeeping and accounting duties and utilizes her good credit and steady income to qualify for long-term financing on their rehabbed projects. Indeed, this real synergy of talents creates a dynamite partnership/company.

In the two years that the group has been working together, they have completed five rehab projects and have placed the properties in their long-term rental portfolio. Cheryl has developed quite a unique method of buying bargain properties. She has gotten to know the city of Milwaukee officials who handle properties that have been condemned or abandoned and that are slated for demolition. She makes purchase offers either directly to the city (if the city has taken ownership) or she will contact the owners and make an offer. In either case, she has little or no competition and the properties can be purchased very inexpensively.

On a recent deal, they purchased a two-unit flat scheduled for demolition, directly from the city for $10,900. Over the following two and one-half months, Charles and his subcontractor crews completed $27,000 in renovations and created a property worth $64,000. Theresa then obtained long-term refinancing and cashed out the short-term lender. With the property now fully rented, the group has approximately $17,000 net equity in a property that generates a $700 monthly positive cash flow.

With five buildings now completed, the group has developed an excellent reputation with city officials, lenders, subcontractors, and tenants. In fact, their finished product is so attractive to tenants that they now have a waiting list for their future apartment units!

How to Buy Bank REO Properties

*Dallas, Texas—*Tim is now an "old pro" in the real estate investment game, having some 20-plus years of experience buying and selling houses and mobile homes. He classifies himself as a "little-deal guy," but he has been remarkably successful in building his investment portfolio. Tim operates primarily in the midcities area between Dallas–Ft. Worth and Denton, Texas, and tends to specialize in acquiring properties and selling on a lease/option basis (also known as rent to own, where the "buyer" actually leases the property with the option to purchase at a later date).

I'm bringing you Tim's story on one particular deal involving a bank REO property because it is the most fascinating story I have yet encountered on the topic. As you recall in Chapter 6, I emphasized the importance of repetitive offers as the key ingredient to success in purchasing these properties. Tim's story puts a big exclamation point on this concept.

One day in March, Tim got a call from the listing agent on a bank REO property. The agent called Tim because he had purchased several other REOs from her in the past. The house was located in the Kessler Park area of Oak Cliff, just south of Dallas. This was a good neighborhood, but the house needed a lot of rehab work. In tip-top shape, the house would be worth about $155,000. But Tim's plan was to buy the house and assign his contract for a few thousand dollars to a friend who specializes in rehab properties. He and his agent worked up an offer for $92,000 and submitted it to the bank. Within a couple of days the offer was rejected, without a counteroffer, not an unusual event in the world of REO properties.

The next month, his real estate agent called and advised him that the house was still on the market. Tim told her to just submit the same offer again and see what happens. Well, the same thing happened–a rejection without a counteroffer. Tim decided to continue the game and gave instructions to his agent to resubmit the same offer each month until the property sold to him or someone else.

In the meantime, the bank decided to begin renovations on the property, hoping to find a buyer for full retail value. The months continued to go by, with Tim's standing offer being rejected each month and the bank continuing to spend money on renovations. Finally, in December he got an excited call from his agent. The bank had made a counteroffer. The bank had countered at the same price Tim had been offering since March ($92,000), but they wanted twice the earnest money. The counteroffer was immediately accepted. But here's the clincher–the bank had spent over $30,000 on renovating the house! It was in almost mint condition by this time–but the bank didn't care. They wanted it off their books by the end of the year!

Shocked and amazed, Tim closed that deal with a big smile on his face. He then spent about $1,500 on the landscaping to create spectacular curb appeal in the front yard. He also spent about $800 on what he calls "foo-foo" items like brass address numbers, all-new electrical switch and outlet covers, 150-watt lightbulbs, and mini-blinds. The masterpiece was now complete. Instead of putting it on the market and selling it outright, he put it on his lease/option program and had a qualified "buyer" within two weeks who agreed to a $162,000 price, a nice, tidy profit of $67,700.

Indeed, a truly incredible story! With this in mind, I'm sure you will never again just submit an offer on an REO property and forget about it if it's not accepted. You may not hit the jackpot like Tim did, but you will certainly land your fair share of good deals. Happy hunting!

Part-Time Wholesale Entrepreneur Tells His Story

Charlotte, North Carolina—Rob is an architect in Charlotte, working mostly on commercial projects. He and his wife had been interested in doing some entrepreneurial real estate investing for quite a while and even purchased the Carleton Sheets material.

"I bought a Carleton Sheets course, which was good, but I finally did some hard self-examination and determined that I did not have the patience or temperament to be a good landlord."

Rob later discovered this book and my *Secrets of the Real Estate Wholesale Business* course. He studied the course material and then went to work. Within four months, Rob wholesaled five properties and earned $15,700 on a part-time basis!

How in the world did he do this so quickly?

"All I did was follow your course instructions. It was so easy!"

Let's take a look at one of Rob's deals to see exactly how he puts together a wholesale project. Keep in mind that this was his most profitable transaction during this initial four month period, and it turns out, his quickest and easiest. Here's his story, in his own words.

In our local legal newspaper, I found a property in a good, older neighborhood that was being cited for housing code violations (the tenants and the owners were at war, so the tenants got the code inspectors involved in retaliation). I sent the owners a form letter explaining my interest in buying the property.

As it turns out, the owners were very motivated. They were a husband and wife, now separated and living in different parts of the state. The tenants had slipped out in the middle of the night, but not before trashing the place—and the bank was sending them hate mail because they were behind on their payments. They wanted to dump the place quickly.

I had already developed relationships with several rehabbers in town and found out what they look for, areas, and price ranges. This place fit the bill. My market research showed the maximum retail value to be $85,000 to $90,000. From there, I backed out all of my acquisition, holding sales, and estimated rehab cost (as if I were going to do the rehab), contingency, the rehabbers profit and my profit.

I negotiated a price of $46,500 and got a signed contract. I then began calling several investors the next day, asking for $56,500. Within three hours, one of them drove by it, and called me back agreeing to my price. We signed a contract the next day and did a double (simultaneous) closing the following week. I had roughly $625 in combined closing costs for the two transactions, leaving me a net profit of $9,375.

All total, I maybe had ten hours of time invested—what a blast!

To date, none of my five transactions have involved real estate agents. It's meant more hustle and work on my part, but many times there just isn't enough room for the agent to get his cut, on top of the rehabber's profit and mine. So I focus on properties where I can deal directly with the owner.

I found my customers, the rehabbers, by calling all the ads around town that basically say: We Buy Houses—Any Condition—All Cash—Quick Closings. There are maybe ten of these guys around town that have billboards, flyers stapled to telephone polls, ads in papers, and the like. I just called them, introduced myself and what I was doing, used the follow-up letter and investor worksheet that came with the course, and within a few days, I had a file of potential customers (rehabbers) to whom I could wholesale my deals with a phone call. I only deal with the ones who can generate cash quickly. I've had to weed out the ones who want to get creative with notes and carrying paper and all the other no-money-down techniques. I want to work with serious people who can follow through.

I basically follow the outline in the course. I find a house in need of significant work, negotiate a rock bottom price, get a signed contract, and fax it to my attorney (I believe that in North Carolina, closings must be handled by an attorney and not a title company). He then handles the rest. While he's researching the title and getting loan payoff information, I'm on the phone getting my rehabber customers out to see the property. In case no one wants it, or if I've failed to get a low enough price, I build in a contingency clause in the contract saying, "offer is subject to buyer's partner inspection and approval of the property and this agreement. If approval is not granted within ten days, either party may terminate this agreement." This weasel clause gives me an out if I can't find an interested buyer. That way, I'm protected. I've never had a seller question it. I explain to them that in order to generate cash on short demand, I won't be going to Bank of America for the loan. I'll be dealing with hard money lenders or partners with cash. They seem okay with it."

To date, I've done four double closings and one assignment. The assignment was great because I didn't have to attend the closing. I just got a $3,000 check in the mail—what a blast!"

It's always a pleasure for me to hear from students who just pick up the ball and run with it. Rob is obviously an individual who has embraced the Just Do It philosophy and, most importantly, he is having great fun!

Well, we've come to the end of our journey together. I've had a lot of fun writing this book and I hope that you have enjoyed reading it. The ball is now in your court. You now have the knowledge and the tools to create the momentum that will lead you to financial security. Pick up the ball and run! And be sure to e-mail me about *your* success story! Send the details success@rehabwiz.com—I'd love to hear from you!

One last point: I do offer a free, online newsletter (ezine) and would be happy to add you to my mailing list. Just go to <www.rehabwiz.com> and sign up—it's *free*!

Best of Success!

Appendix A
Investment Opportunity Worksheet

✏️ **Investment Opportunity Worksheet**

Date: __6-1-03__

Property Address: __9612 Woodland Ave.__ City: __Albuquerque__ State: __NM__

Listing Type: ☐ REALTOR® ☒ FSBO ☐ REO ☐ HUD ☐ VA ☐ Other _____

Property Description: __3__ Bedroom(s) __1__ Bath __Pueblo/Flat__ Style

__1,242__ Sq.Ft. Age: __40+ yrs.__ Garage: __1__ Car ☐ None

Other Information: __Corner lot; nonassumable loan__

_____

Listing/Asking Price $ __70,000__

Rehab Plan Cost Summary

Repair Category	Cost Estimate
Roof	1,800
Foundation	
Site Drainage	
Electrical System	
Heating and Cooling	
Hot Water Heater	200
Concrete	
Fireplace	
Termite Damage	
Exterior Wood	
Stucco or Siding	

Investment Opportunity Worksheet (Continued)

Landscaping	*800*
Junk Removal	
Exterior Paint	*1,000*
Interior Paint	*1,500*
Flooring	*2,000*
Kitchen Rehab	*2,000*
Bathroom(s) Rehab	*1,000*
Interior Walls	
Windows	*800*
Skylights	*500*
Light Fixtures	*300*
Doors	*300*
Security System	
Sizzle Features	*2,500*
Other	
Subtotal	*14,700*
Contingency	*1,000*
Total Estimated Cost	*15,700*

After-Repaired Maximum Retail Value: *$105,000*
  Based on Neighborhood Comparable Sales

Maximum Retail Value	*$105,000*
Subtract the following:	
Purchase Costs	*– 5,000*
Rehab Costs	*–16,000*
Holding Costs	*– 4,000*
Sales Costs	*– 7,000*
Contingency Factor	*– 2,000*
Profit	*–15,000*
Maximum Purphase Price	*$ 56,000*

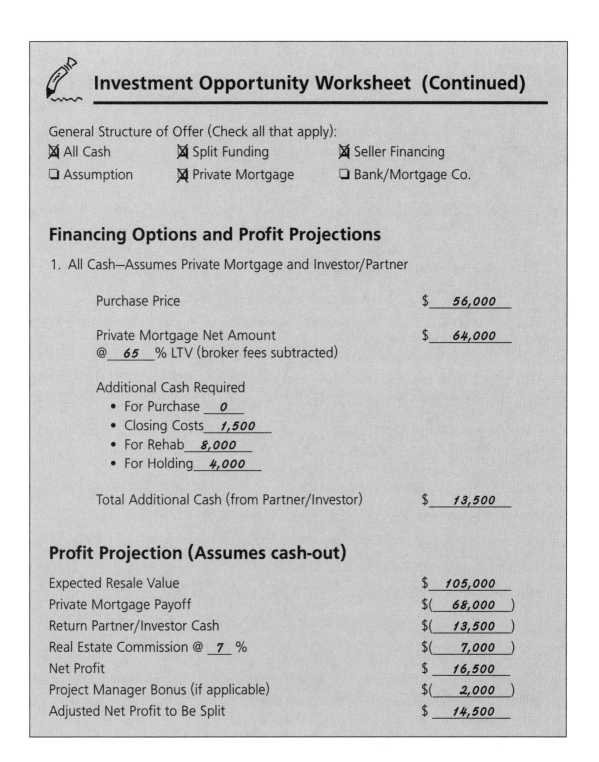

Investment Opportunity Worksheet (Continued)

General Structure of Offer (Check all that apply):

☒ All Cash ☒ Split Funding ☒ Seller Financing

☐ Assumption ☒ Private Mortgage ☐ Bank/Mortgage Co.

Financing Options and Profit Projections

1. All Cash—Assumes Private Mortgage and Investor/Partner

Purchase Price	$ 56,000
Private Mortgage Net Amount @ 65 % LTV (broker fees subtracted)	$ 64,000

Additional Cash Required
- For Purchase 0
- Closing Costs 1,500
- For Rehab 8,000
- For Holding 4,000

Total Additional Cash (from Partner/Investor)	$ 13,500

Profit Projection (Assumes cash-out)

Expected Resale Value	$ 105,000
Private Mortgage Payoff	$(68,000)
Return Partner/Investor Cash	$(13,500)
Real Estate Commission @ 7 %	$(7,000)
Net Profit	$ 16,500
Project Manager Bonus (if applicable)	$(2,000)
Adjusted Net Profit to Be Split	$ 14,500

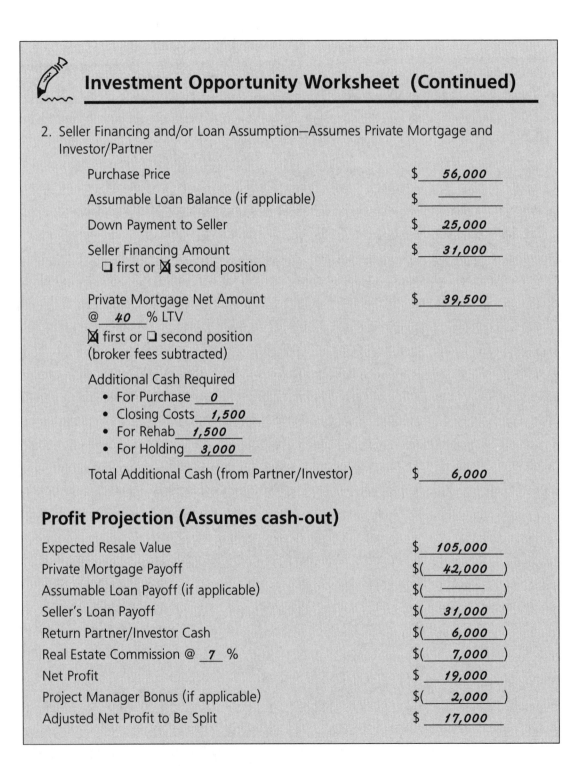

Investment Opportunity Worksheet (Continued)

2. Seller Financing and/or Loan Assumption—Assumes Private Mortgage and Investor/Partner

Purchase Price	$ 56,000
Assumable Loan Balance (if applicable)	$ ——
Down Payment to Seller	$ 25,000
Seller Financing Amount	$ 31,000

   ☐ first or ☒ second position

Private Mortgage Net Amount	$ 39,500

@ __40__ % LTV
☒ first or ☐ second position
(broker fees subtracted)

Additional Cash Required
- For Purchase __0__
- Closing Costs __1,500__
- For Rehab __1,500__
- For Holding __3,000__

Total Additional Cash (from Partner/Investor)	$ 6,000

Profit Projection (Assumes cash-out)

Expected Resale Value	$ 105,000
Private Mortgage Payoff	$(42,000)
Assumable Loan Payoff (if applicable)	$(——)
Seller's Loan Payoff	$(31,000)
Return Partner/Investor Cash	$(6,000)
Real Estate Commission @ _7_ %	$(7,000)
Net Profit	$ 19,000
Project Manager Bonus (if applicable)	$(2,000)
Adjusted Net Profit to Be Split	$ 17,000

Appendix B

State Foreclosure Information

Summary information only—See local attorney for current legal requirements.

Alabama

Type of Security Instrument	Title Mortgage
Legal Action	Nonjudicial
Redemption Period Following Sale	12 months

Alaska

Type of Security Instrument	Lien Deed of Trust
Legal Action	Nonjudicial
Redemption Period Following Sale	None

Comments: If a mortgage is in place, requiring a judicial foreclosure, there is a 12-month redemption period.

Arizona

Type of Security Instrument	Lien Deed of Trust
Legal Action	Nonjudicial
Redemption Period Following Sale	None

Comments: If a mortgage is in place, requiring a judicial foreclosure, there is a six-month redemption period.

Arkansas

Type of Security	Mix
Instrument	Mortgage
Legal Action	Judicial
Redemption Period Following Sale	None

Comments: No redemption if waived in instrument, 12 months if not waived. Mortgage may authorize nonjudicial legal action.

California

Type of Security	Lien
Instrument	Deed of Trust
Legal Action	Nonjudicial
Redemption Period Following Sale	None

Comments: If a mortgage is in place, requiring a judicial foreclosure, there is a 12-month redemption period.

Colorado

Type of Security	Lien
Instrument	Deed of Trust
Legal Action	Nonjudicial
Redemption Period	2.5 months
Following Sale	75 days

Comments: Redemption period is six months if agricultural.

Connecticut

Type of Security	Mix
Instrument	Mortgage
Legal Action	Strict Foreclosure
Redemption Period Following Sale	None

Comments: Redemption depends on equity; set by court.

Delaware

Type of Security	Mix
Instrument	Mortgage
Legal Action	Judicial
Redemption Period Following Sale	None

District of Columbia

Type of Security	Mix
Instrument	Deed of Trust
Legal Action	Nonjudicial
Redemption Period Following Sale	None

Florida

Type of Security	Lien
Instrument	Mortgage
Legal Action	Judicial
Redemption Period Following Sale	None

Georgia

Type of Security	Title
Instrument	Security Deed
Legal Action	Nonjudicial
Redemption Period Following Sale	None

Hawaii

Type of Security	Lien
Instrument	Mortgage
Legal Action	Nonjudicial
Redemption Period Following Sale	None

Comments: Many mortgages foreclose by judicial legislation.

Idaho

Type of Security	Lien
Instrument	Deed of Trust
Legal Action	Nonjudicial
Redemption Period Following Sale	None

Comments: If a mortgage is in place, requiring a judicial foreclosure, there is a six-month redemption period.

Illinois

Type of Security	Mix
Instrument	Mortgage
Legal Action	Judicial
Redemption Period Following Sale	None

Comments: Redemption period precedes sale.

Indiana

Type of Security	Lien
Instrument	Mortgage
Legal Action	Judicial
Redemption Period Following Sale	Three to six months

Comments: Mortgages dated prior to July 1, 1975, have a six-month redemption period; otherwise, three months.

Iowa

Type of Security	Lien
Instrument	Mortgage
Legal Action	Judicial
Redemption Period Following Sale	Six months

Comments: Exceptions are made for agricultural and nonowner occupied properties; waiver of deficiency judgment.

Kansas

Type of Security Instrument	Lien
	Mortgage
Legal Action	Judicial
Redemption Period Following Sale	6 to 12 months

Comments: Redemption period depends on equity.

Kentucky

Type of Security Instrument	Lien
	Mortgage
Legal Action	Judicial
Redemption Period Following Sale	None

Comments: A 12-month redemption period is required if the sale is for less than two-thirds of appraised value.

Louisiana

Type of Security Instrument	Lien
	Mortgage
Legal Action	Judicial
Redemption Period Following Sale	None

Comments: This is an executory process.

Maine

Type of Security Instrument	Title
	Mortgage
Legal Action	Judicial
Redemption Period Following Sale	None

Comments: Redemption period is 12 months if mortgage is prior to October 1, 1975, and is silent on redemption issue.

Maryland

Type of Security Instrument	Title Deed of Trust
Legal Action	Nonjudicial
Redemption Period Following Sale	None

Massachusetts

Type of Security Instrument	Mix Mortgage
Legal Action	Judicial
Redemption Period Following Sale	None

Comments: Entry and possession also are allowed.

Michigan

Type of Security Instrument	Lien Mortgage
Legal Action	Nonjudicial
Redemption Period Following Sale	Six months

Comments: Redemption period is 12 months if mortgage is dated prior to January 1, 1965.

Minnesota

Type of Security Instrument	Lien Mortgage
Legal Action	Nonjudicial
Redemption Period Following Sale	Six months

Comments: Redemption period increases to 12 months if mortgage is dated after July 1, 1967.

Mississippi

Type of Security	Title
Instrument	Deed of Trust
Legal Action	Nonjudicial
Redemption Period Following Sale	None

Missouri

Type of Security	Lien
Instrument	Deed of Trust
Legal Action	Nonjudicial
Redemption Period Following Sale	None

Comments: Mortgagor may, within ten days of sale, give notice of intent to redeem, in which case redemption period is 12 months.

Montana

Type of Security	Lien
Instrument	Deed of Trust
Legal Action	Nonjudicial
Redemption Period Following Sale	None

Nebraska

Type of Security	Lien
Instrument	Mortgage
Legal Action	Judicial
Redemption Period Following Sale	None

Comments: Redemption period precedes sale; deed of trust with nonjudicial foreclosure is also allowed.

Nevada

Type of Security	Lien
Instrument	Deed of Trust
Legal Action	Nonjudicial
Redemption Period	None
Following Sale	

New Hampshire

Type of Security	Title
Instrument	Mortgage
Legal Action	Nonjudicial
Redemption Period	None
Following Sale	

New Jersey

Type of Security	Mix
Instrument	Mortgage
Legal Action	Judicial
Redemption Period	None
Following Sale	

New Mexico

Type of Security	Lien
Instrument	Mortgage
Legal Action	Judicial
Redemption Period	None
Following Sale	

Comments: Redemption period precedes sale.

New York

Type of Security	Lien
Instrument	Mortgage
Legal Action	Judicial
Redemption Period	None
Following Sale	

North Carolina

Type of Security Instrument	Mix Deed of Trust
Legal Action	Nonjudicial
Redemption Period Following Sale	None

North Dakota

Type of Security Instrument	Lien Mortgage
Legal Action	Judicial
Redemption Period Following Sale	Two to six months

Comments: Redemption period is the later of six months from notice of default or 60 days from sale, on mortgages after July 1, 1981.

Ohio

Type of Security Instrument	Lien Mortgage
Legal Action	Judicial
Redemption Period Following Sale	None

Oklahoma

Type of Security Instrument	Lien Mortgage
Legal Action	Judicial
Redemption Period Following Sale	None

Oregon

Type of Security Instrument	Lien Deed of Trust
Legal Action	Nonjudicial
Redemption Period Following Sale	None

Pennsylvania

Type of Security Instrument	Title Mortgage
Legal Action	Judicial
Redemption Period Following Sale	None

Rhode Island

Type of Security Instrument	Title Mortgage
Legal Action	Nonjudicial
Redemption Period Following Sale	None

South Carolina

Type of Security Instrument	Lien Mortgage
Legal Action	Judicial
Redemption Period Following Sale	None

South Dakota

Type of Security Instrument	Lien Mortgage
Legal Action	Judicial
Redemption Period Following Sale	Six months

Tennessee

Type of Security Instrument	Title Deed of Trust
Legal Action	Nonjudicial
Redemption Period Following Sale	None

Texas

Type of Security Instrument	Lien Deed of Trust
Legal Action	Nonjudicial
Redemption Period Following Sale	None

Utah

Type of Security Instrument	Lien Deed of Trust
Legal Action	Nonjudicial
Redemption Period Following Sale	None

Comments: Redemption period precedes sale.

Vermont

Type of Security Instrument	Title Mortgage
Legal Action	Judicial
Redemption Period Following Sale	None

Virginia

Type of Security Instrument	Mix Deed of Trust
Legal Action	Nonjudicial
Redemption Period Following Sale	None

Washington

Type of Security	Lien
Instrument	Deed of Trust
Legal Action	Nonjudicial
Redemption Period Following Sale	None

Comments: VA loans are typically foreclosed judicially.

West Virginia

Type of Security	Lien
Instrument	Deed of Trust
Legal Action	Nonjudicial
Redemption Period Following Sale	None

Wisconsin

Type of Security	Lien
Instrument	Mortgage
Legal Action	Judicial
Redemption Period Following Sale	None

Comments: Redemption period precedes sale.

Wyoming

Type of Security	Lien
Instrument	Mortgage
Legal Action	Nonjudicial
Redemption Period Following Sale	Three months

Comments: Additional redemption periods of 30 days for successive lien holders is allowed.

Glossary of Common Real Estate Terms

acceleration clause a condition in a loan contract or note that permits the lender to require immediate repayment of the entire balance if the contract is breached.

ad valorem tax according to value (Latin); generally used to refer to real estate taxes that are based on assessed property value.

adjustable-rate mortgage (ARM) a mortgage loan in which the interest rate can go up or down based on market conditions. Changes in the interest rate are determined by a financial index. ARM loans have a cap or limit on how much the interest rate can change.

amortization repayment of a mortgage loan with equal periodic payments of both principal and interest. The payments are calculated so that the debt is paid off at the end of a fixed period.

annual percentage rate (APR) a term that expresses the cost of a mortgage as an annual rate. The APR is normally higher than the advertised interest rate because it includes interest, points, and other finance charges. The APR is used to compare different types of mortgages.

appraisal adjustment a decrease or increase in the sales price of a comparable property to account for a feature that the property has or does not have in comparison with the subject property.

appraisal an estimate of value; the process through which conclusions of property value are obtained; also refers to the report.

appreciation an increase in value due to any cause such as inflation, repair, or supply-and-demand factors.

arm's-length transaction a transaction in which both buyer and seller act willingly and under no pressure, with knowledge of the present conditions and future potential of the property, and in which the property has been offered on the open market for a reasonable length of time and for which there are no unusual circumstances.

asphalt shingles roof shingles made of felt, saturated with asphalt, and surfaced with mineral or ceramic granules.

assessed value value given to property that is used *solely* for determining property taxes. Value usually has no direct relationship to fair market value.

backflow preventer in the kitchen context, a device that keeps water in the sink from traveling back into faucets where the spout pulls out and becomes a sprayer.

balloon mortgage a short-term mortgage loan of equal monthly payments in which a large final payment (balloon) is due on a specified date. The final payment is equal to the remaining balance of the loan.

base cabinet a kitchen cabinet that goes on the floor, and usually is deeper and taller than a wall cabinet.

baseboard heating a heating unit comprised of an electric or forced hot-water heating element, located at the base of the interior wall.

batt insulation narrow-width insulating material, usually composed of mineral fibers, used to insulate between framing members.

bay window a window that projects out from a wall and either has its own foundation or is cantilevered.

bearing wall a wall that supports an upper floor or roof loads.

building codes rules of local or state government specifying minimum building and construction standards for the protection of public safety and health.

built-in appliances those that are installed into a run of cabinets in contrast to freestanding appliances that slide into place.

caissons poured-in-place, reinforced concrete pilings.

capitalization rate the percentage rate applied to the income a property is expected to produce to derive an estimate of the property's value; includes both an acceptable rate of return on the amount invested (yield) and return of the actual amount invested (recapture).

cash flow the net spendable income from an investment, determined by deducting all operating and fixed expenses from gross income. If expenses exceed income, a *negative* cash flow is the result.

closing costs fees paid by either buyer or seller at closing of the mortgage loan. Fees usually are in the range of 3 to 6 percent of the mortgage amount. Typical closing costs are agent fees, appraisal fees, and prepaid insurance and taxes.

cloud on title a claim or encumbrance that impairs the owner's title, if valid.

collateral property pledged as security for repayment of the mortgage loan.

comparables properties that are substantially equivalent to the subject property.

compound interest interest paid on both the original investment and accrued interest.

condominium type of ownership of a multiunit property in which the owner holds title to an individual unit and a percentage of common areas.

consideration anything given as an inducement to enter into a contract, such as money or personal services.

contingent dependent upon conditions or events specified, but not yet accomplished. Property may be sold contingent upon the seller or buyer meeting specified predetermined conditions.

contractor overhead the contractor's operating expenses, including insurance, equipment, and any temporary facilities that cannot be prorated to a specific category.

contractor profit the compensation accrued for the assumption of risk in constructing or rehabbing a building.

conventional loan a mortgage loan made by an approved lender in which the borrower's ability to repay the debt is not insured by a government agency such as FHA or VA.

conveyance a written instrument, such as a deed or lease, by which title or an interest in real estate is transferred.

corporation an association of shareholders, created under law, having a legal identity separate from the individuals who own it.

cost approach the process of estimating the value of a property by adding the appraiser's estimate of the reproduction or replacement cost of property improvements, less depreciation, to the estimated land value.

covenant an agreement written into deeds and other instruments promising performance or nonperformance of certain acts or stipulating certain uses or nonuses of property.

crawl space a space of limited height but sufficient to allow access to piping or wiring underneath the floor of a raised floor structure.

custom cabinets cabinets that are made to order to a customer's exact specifications. Usually constructed of better-quality wood with an emphasis on craftsmanship.

deed of trust an instrument used to create a mortgage lien by which the borrower conveys title to a trustee, who holds it as security for the benefit of the note holder (the lender).

deed restrictions provisions in a deed limiting the future uses of the property. Deed restrictions may take many forms: They may limit the density of buildings, dictate the types of structures that can be erected, and prevent buildings from being used for specific purposes or used at all.

deed a written instrument that conveys title to or an interest in real estate when properly executed and delivered.

default failure to perform a duty or meet a contractual obligation.

deficiency judgment when the security for a loan is sold for less than the amount of the loan, the deficiency amount is held by law to be a judgment and is the liability of the borrower unless the new owner has assumed the debt.

discount points also called *points*. A one-time charge paid to the lender at closing to obtain a lower interest rate. One point is equal to one percent of the loan amount. Points are collected by lenders to increase the yield on their investment.

discount to sell a promissory note for less than its face value.

dormer an outward projection from a sloping roof used to allow headroom under the roof and allow placement of a window.

double-hung window a window with an upper and lower sash, each balanced by springs or weights to allow vertical movement.

dry wall a finish material applied to an interior wall in a dry state, in contrast to a wet plaster. Also known as gypsum board or Sheetrock.

ducts enclosures for distributing warm or cool air from the central unit to various rooms.

due-on-sale clause also known as an *alienation clause,* this provision allows a lender to demand full payment of the loan balance if the property is sold.

earnest money the down payment made by a purchaser of real estate used to demonstrate good faith in the transaction.

easement a right to use the land of another for a specific purpose, such as a right of way or for utilities.

economic life the period during which a structure may reasonably be expected to perform the function for which it was designed or intended.

elevated slab a horizontal, reinforced concrete foundation that is formed and poured in-place above the ground.

eminent domain the right of a federal, state, or local government or public corporation, utility, or service corporation to acquire private property for public use through a court action called *condemnation,* in which the court determines compensation to the owner.

encroachment a building, wall, or fence that extends beyond the land of the owner and illegally intrudes on land of an adjoining owner.

encumbrance a lien (such as a mortgage, tax, or judgment lien), easement, restriction on the use of land, outstanding dower right, or other interest that may diminish the value of property to its owner.

equity the amount of the home that you actually own. Equity is the difference between the market value of the home and what you still owe on it.

escrow account an account required by the lender to pay taxes and insurance. When each mortgage payment is made, a portion goes into the escrow account.

escrow the closing of a transaction through a disinterested third person called an *escrow agent,* who holds funds or documents, or both, for delivery on the performance of certain conditions.

evaporative cooler an air-conditioner that cools the air by water evaporation.

exclusive right to sell a written agreement that gives a real estate broker the exclusive right to sell a property for a specified period. If a sale is made by the owner or any other broker during the time period, the broker holding the exclusive right is entitled to compensation, unless the provision has been modified by a buyout agreement.

Fannie Mae (FNMA) the Federal National Mortgage Association, a government-chartered private company that buys large blocks of mortgage loans from lending institutions, and obtains its money by selling securities in the open market to investors.

feasibility study an analysis of an existing or proposed property with emphasis on the attainable income, probable expenses, and most advantageous use and design. The purpose of such a study is to ascertain the probable success or failure of the project under consideration.

federal reserve bank system the central bank of the United States, established to regulate the flow of money and the cost of borrowing.

federal tax lien an obligation to the U.S. government as a result of nonpayment of federal taxes.

fee simple the greatest possible estate or right of ownership of real property, continuing without time limitation.

FHA the Federal Housing Administration; insures loans made by approved lenders in accordance with its regulations.

final value estimate the appraiser's estimate of the defined value of the subject property, arrived at by reconciling (correlating) the estimates of value derived from the sales comparison, cost, and income approaches.

finish hardware all exposed hardware in a house, such as doorknobs, door hinges, locks, clothes hooks, and so on.

first mortgage a mortgage that has priority as a lien over all other mortgages.

fixture anything affixed to land, including personal property attached permanently to a building or to land so that it becomes part of the real estate.

forced-air heating a warm-air heating system that circulates air by a motor-driven fan and includes air-filtration devices.

foreclosure a court action initiated by a mortgagee or lienor for the purpose of having the court order that the debtor's real estate be sold to pay the mortgage or other lien.

functional obsolescence defects on a building that detract from its value or marketability, usually the result of layout, design, or other features that are less desirable than features designed for the same function in newer property.

GFCI abbreviation for ground-fault interrupter. A type of electrical outlet that shuts itself off automatically if it gets wet, thereby avoiding shock or fire.

gable roof a ridged roof that slopes up from only two walls. A gable is the triangular portion of the end of the building, from the eaves to the ridge.

gambrel roof a type of roof that has its slope broken by an obtuse angle, so that the lower slope is steeper than the upper slope; a roof with two pitches.

general contractor a person or business entity that supervises all work in a building or structure, usually licensed and bonded by a state regulatory agency.

good faith estimate an estimate of the fees you will be required to pay at closing. It is required by law that the lender provide the good faith estimate within three days of your initial loan application.

grant deed a type of deed in which the grantor warrants that he or she has not previously conveyed the estate being granted to another, has not encumbered the property except as noted in the deed, and will convey to the grantee any title to the property the grantor may later acquire.

gross living area the total finished, habitable, above-grade space, measured along the building's outside perimeter; the square footage of a house for appraisal purposes.

highest and best use the use most likely to produce the greatest net return to the land or building over a given period.

homestead a home upon which the owner has recorded a declaration of homestead, which protects the home against judgments up to a specified dollar amount.

income capitalization approach the appraisal process of estimating the value of an income-producing property by capitalization of the annual net operating income expected to be produced by the property during its remaining economic life.

independent contractor a person who contracts to do work for another by using his or her own methods and without being under the control of the other person regarding how the work should be done.

installment contract a contract for the sale of real estate by which the purchase price is paid in installments over an extended period of time by the purchaser, who is in possession of the property, but with the title retained by the seller until a certain number of payments are made. The purchaser's payments may be forfeited upon default.

institutional lender financial institutions whose loans are regulated by law. The category includes banks, savings and loans, thrifts, insurance companies, credit unions, and commercial loan agencies.

joint venture the joining to two or more people to conduct a specific business enterprise. A joint venture is similar to a partnership in which it must be created by agreement between the parties to share in the losses and profits. It is unlike a partnership in which the venture is for one specific project only, rather than for a continuing business relationship.

junker a house in need of extensive repairs to bring it up to the average condition of comparable properties in the neighborhood.

laminate typically referred to as the trade name *Formica*. A countertop surfacing material consisting of paper and plastic pressed together under heat.

land contract see *installment contract.*

land trust a trust originated by the owner of real property in which real estate is the only asset. Because the interest of a beneficiary is considered personal property and not real estate, a judgment against the beneficiary will not create a lien against the real estate; used as an asset protection tool and as a means of taking control of a property anonymously.

letter of opinion report of property value that states the appraiser's conclusion of value or a range of values and provides only a brief summary of the supporting data and appraiser's analysis.

lien a right given by law to certain creditors to have their debts paid out of the property of a defaulting debtor, usually by means of a court sale.

loan origination fee a fee that the lender may charge the borrower for the service of creating the mortgage loan. This fee is usually stated as a percentage of the loan amount.

loan-to-value ratio (LTV) the ratio of the amount of a loan on a property divided by the value of the property. A loan of $65,000 on a house valued at $100,000 results in an LTV of 65 percent.

lot-and-block system method of legal description of an individual parcel of land by reference to tract, block, and lot numbers by which the parcel is identified in a recorded subdivision map.

market value the most probable price real estate should bring in a sale occurring under normal market conditions.

masonry or block construction a type of construction with concrete, concrete block, or brick used for load-bearing exterior walls.

mechanic's lien a lien created by statute that exists in favor of contractors, laborers, or material suppliers who have performed work or furnished materials in the erection or repair of a building.

millwork wooden portions of a building that have been prebuilt and finished in a shop and brought to the site for installation such as cabinets, door jambs, molding, and trim.

monolithic one piece. Monolithic concrete is poured in a continuous process so there are no separations.

mortgage broker an individual who brings together borrowers and lenders and is paid a fee for the service.

mortgage note a document that you sign at closing that states your promise to pay a sum of money at a specified interest rate for a fixed period of time.

mortgage a legal document that pledges your property as security for repayment of the loan.

mortgagee the lender in a loan transaction secured by a mortgage.

mortgagor an owner of real estate who borrows money and conveys his or her property as security for the loan.

mullion a cabinet door with glass panes installed.

Multiple Listing Service (MLS) a computerized database of property listings compiled by member brokers to announce the availability of property for sale.

neighborhood a residential area with similar types of properties, buildings of similar value or age, predominant land use activities, and natural or fabricated geographic boundaries, such as highways or rivers.

nonqualifying assumption a mortgage or deed of trust that allows the transfer of title freely without permission of the lender and without an acceleration of the loan balance. The loan document does not contain a due-on-sale clause.

nonjudicial foreclosure power of sale is allowed in certain states, which gives the lender or trustee the right to sell the property without requesting a court proceeding, after advertising the notice for sale.

notice of default a notice filed to show that the borrower under a mortgage or deed of trust is in default on the payments.

notice of trustee's sale the final step before the foreclosure auction. Recorded in the county recorder's office, the document is advertised and posted. It gives the time and location of the sale.

partnership an association of two or more individuals who carry on a continuing business for profit as co-owners. Under the law, a partnership is regarded as a group of individuals rather than as a single entity.

pier the short, individual concrete or masonry foundation supports for the post and girder underpinnings of a raised floor structure.

plat a map representing a parcel of land subdivided into lots, showing streets and other details or a single site.

prepaid items of expense expense items, such as insurance premiums and tax reserves, that have been paid in advance of the time that the expense is incurred. Prepaid expenses are typically prorated and credited to the seller in the preparation of a loan closing statement.

prepayment clause a clause in a loan document that gives the borrower the privilege of paying the indebtedness before it is due. Some loans include a prepayment penalty.

private mortgage insurance (PMI) insurance that protects the lender in case the house payments are not made. Typically, you would be required to pay a monthly fee for PMI if your down payment is less than 20 percent.

private mortgage same as a typical bank mortgage, except that the lender is a private individual rather than an institution.

purchase money mortgage a note secured by a mortgage or trust deed given by the buyer, as mortgagor, to the seller, as mortgagee, as part of the purchase price of real estate.

quantity survey a method of cost estimation that considers a detailed count of all materials going into a structure together with the cost of labor to install each unit of material.

quitclaim deed a conveyance by which the grantor transfers whatever interest he or she has in the land, without warranties or obligations; generally considered inadequate except when interests are being passed from one spouse to the other.

R-value the standard measurement of resistance to heat loss related to a given thickness of insulation required by climatic demands.

real estate land and fixtures permanently attached thereto by nature or by man, anything incidental or appurtenant to land, and anything immovable by law.

real property the rights of ownership of real estate, often called the *bundle of rights;* for all practical purposes, synonymous with the term *real estate.*

rehab the rehabilitation or restoration of a property to satisfactory condition without drastically changing the plan, form, or style of architecture.

REO (real estate owned) property obtained by a lender through foreclosure and held in inventory.

request for notice of default a recorded notice requesting that a person be notified in the event that foreclosure proceedings are commenced on a specific mortgage or deed of trust; most often used by a junior lien holder so he or she can act to protect his or her interest should a senior lien be delinquent.

restraint of bidding an illegal agreement by two or more people to not raise the bidding on a property being sold at a foreclosure auction.

right of redemption the right of an owner to recover property lost in a foreclosure action; requires that the debt be paid off either before or after the foreclosure, within a specified period of time.

right-of-way the right that one has to travel over the land of another; an easement.

RTC (Resolution Trust Corporation) the federal agency created by the Financial Institutions Reform, Recovery, and Enforcement Act of 1989 to oversee management and liquidation of assets of failed savings and loan associations.

sales comparison approach the process of estimating the value of property through examination and comparison of actual recent sales of comparable properties.

second mortgage a mortgage loan secured by real estate that has an existing first mortgage. Also called a *junior mortgage* or *junior lien.* The order or recording (in time) determines the seniority or the lien.

septic tank a watertight settling tank in which solid sewage is decomposed by natural bacterial action. Typically associated with an adjacent leach field.

setback the distance from the curb or other established line, within which no buildings can be constructed.

sheriff's deed a deed given by a court to effect the sale of property to satisfy a judgment.

skylight an opening in a roof, covered with plastic or glass, used for light and ventilation.

soffit the underside of a building member; for example, the underside of a roof overhang. In kitchens, the area above the wall cabinets.

special assessment a charge against real estate made by a unit of government to cover the proportional cost of an improvement such as a street or sewer.

split funding refers to a buying technique wherein an investor provides a small downpayment to close the purchase with the balance due at a later date, usually as a balloon payment.

stock cabinets cabinets that come in a set number of widths, finishes, and door styles. Lack of options allows retail outlets to keep many in stock for quick delivery. Usually the least expensive cabinets available.

storm window a window placed outside an ordinary window for additional protection against severe weather.

stucco a coating for exterior walls in which cement is applied in wet layers and when dry, becomes exceedingly hard and durable.

subdivision a tract of land divided by the owner into blocks, building lots, and streets by a recorded subdivision plat.

subordination clause a clause in a mortgage that gives priority of a mortgage taken out at a later date, thus allowing the placement of a new loan in senior position.

supply and demand the economic principle that the value of a commodity will rise as demand increases or supply decreases.

survey the process of measuring land to determine its size and area; also a map or plat showing the results.

tax deed the instrument used to convey legal title to property sold by a government agency for nonpayment of taxes.

tenancy by the entirety the joint ownership of property acquired by husband and wife during marriage. Upon death, the surviving spouse becomes the owner.

tenancy in common a form of co-ownership by which each owner holds an interest in the property as if he or she were sole owner. No right of survivorship but right of inheritance is granted.

thermal window a double glass pane window (also known as double glazed) with an air space between the two panes, which may be hermetically sealed to provide insulation from heat loss.

third-party administrator (TPA) an entity that is approved to administer funds for a self-directed IRA retirement program.

title insurance an insurance policy that insures the homebuyer against errors in the title search. The fee for the title insurance policy is paid at loan closing.

title search an examination of officially recorded documents to determine the legal ownership of property.

title the evidence of a person's right to the ownership and possession of property.

trap the s-shaped pipe below a sink or in a toilet that traps water to create a seal between the house and the sewer system.

trust a fiduciary arrangement whereby property is conveyed to a person or an institution, called a *trustee,* to be held and administered on behalf of another person or entity, called a *beneficiary.* The one who conveys the trust is called the *trustor.*

unlawful detainer action a lawsuit to evict a tenant or former owner who unlawfully remains in possession of real property.

usury the lending of money at a rate of interest greater than that permitted by law.

VA mortgage a mortgage loan on approved property made to a qualified veteran by a lender and guaranteed by the Department of Veterans Affairs to limit possible loss by the lender.

wall cabinet a kitchen cabinet mounted to the wall, usually shallower than a base cabinet.

waterproofing any material used to stop the passage of water. Plastic sheets of treated papers and asphalt are used for membranes, while various chemical sealants and asphalt applications are used to seal pores and cracks.

weather stripping strips of felt, rubber, metal, or other material attached along the edges of a door or window to keep out drafts and reduce heat loss.

whirlpool bath a tub fitted with jets that circulate water or air. Sometimes referred to as a *Jacuzzi.*

wraparound mortgage A new loan that encompasses any current mortgages and is subordinate to them. The wraparound mortgage is written for the total of the existing mortgages plus the amount being financed by the lender, who may be the seller. A single mortgage payment amount and interest rate is specified.

yield the total income produced by an investment, usually expressed as an annual percentage.

zoning ordinance regulation of the character and use of property by a municipality or other government entity through the exercise of its police power.

Index

The Wholesale Real Estate Advisor

Your Online Investment Success Newsletter

*Every issue is jam-packaged with information
you won't find anywhere else:*

◆ **How to find foreclosure properties before any other investors**

◆ **How to win with short sale techniques when dealing with lenders**

◆ **How to wholesale properties to other investors for quick profits**

◆ **How to find and work with private mortgage lenders**

◆ **How to sell your properties FSBO and save a fortune on each deal**

◆ **How to find the best HUD and bank REO properties in your area**

◆ **How to create and use real estate notes to maximize your success**

◆ **More success stories from the field**

To subscribe, Just Go to <www.rehabwiz.com>
and Sign Up — It's **Free!**

Share the message!

Bulk discounts
Discounts start at only 10 copies. Save up to 55% off retail price.

Custom publishing
Private label a cover with your organization's name and logo.
Or, tailor information to your needs with a custom pamphlet
that highlights specific chapters.

Ancillaries
Workshop outlines, videos, and other products are available on
select titles.

Dynamic speakers
Engaging authors are available to share their expertise and insight
at your event.

Call Dearborn Trade Special Sales at
1-800-245-BOOK (2665)
or e-mail trade@dearborn.com